THE CHANGING BOUNDARIES
OF THE FIRM

The Changing Boundaries of the Firm offers a distinctive analysis of the relations and interplay between the intramural activities of firms, their changing boundaries, and increasing reliance on networks and alliances with other firms.

The volume is the result of works conducted in connection with the research programme of the European Science Foundation on 'European Management and Organization in Transition', devoted to the analysis of changing forms of economic organization in Europe. The contributors offer a blend of theoretical and empirical studies; they are based on a set of related perspectives in modern economics, including transaction cost economics, competence and resource-based theories of the firm, evolutionary economics, and theories of foreign direct investments and the multinational enterprise. The unifying concern shared by the different studies is the need to model firm behaviour and inter-firm co-operative activities in terms of knowledge growth and competence building rather than merely in terms of cost reduction; they emphasize learning processes and dynamic efficiency rather than the efficient allocation of given resources.

Massimo G. Colombo is Full Professor of Applied Economics at the Università di Pavia. He is also Professor of Economics of Technical Change at the Politecnico di Milano. He is the author of numerous publications in the fields of industrial economics, economics of innovation and the theory of the firm in established international journals.

ROUTLEDGE STUDIES IN BUSINESS ORGANIZATIONS AND NETWORKS

THE CHANGING BOUNDARIES OF THE FIRM

Explaining evolving inter-firm relations

Edited by Massimo G. Colombo

London and New York

First published 1998
by Routledge
11 New Fetter Lane, London EC4P 4EE

Simultaneously published in the USA and Canada
by Routledge
29 West 35th Street, New York, NY 10001

Typeset in Garamond by Routledge
Printed and bound in Great Britain by TJ International Ltd, Padstow, Cornwall

British Library Cataloguing in Publication Data
A catalogue record for this book is available from the British Library

Library of Congress Cataloging in Publication Data
A catalogue record for this book has been requested

ISBN 0–415–15470–7

CONTENTS

CONTENTS

ILLUSTRATIONS

Tables

ILLUSTRATIONS

Figures

CONTRIBUTORS

John Cantwell is Professor of International Economics at the University of Reading. He has been a Visiting Professor of Economics at the University of Rome 'La Sapienza', the University of the Social Sciences, Toulouse and Rutgers University, New Jersey, and is a former President of the European International Business Association. He is the author of numerous articles and books on foreign direct investments, multinational enterprises, and the economics of innovation.

Massimo G. Colombo is Full Professor of Applied Economics at Università degli Studi di Pavia. He also is Professor of Economics of Technical Change at Politecnico di Milano. He is a member of the Scientific Advisory Boards of CIRET (Interdepartment Research Centre on the Economics of Telecommunications), Politecnico di Milano and DRUID (Danish Research Unit on Industrial Dynamics), Copenhagen. He is the author of over seventy articles in international and Italian journals and books on issues related to strategic alliances, the organization of business groups, firms' innovation strategies, the diffusion of innovations, and the economics of information and communication technologies.

Michel Delapierre is Chargé de Recherches au CNRS (National Centre for Scientific Research) and Head of the Centre d'Etudes et de Recherches sur l'Entreprise Multinationale (FORUM/CEREM) at Paris-X University. His main research interests are in globalisation, foreign direct investments, multinational enterprises, and the economics of innovation.

John Dunning is State of New Jersey Professor of International Business at Rutgers University. He is probably the best known scholar in the world in the field of foreign direct investments and the multinational enterprise, having published extensively in this area since his pioneering study of American investments in Britain in the 1950s.

Emilio Esposito is Associate Professor of Business Economics and Organization at the Faculty of Engineering, Università di Napoli 'Federico II'. He is a research associate with ODISSEO-DIS (Centre for Organization and

Technological Innovation), Department of Computer Science and Systems, Università di Napoli 'Federico II'. His research interests focus on the analysis of subcontracting relations.

Paola Garrone is Associate Professor of Business Economics and Organization at Politecnico di Milano. Her main research interests are in the economics of technical change (determinants, effects, and dynamics of innovations and innovation strategies) and the economics of communication industries.

Susan Helper is Associate Professor of Economics at Case Western Reserve University in Cleveland, Ohio. She is also a research associate at the MIT International Motor Vehicle Program. Her research interest is in the impact of long-term, information-rich relationships on economic performance. She has published in journals such as Sloan Management Review, Strategic Management Journal, and the Journal of Economic Behavior and Organization.

Jean-François Hennart is Professor of International Business and Director of the Ph.D. program in International Business at the University of Illinois at Urbana-Champaign. His main research focus has been on the transaction cost theory of the multinational firm and of its alternatives, and on the theory and empirical analysis of modes of entry into foreign markets. He is the author of A Theory of Multinational Enterprise (University of Michigan Press, 1982) and of more than 20 articles in international journals.

Neil Kay is Professor of Business Economics. He has held two Visiting Associate Professorships in the University of California at Irvine and was Visiting Professor at the European University in Florence. He has been a member of ACOST (Cabinet Office) and DTI working parties. He has published three books and numerous articles on industrial economics and corporate strategies, particularly on topics of diversification, multinationalism and innovation.

Lynn Krieger Mytelka is currently Director of the Division on Investment, Technology and Enterprise Development at the United Nations Conference on Trade and Development (UNCTAD) in Geneva (Switzerland). She is on leave from her positions as Professor in the Institute of Political Economy at Carleton University, Ottawa (Canada) and Director of Research, at the Centre d'Etudes et de Recherches sur l'Entreprise Multinationale (FORUM-CEREM), Université de Paris-X, Nanterre (France). She has held visiting Professorships at the Universities of Lille, Paris-X, Paris-I, Yale and Queens. She currently serves on the board of the International Studies Quarterly, the International Political Economy Yearbook and the Canadian Journal of Development Studies. Professor Mytelka is the author of numerous books and articles on learning, innovation, strategic partnerships and industrial policy.

Bart Nooteboom is Professor of Industrial Organization at the Faculty of Management and Organization, Gröningen University. He also is the Scientific Director of the Research Institute for Small Business in The Netherlands. He published about 150 articles in international and Dutch journals and books on: retailing, small business and entrepreneurship, economies of scale, price setting, technology and industrial policy, innovation and diffusion, transaction cost theory, subcontracting, inter-firm alliances, organizational learning, ethics, methodology and philosophy of economics and management.

Ivana Paniccia is a Ph.D. candidate at the University of Reading, Department of Economics. She presently is a research associate with the Italian Regulatory Authority for Energy, Research and Documentation Department. Her research interests are in the fields of industrial districts, theory of the firm, and regulation.

Christos Pitelis is at the Judge Institute for Management Studies, Cambridge University. He is University Lecturer (Barclays Bank) and Director of Studies in Economics, Queens' College (Industrial and Business Strategy). He has published extensively on industrial organization and political economy and its applications to business strategy, industrial strategy and international business. His books include Corporate Capital (Cambridge University Press, 1987), The Political Economy of Privatization (with T. Clarke, Routledge), Market and Non-Market Hierarchies (Blackwell, 1991) and The Nature of the Transnational Firm (with R. Sugden, Routledge, 1991).

Mario Raffa is Full Professor of Business Economics and Organization at the Faculty of Engineering, Università di Napoli 'Federico II', and Scientific Director of ODISSEO-DIS (Centre for Organization and Technological Innovation), Department of Computer Science and Systems, Università di Napoli 'Federico II'. He is the author of numerous publications related to supply relations and the organization of innovation and technology transfer in small high-tech firms.

Sabine Reddy is Assistant Professor at the Department of Management and Organization Sciences, School of Business at Wayne State University. Her areas of specialization include business strategy, international business and organizational theory.

PREFACE

This book offers a distinctive analysis of firm boundaries and inter-firm co-ordination, based on an integration between a set of forefront research programmes in economics, organization and management, including transaction cost economics, competence and resource-based theories of the firm, evolutionary economics, learning based theories of technological change and theories of international production and foreign direct investment. If it is an eclectic endeavour, it is so in the sense of a fruitful integration between complementary and related perspectives into a wider 'eclectic theory', the sense advocated by one of the leading scholars who have contributed to the book (Dunning, this volume).

The volume is the result of one of the international workshops organized within the research programme of the European Science Foundation on 'European Management and Organization in Transition' (EMOT), devoted to the integration between European researches conducted on a set of selected research questions on the changing forms of economic organization in Europe. These questions have been organized into various themes, articulating the general research interest in understanding and assessing the nature and properties of the differentiation between European business systems and the organization and management arrangements that can contribute to their effective integration. This book is relevant for both the main themes in which the problem of integration between European economic activities has been addressed in the EMOT programme: the theme focused on the nature and role of firms as cross-boundaries integrating actors; and the theme on the nature and role of inter-firm networks and alliances as integrating mechanisms.

Massimo Colombo, of the Università di Pavia, has been the entrepreneur and the architect of this very successful workshop, in which he brought together leading and younger researchers, students of multinational corporations and network researchers, from both Europe and the US, in an effort to understand the interplay between firms' intra-mural activities, firm boundaries and inter-firm linkages. According to EMOT practices and purposes, contributions were carefully selected both *ex ante* and *ex post* of the workshop as relevant and pertinent responses to a set of specific research questions, so as to produce the sought confrontation and integration among potentially connected researches, and some conclusive points about the theory and practice of economic organization.

I would like to signal three substantive points that emerge from the whole effort and that can be particularly fruitful in future research. As Massimo Colombo observes in his introduction, the principal unifying concern in the selected contributions is the need for modelling firm and inter-firm co-operative activities in terms of knowledge growth and competence acquisition and not only in terms of cost reduction; a concern that drives a research interest in the learning processes on which economic activity is based rather than only in efficient resource allocation processes. I would like to point out here some further implications of these two key concerns on *competence* and *learning*, besides the often stressed advantage of providing dynamic rather than static accounts of firms' changing boundaries and alliances.

From transaction costs to relational benefits   A competence-based view of inter-firm co-operation may restore the deserved attention to the *benefits* of co-operation, in addition to the much analysed costs of co-ordination and transaction. In fact, the argument that competence and resource complementarities are an important *raison d'être* for inter-firm collaboration under various forms, emphasizes the creation of new value, the 'enlargement of the pie', the generation of quasi-rents to be divided among the partners. For finding these Pareto-superior combinations of competencies and resources, 'investments' in costly search, problem solving and negotiation processes may be well deserved. Let me reinforce this contention, reached here through a competence-based argument, by mentioning that it has emerged also in another EMOT workshop on inter-firm networks, through a negotiation and opportunity cost analysis of inter-firm co-ordination (Ring 1996; Grandori and Neri forthcoming).

From structural alternatives to structural complements   Analyses of firm boundaries and inter-firm co-ordination, not only among economic approaches, have privileged a view of firms, markets and networks as alternative forms of regulation of economic life, that are effective under different circumstances. The studies of this volume emphasize, instead, the implications of the use of these forms for each other rather than their connection with external variables. The nexus turns out to be quite complicated. On one side, the more a firm has built competencies internally in a certain activity, the more likely it is that it can become a valuable partner in an alliance, thereby configurating a possible mutual reinforcement between the use of internal hierarchy and that of external networking. Many essays in the volume stress this effect of competence building and learning processes on organizational arrangements. On the other side, a collaboration with a partner may be established just for the opposite reason, the lack of internal competence; or, vice versa, the lack of partners with sufficient competencies, may force a firm to develop activities internally. Even though we can not therefore hypothesize a simple or direct relationship between the internal and external governance of competencies and activities, we can observe that they are related and that the initial configuration and distribution of internal and external competencies does help in predicting and evaluating changes in firm boundaries and inter-firm networks. A more general methodological implication of this contention is that the approach to the analysis of inter-firm boundaries and networks needs to become more configurational and relational, rather than to persevere in the track of a contingency approach linking structural solutions to given attributes of activities and exchanges (Ebers and Grandori 1997).

Back from property arrangements to organizational arrangements   The conceptualization of networks as hybrids between markets and hierarchies, especially diffused in economic perspectives, has led to the expectation that the set of co-ordination mechanisms employed in inter-firm relations is a sum, or a mixture, or a mean of the mechanisms employed in markets and in hierarchies. In opposition to this view, other scholars, especially in management and organization, have conceptualized the network as an independent third type located outside of the market to hierarchy continuum, being therefore led to look for different and distinctive mechanisms of co-ordination that are not present either in markets or hierarchies. A learning interpretation of inter-firm co-operation seems to lead to a still different approach. In the first place it may lead to recognize that not all firms and not all networks are geared at innovation, and that not all firms or all networks learn in the same way. There are both firm and network types (and stages in their life cycles) that are oriented to and capable of 'exploratory learning', or oriented to 'exploitative learning', or capable only of incremental learning, or even blocked into homeostatic learning cycles (March 1991; Nooteboom, Chapter 9 this volume; Grabher 1993). Therefore it is very difficult to assess the learning properties of firms and networks, of internal and external organization as such. Rather than the internal–external divide other organization dimensions seem to be critical for understanding the learning capabilities of governance structures.

For example, whereas exploratory learning based on cross fertilization of competencies is sought, the most important feature of an organizational arrangement is to allow confrontation, reciprocal transfer of complex and tacit know-how, group problem solving, and an evaluation and reward system that 'problematizes' rather than punishes errors. Therefore, a crucial feature of the governance system is that it provides occasions in which a set of differentiated actors can participate on a parity basis to problem solving with the appropriate guarantees. This feature can be possessed either by a firm, provided that it is organized as a flexible 'organic system' and that unified property does not mean unified decision making; or by a multilateral contractual agreement among firms, provided that the contract does not incorporate too many obligational rules, procedures and hierarchical interventions. Both internal and external organization needs to become significantly decentralized, *ad hoc*, and densely connected in terms of their communication and decision network structure (at least periodically) if it is to be highly conducive to innovation and exploratory learning.

Received organization theory would suggest to connect exploitative learning, focused on resource rationalization, to more mechanistic organizational arrangements, which may be found both within firms with unitary and functional organization forms and in highly formalized, hierarchical obligational contracts among firms. A task for future research may be to understand better these relationships between governance forms and learning, opening up variety in our conceptualizations of forms of learning as well as of forms of organization.

Anna Grandori
EMOT Co-director
Università di Modena and Università Bocconi, Milan
April 1997

References

Ebers, M. and Grandori, A. (1997) 'The forms, costs and development dynamics of inter-organizational networks', in M. Ebers (ed.) *The Formation of Inter-Organizational Networks*, London: Routledge: 265–86.

Grabher, G. (1993) 'The weakness of strong ties', in G. Grabher (ed.) *The Embedded Firm*, London: Routledge: 255–77.

Grandori, A. and Neri, M. 'The fairness properties of networks', in A. Grandori (ed.), 'Inter-firm networks: negotiated order and industrial competitiveness, London: Routledge (forthcoming).

March, G.J. (1991) 'Exploration and exploitation in organizational learning', *Organization Science* 2: 71–87.

Ring, P. Smith (1996) 'The costs of networks', EMOT Conference 'Inter-firm networks: outcomes and policy implications', Modena, September.

ACKNOWLEDGEMENTS

The book has its origin in a workshop I organized in Como within the framework of the research programme of the European Science Foundation on 'European Management and Organisation in Transition'. I am indebted to the European Science Foundation, the Italian Consiglio Nazionale delle Ricerche and Politecnico di Milano for financial support to the organization of the workshop.

I am particularly grateful to Anna Grandori, co director of the EMOT programme, Ash Amin and Arthur Francis, who co-ordinated EMOT theme 5 on 'Internationalization and the management of strategic corporate change', for suggestions and encouragement during the realization of the volume. I would also like to thank John Cantwell and Patrick Cohendet for discussion on the design of the volume. In addition, the volume greatly benefited from referee work provided by participants in the workshop.

Lastly, I thank the *Journal of International Business Studies* for granting permission to reprint in Chapter 2 the article by John Dunning on 'Reappraising the eclectic paradigm in an age of alliance capitalism', the only one of the studies included in the book which was not originally presented in the Como workshop.

1

SOME INTRODUCTORY
REFLECTIONS[1]

Massimo G. Colombo

Introduction

Economists have long been interested in co-operation among firms.
Nonetheless, in the recent period, scientific work on this topic has been
rapidly growing, both at the theoretical and (to a more limited extent) empirical level. This probably is a consequence of the surge in the number of
co-operative arrangements concluded by firms in the 1980s and 1990s, which
is documented by various sources (see the references in the studies by Dunning,
and Delapierre and Mytelka in Chapters 2 and 4, respectively).

The studies included in this volume belong to this stream of literature. All
of them deal with use by firms of co-ordination mechanisms which differ from
both arm's length transactions and hierarchical arrangements. They analyse
their relative advantages (and disadvantages) from different perspectives and
highlight their implications for firms' organization and conduct, market
structure and industrial policy. Although their individual contribution is
valuable, I believe that there is some additional value when they are considered together. This actually is the main reason for the publication of this
volume. The aim of this introductory chapter is to provide support for this
argument. More specifically, I will try to explain my personal view as regards
the relation of the volume to the current scientific debate on the changing
boundaries of the firm, and the specific lessons which can be obtained from
reading all the chapters it includes. For this purpose, I will firstly summarize,
in a very brief and probably quite partial manner, the main differences
between the approaches to the study of co-operation among firms of mainstream (i.e., neo-classical) economics on the one hand and heterodox schools
of thought (mainly evolutionary and competence-based theories of the firm)
on the other. Subsequently, I will propose a competence-based view of co-
operation, which I think is shared to a large extent by the various studies
presented in the following chapters. This will offer a general framework
allowing to point out the main theoretical arguments and empirical findings
provided by the volume.

Co-operative agreements among firms and the internalization of externalities

In general terms, neo-classical economics tends to explain the establishment of co-operative arrangements as the attempt of profit maximizing firms to internalize externalities. From this standpoint, it is useful to make a distinction between: (a) horizontal competitive externalities; (b) technological externalities; (c) vertical externalities; and (d) network externalities.

Co-operative agreements and the internalization of horizontal competitive externalities

Oligopoly theory has long recognized that firms have an incentive to co-operate as far as their decisions when they act independently (that is non co-operatively) are detrimental to one another. As is noted by Jacquemin and Slade (1989: 418), 'in a static framework with costless collusion, firms can do at least as well when colluding as when acting non co-operatively . . . because the non co-operative solution is always a feasible collusive outcome'. Of course, even though co-operation increases firms' profits, it also decreases consumers' surplus, thus negatively affecting social welfare. This holds true unless the agreement has positive implications on the demand and/or supply sides, for instance because it results in an increase in product variety or a decrease in production cost due to economies of scale or rationalization of investments.

The problem with collusion is that reaching an agreement may turn out to be difficult. In other words, negotiation and bargaining costs may be substantial. This especially applies when there are (exogenous) asymmetries among firms due to product and/or cost heterogeneity or different expectations about future market and technological conditions. In addition, when a collusive agreement has been reached, there are incentives for the parties to cheat (i.e., to cut prices or increase output). Actually, the decision whether to cheat or not can be modelled as a prisoner's dilemma game. In a static framework, cheating proves to be the dominant strategy. This would explain why cartels tend to be unstable.[2]

In a similar vein, numerous theoretical contributions have highlighted the anti-competitive effects of horizontal minority shareholdings and joint-ventures in non co-operative oligopolies. By linking the profits of competitors, such arrangements lessen their incentives to compete, leading to output reductions and higher prices.[3]

Co-operative agreements and the internalization of technological externalities

In an oligopolistic industry, a firm's research and development (R&D) expenses may have either a positive or a negative impact on the cost (and/or demand conditions) of rival firms, therefore engendering a positive or a negative externality, respectively.

Negative technological externalities are the result of technological competition. Investments in R&D may allow a firm to obtain process or product innovations, which lower operating costs or improve the product mix. In so far as there is strong protection of intellectual property, the innovator will increase its output and profits to the detriment of those of rival firms. The closer firms' products substitute for one another, the larger is the negative effect of R&D investments upon competitors. In addition, if a firm devotes a larger amount of resources to R&D, it is more likely to obtain patentable intermediate results that render costlier and/or more hazardous innovation activity by other firms.

Positive technological externalities arise from spillovers. If the appropriability regime is weak, for instance due to the limited effectiveness of patent and copyright laws, the results of a firm's innovative activity have public good nature. Rival firms may employ them without purchasing the right to do so, therefore incurring negligible imitation costs. Under such circumstances, the private incentives to R&D are too low, as firms do not consider spillovers in their profit function.

A growing body of contributions in industrial organization sharing a game-theoretic approach, has pointed out that co-operation among firms may be instrumental to the internalization of (negative and positive) technological externalities. By means of multi-stage models of oligopolistic competition, authors in such tradition examine the influence that the decision of firms to collaborate in the research, development and/or production stages exerts on the level of R&D expenses, the equilibrium output and price, and social welfare.[4] The main results can be synthesized as follows.

- Co-operation in R&D increases the amount of R&D investments by firms, with beneficial implications for social welfare, if the effect of the positive externalities connected with spillovers dominates the one arising from the negative externalities due to technological competition. The effect is larger if co-operation not only involves *ex ante* co-ordination of partners' decisions concerning R&D expenses, but also results in *ex post* exchange of R&D results (see Kamien *et al*. 1992).
- If co-operation extends forward to the production stage, the increase of R&D expenses is larger. Nevertheless, if firms' products are close substitutes, the output reduction due to collusion engenders a loss of consumers' surplus which generally is not compensated by the greater profits of firms. Consequently, social welfare is negatively affected.

Co-operative agreements and the internalization of vertical externalities

When an imperfectly competitive downstream industry purchases an essential component from an upstream monopolist who owns a 'bottleneck' facility, a negative vertical externality connected with the 'double marginalization' effect, arises. Such effect was originally highlighted by Cournot ([1838] 1927). He considered two monopolists producing complementary components that need to be combined in fixed proportions to obtain a composite good. He showed that joint ownership of the two units reduces the equilibrium price consumers pay for the composite good, and increases both producers' and consumers' surplus. The reason lies in the fact that the two independent firms ignore the negative effect of their own mark up on each other, while the integrated monopolist internalizes such externality.

Similarly, the above mentioned negative vertical externality between the upstream monopolist and the downstream oligopolists can be internalized (with a beneficial effect on social welfare) if the latter firms jointly own the upstream bottleneck facility.[5]

Nevertheless, one should also acknowledge that both vertical mergers,[6] and vertical co-operative arrangements, may well have anti-competitive effects. In particular, the set up of an upstream joint venture may well be instrumental to collusion among downstream oligopolists, favouring information sharing, co-ordination of conducts, and side payments. Under such circumstances the impact on social welfare may well turn out to be negative.[7]

Co-operative agreements and the internalization of network externalities

There are (positive) network externalities when the value of a unit of a good increases with the number of units which have been previously sold. Network externalities may be direct or indirect (see for instance Katz and Shapiro 1994, Economides 1996). The former refer to the case, typical of two-ways communication networks, when the value of subscription to any user is positively affected when an additional user joins the network.[8] The latter arises in the so-called hardware–software paradigm, when customers must buy two compatible components to consume a service (for instance, computer hardware and software or TV-set and video programming).[9] Network externalities are characteristic of network industries and industries where system goods (i.e., goods composed of complementary components) are produced.

In network and system industries, co-ordination among suppliers is crucial. Co-operative arrangements may serve the purpose of assuring inter-operability among networks, defining common standards for hardware platforms, or making platform-specific software available (see again Katz and Shapiro 1994).

Some critical comments

Generally speaking, the vision of the co-operation phenomenon proposed by neo-classical economics is a very stylized one. Its major shortcoming is that it fails to provide clear insights into the determinants of collaborative ventures among firms.[10]

First, in neo-classical theoretical models, the decision by a given firm to enter into a co-operative arrangement with another firm is *exogenous*. In other words, such literature does not offer any indications on such crucial issues as which firms are likely to co-operate and which ones are not, and how firms select partners for collaboration. The implicit assumption is made that *ex-ante* all firms have private incentives to co-operate; the analysis focuses on the effects of co-operation on the equilibrium price and output of industries, and on the implications for industrial and competition policy.

Second, from an empirical standpoint, the explanatory power of the neo-classical literature is confined to a quite negligible, even though conceptually important portion of the collaborations undertaken by firms. Namely, the internalization of externalities figures prominently in explaining (a) cartels and other (tacit or explicit) collusive arrangements aimed at market sharing or price fixing, (b) research consortia coping with the free rider problem that characterizes the production of scientific knowledge and basic research, (c) vertical relationships allowing to internalize vertical externalities, and (d) standard setting agreements and other collaborative arrangements which allow firms to take advantage of network economies.

Third, it is fundamental to recognize that if the aim of collaborative agreements is the internalization of externalities, the same benefits could be captured through mergers and acquisitions (M&As). If the alleged greater administrative costs of co-operative agreements are taken into account, they always are inferior to M&As;[11] in other words, they represent a second-best solution, to which firms would only resort when M&As are prevented by regulatory constraints (antitrust rules, limits to foreign direct investments, etc.).

Lastly, neo-classical economics provides a *static* framework to analyse the effects of co-operation. Such effects are shown to differ according to the different, exogenously determined characteristics of the competitive, technological and institutional settings in which firms are embedded. It follows that the decisions of policy makers to favour or impede co-operative arrangements also come to depend on such static characteristics. Feedbacks related to the dynamic impact of co-operation on firms' own characteristics and those of their environment, are not considered.

Technology, knowledge, the nature of the firm and the dynamics of competition

I now claim that in order to improve our understanding of the co-operation phenomenon, we need a more articulated view of the characteristics of technology, the role of knowledge, the nature of the firm, and the dynamics of competition than the one provided by mainstream economics.

Technology as knowledge

Neo-classical economics considers technology as 'information' (see Arrow 1962). Accordingly, differences among firms in innovative performances are merely to be traced to asymmetries in the available information. Such a view also implies that once technology has been discovered, it is easy to apply and inexpensive to transfer and reproduce in comparison with the costs incurred by the innovator. In the absence of regulatory mechanisms designed to inhibit spillovers, technology basically is a public good, as was pointed out previously.

Such conceptualization of technology seems not to be supported by the available empirical evidence on the nature of the innovation process (see Dosi 1988), and has been questioned by a series of contributions in the economics of technical change.[12] One of its major drawbacks is that it completely rules out the *cognitive dimension* of the innovation process.

In order for valuable technological results to be produced, information needs to be collected, selected, processed, interpreted, compared and put to a finalized use. In other words, information needs to be transformed into *knowledge* through a cognitive activity which relies on agents' frames of reference and systems of beliefs. These latter play a fundamental heuristic function in orienting the search for useful information and the disregard of irrelevant ones. As was already noticed by Simon (1959), the information set as perceived and used by economic agents in their decision making activity does not coincide with the 'objective' information set present in their environment.[13] There is a much looser relation between the real world and agents' representations of it than is acknowledged by mainstream economics. It follows that when agents operate in environments where the possible courses of actions and their consequences are surrounded by ambiguity and uncertainty, they may develop different sets of knowledge from the very same set of information.[14] In addition, as the cognitive patterns of individuals evolve over time (see below), the same set of information may lead to different sets of knowledge in different times (see Nooteboom 1996).

Firms are multi-agent economic institutions which possess their own frames of reference and systems of belief. These latter are contingent on (a) those of the individuals who are in charge of making relevant decisions at the various levels in the organization and (b) the interactions between and the co-ordination of the behaviour of such individuals. In other words, the production of knowledge is a collective (i.e., social) activity which requires the representations of the world of the different agents within a firm to be harmonized and possible conflicts to be reconciled.[15]

Both individual and collective cognitive mechanisms are path-dependent. They are shaped by the context-specific problem solving activity of individuals and organizations, and are nurtured by their previous experiences of successes and failures. They evolve in an incremental and cumulative way as a consequence of the interaction with the physical and social environment.

According to such perspective, technological differences among firms at any given time are mainly to be explained as the result of differences in cognitive patterns rather than as a consequence of the asymmetric distribution of relevant information.

The notion of technology as 'knowledge' requires some further specifications. Various classifications of knowledge have been proposed in the literature, with each one emphasizing different characteristics which affect its generation, storage and transmission.[16] In general terms, a distinction can be made between:

- embodied knowledge in parts, components, software packages, capital equipment, and final products; it is a form of ready-to-use knowledge, as its use does not require any understanding of its inner properties, except its interface characteristics;
- disembodied codified knowledge: this is the part of knowledge that can be written down in a 'blueprint' form, and thus it is easy to transmit and reproduce;
- disembodied tacit knowledge; it can be defined as the ability to do something well without being able to precisely tell how.[17] It usually is the result of a process of learning of a set of skills and of their subsequent fine-tuning and improvement through practice; it is largely idiosyncratic and non-decomposable. Hence, it is difficult to reproduce in and tailor to an application environment different from the one where it was developed. Due to the difficulty of expressing it in verbal, articulated and unambiguous form, so as to make it understandable to others who didn't contribute to its development, its transfer mainly takes place by imitation; moreover, it often requires the physical transfer of individuals or groups of individuals and the realization of substantial relation-specific investments on the part of both the provider and the recipient.[18]

The taxonomy proposed above does not make justice of the fact that in most circumstances what really matters is the *degree* of tacitness of knowledge.[19] However, it is instrumental to pointing out that there are inherent limits in the extent to which knowledge can be articulated, verbalized and transmitted, independently of economic forces and notably the structure of incentives that economic agents face.[20]

The firm as a repository of competencies

In mainstream economics the firm essentially is a 'processor of information'. On the basis of market signals relating to the demand for its products and the supply of production factors, of information concerning the production function, and of expectations on the behaviour of competitors, firms make subjectively optimal decisions as to the output quantity they will produce or the price of their products. They may also make decisions concerning other variables such as the level of R&D and marketing expenses, which modify technology and/or demand conditions. Firms are considered as substantially rational,[21] with their decision-making activity being only constrained by the amount and quality of the available information. Uncertainty is confined to 'risk', in accordance with Frank Knight's well-known definition, and involves probabilistic description of the different states of nature and the outcomes of the possible courses of actions under those states of nature. In other words, uncertainty originates from lack of information. Accordingly, learning is merely regarded as Bayesian updating of subjective probabilities by economic agents as additional information is made available over time.[22]

The vision of the firm as a 'processor of information' is basically shared by what are commonly referred to as the contractual theories of the firm, a stream of literature which includes transaction-cost theory (Coase 1937; Williamson 1975, 1985), agency theory (Jensen and Meckling 1976) and incomplete contracts theory (Alchian and Demsetz 1972; Grossman and Hart 1986). In spite of remarkable differences between the various contributions, it is fair to state that they tend to consider the origin and nature of the firm as a (more or less efficient) response to information-related problems.[23]

In contrast, following the seminal works by Knight (1921), Alchian (1950) and Penrose (1959), the firm may be regarded as a 'repository of assets'.[24] From this standpoint, the most important activities in which the firm is involved relate to the disposal of assets between different uses, maintenance of existing assets and building of new ones. Some of these assets are of a physical nature: general-purpose and specialized capital equipment, distribution networks, research laboratories, etc. Other assets are of intangible nature: resources such as a firm's brand name, its goodwill among customers and suppliers, and its stock of patented knowledge belong to this category. Among a firm's intangible assets, *core competencies* play a crucial role (see Prahalad and Hamel 1990).[25] They can be defined as a firm's ability to select, mobilize and use other tangible and intangible assets to perform tasks in a unique way. They express what a firm is able to do better than other firms. In light of the discussion in the previous section, a firm's distinctive capabilities constitute an essential part of its stock of disembodied tacit knowledge. Accordingly, they are contingent on firm's frames of reference and systems of belief.

For the purposes of the present analysis, there are a number of characteristics of a firm's core competencies which are worth being emphasized.[26] First, even though they take advantage of the skills of the individual members of an organization, core competencies have a collective, non-decomposable nature. This means that they cannot be reduced to the sum of individual skills. On the one hand this feature can be traced to the social nature of a firm's cognitive patterns, as was mentioned in the previous paragraph; on the other it relates to the role of the firm's specific organizational structures and co-ordination processes in assuring effective performances. Second, core competencies are the legacy of a firm's own history: they are built through a cumulative process based on a firm's problem solving activity through trials, errors, and (mostly incremental) adjustments. Hence, they are path-dependent and context-specific. The path-dependent and collective nature of core competencies makes them rather difficult to imitate outside a firm's boundaries. It is this characteristic that renders core competencies crucial in obtaining sustainable competitive advantages. It also implies that there likely is no market for their services, even though in principle they may be acquired through the market for corporate control. Third, core competencies are subject to a routinization process, in the sense that they tend to involve automatic, co-ordinated responses to specified signals from the firm's environment. When successful solutions to given problems have been found (how to solve a production scheduling problem, how to convey a given promotional message through the packaging of a good, how to differentiate products so as to target specific niche markets, how to effectively exchange design specifications with suppliers, etc.), they can be applied repeatedly to similar problems within the firm while incurring limited (and decreasing) marginal costs.[27] The routinization of core competencies has two corollaries. On the positive side, routines act as the memory where an organization stores its knowledge; they are responsible for the preservation of distinctive capabilities in spite of the fact that individual members of the organizations come and go (see Winter 1988). On the negative side, the routinization process may lead to lock-in effects; a successful organization will tend to conserve its routinized distinctive capabilities even if a shift in the business environment would require their adjustment or replacement. Lastly, in spite of the context-specific nature of a firm's core competencies, they are fungible to some extent; this means that they can be successfully used by the firm in situations which differ from, but share some common traits with the ones from which they originated.

The routinization of a firm's distinctive capabilities plays a prominent role in influencing strategic behaviour. Routinization implies that excess managerial and organizational resources are continuously created within a firm so as to be put to new productive uses. To the extent that core competencies are fungible, this lays the ground for firm's product and/or geographic diversification beyond its current businesses (see for instance Teece *et al*. 1994). In addition, excess resources can be invested in the search for new core competencies. This is especially important in situations where there is a substantial mismatch between the observed results from the use of the current set of capabilities and those that were expected by the firm on the basis of previous experience. Hence, the behaviour of firms can be described in terms of both competence exploiting and competence exploring activities.

In the light of the above reasoning, the mechanisms which allow a firm to modify the set of routinized core competencies, deserve some further explanations. They include different types of learning processes oriented towards competence exploitation, competence exploration, or both.[28] A distinction can be made between the following forms of learning (see also Malerba 1992).

- Learning from experience: learning-by-doing and learning-by-using are the key mechanisms for the fine-tuning of given capabilities, leading to incremental productivity improvements.
- Learning by searching: it consists in an autonomous problem solving activity stimulated by the inconsistencies between actions suggested by the current stock of competencies and the outcome of those actions. It is based on autonomous investments in the development and experimentation of new solutions: examples are provided by investments in new research projects, in the deployment of innovative capital equipment, or in the development of a new marketing mix to support the introduction of new products.
- Learning through imitation: this is the only mechanism which may possibly allow a firm's distinctive capabilities to be (partially) replicated by other firms. However, as was pointed out above, imitation generally is difficult due to the tacit, context-specific and social nature of a firm's capabilities. For the same reasons, it usually requires substantial investments on the part of the imitating firm.
- Learning through interacting: as was said earlier, core competencies reflect the cognitive characteristics of a firm; the interaction with other agents allows firms to enhance their own capabilities, as they are positively influenced by exposition to different, possibly complementary representations of the environment.[29]

Competition

As is well known, in *Capitalism, Socialism, and Democracy* Schumpeter provides a vision of competition as a 'process of creative destruction' capable of assuring dynamic efficiency within the economic system (Schumpeter 1950). Evolutionary theories emphasize two fundamental elements of such dynamic process: variety and selection (see again Nelson and Winter 1982).

Competitive rivalry operates as a selection device among a population of firms which are equipped with different collections of specific assets and distinctive capabilities. Heterogeneity is endogenously assured by the context-specific and path-dependent nature of firms' resources. Firms with different capabilities interpret and react differently to the signals and stimuli from the environment. In addition, firms differ in their aptitude to modify and improve their set of core competencies.

Competition tends to reduce variety through both Darwinian and Lamarckian mechanisms (see Hodgson 1994b). In a Darwinian perspective, long-term survival is guaranteed only for the fittest firms, that is the firms that possess the set of specific assets and core competencies most suitable to the characteristics of the competitive environment. Unfit firms progressively decline and are finally eliminated from the market. However, Lamarckian mechanisms also are at work: unsuccessful firms struggle to modify their assets and competencies so as to adhere to what they consider as the dominant pattern of success. This adjustment process in turn changes the characteristics of the economic environment and influences the outcome of the competitive game.

A competence-based view of co-operation among firms

In a seminal paper, Richardson (1972: 889) pointed out that 'organizations will tend to specialize in activities for which their capabilities offer some comparative advantage, i.e., in similar activities . . . . But the organization of industry has also to adapt itself to the fact that activities may be complementary, in the sense that they represent different phases of a process of production and require in some way or another to be co-ordinated'. Richardson also suggested that, under some conditions (see below), co-operative agreements among firms may be instrumental to efficiently co-ordinating complementary but dissimilar activities.

This conceptualization of co-operation is in line with the previous discussion of the nature of the firm and the process of competition. Both competition and co-operation rest on the variety of firms which originates from the uniqueness of (some of) their assets and capabilities. According to such viewpoint, the main reason why firms engage in collaborative ventures is the desire to combine their own specific assets and core competencies with others which are possessed by other firms and cannot be reproduced autonomously. Such collaborative activity plays a crucial role in protecting and reinforcing firms' existing competitive advantages, and creating new ones. This is one of the key characteristics of what John Dunning calls 'alliance capitalism' in Chapter 2. It also explains the spectacular growth of the formation of co-operative relations since the early 1980s, as competitive enhancing alliances can be regarded as one of the most significant outcomes of recent technological advances and the globalization of the economy.[30]

It should nonetheless be acknowledged that in order to gain access to the required assets and capabilities, firms can also resort to other mechanisms, namely arm's length relations and hierarchical mechanisms, which rely on the price system and the use of administrative authority as a co-ordination tool, respectively.

The issue of when and why co-ordination through the price system may be inefficient, has been extensively examined by transaction cost theory (see Williamson 1975, 1979, 1981). This stream of literature has shown that when firms need the services of specific resources, arm's length relations may engender substantial (static) transaction costs.

In spite of its interest, transaction cost economics suffers from a series of shortcomings that limit its explanatory power.[31] One of its most serious drawbacks is its reliance on a *static* framework of analysis: the given characteristics of the given collection of firms' resources the services of which are required to accomplish an economic transaction, would determine the nature of the most efficient co-ordination mechanism. As is pointed out by Cantwell and Paniccia in Chapter 8, the fact that firms often face the problem of organizing activities aimed at enhancing existing capabilities or building new ones, is not adequately considered.[32] If this happens to be the case, the choice of the institutional arrangement is primarily driven by the need to minimize *learning costs* instead of (static) transaction costs. Besides the costs of alerting contractors to and persuading them of the benefits of an innovation, learning costs include both the costs of transferring capabilities and those involved by the individual (i.e., within a given firm) and joint (i.e., through the interaction with other firms) development of new expertise. They arise whenever the firm is engaged in the process of upgrading its knowledge and capabilities (Cantwell and Paniccia, Chapter 8).[33] According to such standpoint, learning costs consist in investment costs which have a positive impact on the value of the underlying activities, while (static) transaction costs are simply to be subtracted from that value.

In a more general perspective, the implications of the choice of different institutional arrangements for the evolution of firms' assets and capabilities are not taken into due account by transaction costs theory. For the purpose of the present analysis, it is especially important to emphasize that such an approach provides a very partial and biased view of the co-operation phenomenon. Actually, there may be important feedbacks between the collaborative ventures firms have entered into and the nature and evolution of firms' capabilities which can be assessed only in a dynamic framework. The set up of co-operative relations with other firms, and the interactive learning process they entail, are likely to modify, improve and extend the collection of assets and core competencies of the participating firms. This also means that both variables, that is the co-ordination mechanisms chosen by firms and their stock of resources, are endogenous; their evolution should be jointly studied.

In addition, studies inspired by transaction costs economics originally focused on the advantages of vertical and horizontal integration as a response to market failures; less attention has been devoted to the efficiency properties of collaborative arrangements, in spite of recent effort in this direction (see for instance Williamson 1985, Teece 1986). In particular, the dynamic relationships between and respective advantages of collaborative ventures and hierarchical co-ordination mechanisms (i.e., both internal development of assets and competencies and access to them through mergers and acquisitions) have gone quite unexplored in this stream of literature. In my opinion, one of the most important contributions of this volume to the economic debate on co-operation among firms resides in the attempt to enhance our understanding of this fundamental issue. In this regard, the main arguments and empirical evidence set forward in the volume can be synthesized as follows.

In the first place, it was suggested above that a firm resorts to collaborative arrangements with other firms mainly to obtain the services of resources which it lacks and is not able to build economically with no external help. However, one should stress that it is the combination of such unique assets and capabilities with its own ones that provides the firm with a sustainable competitive advantage. Absent the latter, trying to gain access to the former makes no sense. It follows that collaborative ventures are *complementary* to the autonomous development by firms of specific assets and core competencies, in the technological, productive, marketing and managerial spheres.

The empirical study by Colombo and Garrone of technological co-operative agreements in information technologies in Chapter 7, clearly supports such argument. After controlling for other firm-, industry- and country-specific variables, the estimates of a simultaneous two equation panel type econometric model show that in the 1980s, firms with higher R&D intensity did conclude a larger number of agreements aimed at developing new product and process technologies. The specific reasons why firms with considerable autonomous R&D expertise are more prone to technological co-operation are explained as follows. For one thing, R&D expenses are a pre-requisite for building an 'absorptive capacity' (Cohen and Levinthal 1989) which enables firms to take advantage of the benefits of collaborative R&D and transform it in a capabilities enhancing activity (see also Mowery and Rosenberg 1989). In addition, as substantial uncertainty surrounds innovative activity, autonomous technological capabilities are essential to effective decision-making as regards the collaborations in which a firm is involved.[34] In this sense, an autonomous expertise also contributes to limit the (static and dynamic) transaction costs typical of R&D agreements. First, a firm's switching costs to replace an underperforming partner decrease with their own stock of knowledge in the specific field of the co-operation. Second, the ability to evaluate the resources a partner brings to the venture and to monitor its behaviour increases; this in turn reduces adverse selection and moral hazard problems. Third, learning costs are likely to decrease with partners' prowess in R&D. The findings of Colombo and Garrone are confined to technological agreements. Nevertheless, the above arguments are quite general. I guess that they could be extended beyond the sphere of technology, to marketing, production and general management capabilities. Additional evidence on other types of agreements, in the same or other industries, would indeed provide further valuable insights into this quite under-researched issue.[35]

A second domain where this volume offers a significant addition to the economic debate concerns the relationships between co-operative agreements and M&As, an issue addressed in studies by Kay in Chapter 5 and Hennart and Reddy in Chapter 6. In so far as corporate strategy is concerned, alliances can be considered as *complementary* to M&As, a claim which is clearly made by John Dunning in Chapter 2. The reason is that the general rationale for them basically is the same.[36] As was explained earlier in this paragraph, both alliances and M&As originate from the desire of firms to get access to specific assets and non reproducible capabilities possessed by other firms when there is no market for their services. Nevertheless, the contributions included in this volume highlight that there are significant distinctions to be made between alliances and M&As if one wants to understand under which circumstances each institutional arrangement is preferable to the other one.

In Kay's study, the argument is set forward that at the *business unit* level, a strategy based on joint ventures represents a second-best solution with respect to one which relies on M&As.[37] Actually, joint ventures do not provide a firm's business units with any additional advantages which could not be captured by M&As. However, they do entail greater administrative and transaction costs. First, the set up of a new organizational unit is costly and there are inherent inefficiencies in joint ownership due to the greater complexity of the control chain, problems of conflicting objectives between the partners, and imperfect co-ordination. Second, there is the danger of spillovers: thanks to the intimacy gained through the joint venture, a firm's partner may be able to appropriate additional knowledge than set out in the agreement, threatening the firm's sources of competitive advantage. It follows that in order to understand why firms resort to co-operative ventures, one should turn to considering a firm's corporate strategy. At the *corporate* level, there are two situations where alliances are likely to be a first-best solution:

- when the marginal organizational costs of a merger or an acquisition for the partners are greater than those involved by an alliance, due to the inefficiencies of large bureaucratic organizations and the difficulty of co-ordinating a complex internal managerial hierarchy;
- when the assets and capabilities a firm is looking for constitute a small and inseparable part of the collection of resources possessed by the target partner; if this were the case, an acquisition would not be viable, as the acquiring firm would experience serious difficulties in disposing of the acquired and unwanted resources.

The above arguments imply that everything else being equal, one should expect large, highly diversified and internationalized companies to resort to co-operative arrangements to a larger extent than to M&As.[38] As is well known, large, complex organizations suffer from substantial bureaucratic inefficiency which imposes a limit to hierarchical growth (see Williamson 1975). This applies particularly to industries characterized by rapidly changing technological and market conditions. In addition, large firms which extensively rely on centralized, discretionary decision-making power, are likely to suffer from greater influence costs than their smaller rivals due to political activities performed within the organization and detrimental to the pursuit of profits.[39] The findings of Colombo and Garrone's study provide empirical evidence supporting such a view, though in a rather indirect way (see also Colombo 1995 and the references mentioned there). Actually, the number of technological agreements concluded by the firms included in their sample turns out to increase with firm size, the degree of diversification and that of internationalization; however, no comparison is made with the number of M&As.

More direct support to Kay's arguments is provided by Hennart and Reddy's analysis of Japanese investments in the USA over the period 1978–89, in Chapter 6. They highlight that the likelihood for a Japanese investor to resort to a greenfield joint venture with an American partner rather than to an acquisition as an entry mechanism in the USA market, significantly rises when the American target is a large, not divisionalized enterprise. According to Hennart and Reddy, the reason is that acquisitions of large, not divisionalized firms become problematic as it is difficult to separate the desired from the non-desired assets and the resulting firm would operate in industries and at a scale which do not fit well with the characteristics of the acquirer.

It is fundamental to emphasize at this stage that the conceptualization of co-operative agreements which I have proposed, is neutral from the standpoint of social efficiency. Joint ventures and other collaborative agreements are institutional arrangements aimed at combining the idiosyncratic assets and capabilities possessed by different firms, for the services of which there is no market. Everything else being equal, this has a positive impact on the efficient use of the available resources within the economic system. However, this statement requires some specifications. For one thing, as is argued in the study by Pitelis in Chapter 3, one cannot separate the consideration of efficiency from that of power, as it is through efficiency improvements that power is often obtained.[40] In particular, Pitelis claims that power is a driving force, complementary to knowledge, in explaining subcontracting agreements, joint ventures and strategic alliances. In addition, earlier in this chapter I mentioned that the available empirical evidence seems to suggest that co-operative relations are predominantly used by large oligopolistic firms to deal with rapid technical advance and the globalization of markets. Even though such collaborations are likely to increase the efficiency and flexibility of the operations of those firms, they may also lead to an increase in market power. Hence, whether co-operative relations have the effect to step up or reduce competition is an open question which is waiting for additional research work. Nonetheless, that a network of alliances may help leader firms protect and consolidate their dominant position is quite likely. Looking at the high definition TV, computer and pharmaceutical industries, Delapierre and Mytelka show in Chapter 4 that the establishment of a network of alliances among incumbent firms in those industries in the 1980s resulted in the set up of new entry barriers by setting industry standards and enabled participating firms to reduce the shocks of radical technical change and maintain their competitive position in the global oligopoly.

Furthermore, it should be emphasized that even if one focuses on private efficiency, there may be a trade-off between static and dynamic efficiency. As was stated earlier, institutional choices concerning the boundaries of the firm (that is, use of collaborative agreements instead of other institutional arrangements) are to be related to firms' attempt to gain access to and combine heterogeneous distinctive capabilities. In turn, such choices do influence the evolution of firms' own set of capabilities. Accordingly, decisions which conform to allocative efficiency criteria (i.e., minimizing the costs and maximizing the rewards from use of a given set of capabilities) may turn out to be inefficient in the light of the goal of improving and extending a firm's expertise. More importantly, the relative (static and dynamic) efficiency of the different institutional arrangements to which a firm may resort, depends on the evolving and partly endogenous characteristics of the firm and its environment. In other words, a firm's institutional choices at a given time are contingent on (a) the nature of the assets and core competencies the firm is equipped with, (b) the nature of the resources possessed by potential partners/targets, and (c) the characteristics of the technological, economic, and institutional setting in which the firm is embedded. However, such decisions do have a bearing on the characteristics of economic agents and their environment in a subsequent period. This means that the boundaries of the firm are path-dependent and possibly subject to lock-in effects. This approach has a number of interesting implications.

First, the level of specificity of the assets required for efficient operation and the role played by firms' unique capabilities in assuring sustainable competitive advantages depend on sector- and time-specific factors. *Ceteris paribus*, their importance is greater in industries where the tacit, context-specific component of knowledge prevails over the codified one and in stages of industry evolution when radical technical and/or institutional changes create substantial uncertainty as to the winning technological solutions and the characteristics of market demand. Under such circumstances, one should expect organizational patterns to emerge which extensively rely on both vertical and horizontal integration and use of co-operative arrangements.[41]

Second, adoption by firms of an emerging organizational pattern of success is constrained by the contingent factors mentioned above. Therefore, it involves an evolutionary Lamarckian process of adaptation, which takes time as it requires the progressive modification of firms' routinized capabilities and may even be inhibited by lock-in effects. In addition, the organizational pattern of success must be adapted to the specificities of firms, industries, and countries. This is quite apparent from the theoretical and empirical studies in the section of the volume devoted to subcontracting relations. In Chapter 9, Nooteboom analyses different stylized organizational patterns of subcontracting relations: adversarial, co-operative bilateral and co-operative multilateral relations.[42] Such subcontracting systems differ on the basis of the degree of co-operation between buyers and suppliers and the characteristics of the learning processes involved in supply relations. When relations are adversarial, actors focus on independence and the benefits of multiple sourcing; suppliers can capture economies of scale and buyers can ask for competitive prices; co-operation and learning are sacrificed. With co-operative bilateral relations, partners take advantage of mutual learning and a co-operative attitude to price setting; in addition, exclusivity reduces the risks of spillovers. With co-operative multilateral relations, firms enjoy the additional benefits arising from exposure to a variety of learning sources, even though spillovers need to be prevented by use of sophisticated monitoring and opportunism deterring devices. The performances of the different systems depend on exogenous conditions concerning the relative importance of economies of scale on the one hand and relation-specific investments, learning processes between buyers and suppliers and mechanisms aimed at blocking spillovers on the other. However, Nooteboom's game-theoretic model also shows that such organizational patterns are self-enforcing: even though a particular organizational arrangement may be more efficient than the others under some circumstances, there is no guarantee that the corresponding strategies will be adopted by buyers and suppliers. 'Autonomy breeds autonomy, and co-operation breeds co-operation'. In other words, lock-in effects into existing practices may prevent the emergence of the most efficient solution. This holds true especially when changes in the characteristics of firms and their environment induce a change in the relative performance of different organizational solutions.

Empirical evidence in line with Nooteboom's core arguments, is provided in Chapters 10 and 11 by Helper's, and Esposito and Raffa's studies. They concern the adoption by Western enterprises (US component firms in the automobile industry and Italian subcontractors in various metalworking industries, respectively) of Japanese so-called best-practices in supply relations.[43] Helper's findings basically are in support of the transferability of Japanese organizational pattern to Western economies. Nonetheless, they also witness that imitation requires time and sequential adjustments of firms' routines through the set up of specific learning mechanisms. For this purpose, imitation of the transplants of Japanese component firms by US component firms is shown to be far less efficient than the establishment of co-operative subcontracting relations with the transplants of Japanese car assemblers. In addition, adoption of Japanese-style supply relations proves to be far from ubiquitous in the US car industry. Esposito and Raffa describe the recent evolution of Italian subcontracting; in accordance with the characteristics of the Japanese model, they highlight the greater importance of vertical (i.e., between the buyer and the suppliers) and horizontal (i.e., among the suppliers of a given buyer) transfers of technology. These relate especially to the intangible, tacit component of firms' knowledge. Nonetheless, the intensity of the transfers and the kinds of assets and capabilities which are transferred, turn out to depend crucially on the characteristics of the firms and the sectors in which they operate.

Notes

1 The financial support of 1996 FAR funds is gratefully acknowledged. I would like to thank Sergio Mariotti for helpful discussion of the topics covered in this work. Responsibility for any errors lies solely with the author.

2 There are a number of mechanisms that can be used to prevent firms – participating in collusive agreements – from cheating. Their consideration goes beyond the purposes of the present work. See again Jacquemin and Slade (1989).

3 See for instance Reynolds and Snapp (1986), Bresnahan and Salop (1986), Kwoka (1992), Reitman (1994).

4 The seminal works are Brander and Spencer (1984), Spence (1984), Katz (1986), D'Aspremont and Jacquemin (1988). More recent contributions are surveyed by De Bondt (1996). These issues have also been addressed by works in the 'patent races' literature. For a general analysis, see Katz and Ordover (1990). For a survey, see Reinganum (1989).

5 For instance, arrangements of this kind are common in the oil industry, where oil companies jointly own pipeline facilities and/or exploration fields.

6 The main reference is the literature on 'vertical foreclosure'. See for instance Hart and Tirole (1990).

7 Fusfeld (1958), in probably the first empirical study on this issue, emphasized the anti-competitive practices associated with the establishment by US large firms in the iron and steel industry of a considerable number of joint subsidiaries, aimed primarily at backward vertical integration in iron and/or coal mining.

8 In a two-ways communication network, the n-th customer provides a positive externality to all other $(n-1)$ customers by adding $(n-1)$ additional links to the network, thus creating $2(n-1)$ potential new goods.

9 In this case, if (a) users make their purchases over time, (b) complementary components are specific (for instance, the software is platform-specific), and (c) the production of the component whose purchase is delayed (i.e., the software) enjoys economies of scale, consumers will tend to prefer in time t the hardware platform for which the less expensive software will be available in time $(t+1)$. This means that consumers will stay with a technologically inferior platform with a larger installed base, if they expect the larger installed base to lead to a lower price for software.

10 Mainly for the sake of synthesis, I have neglected to discuss the contributions of incomplete contract theory and repeated game theory, which are to be considered as germane to the neo-classical tradition. As to the former, suffice here to say that in spite of its interest, studies in this literature are mainly oriented to understanding the contractual characteristics and the incentives embodied in different contractual arrangements. As to the latter, its main contribution resides in suggesting mechanisms to structure alliances so as to promote robust cooperation. Hence, their consideration does not substantially alter the essence of my arguments.

11 On this issue see the study by Neil Kay in Chapter 5.

12 Among the pioneering contributions see Rosenberg (1976), Nelson and Winter (1977), Nelson and Winter (1982), Dosi (1982) and Pavitt (1984). Recent surveys include Dosi and Nelson (1994) and Nelson (1995).

13 Simon (1959: 273) emphasizes the selection role played by the 'bottleneck of the perceptual apparatus' which performs 'an active process involving attention to a very small part of the whole and exclusion, from the outset, of almost all that is not within the scope of attention'. For a criticism of the failure by mainstream economics to recognize the subjective nature of knowledge, as opposed to the objective one of the externally available information, see for instance Hodgson (1988).

14 Fransmann (1994: 716) uses the term 'interpretative ambiguity' to characterize such situations.

15 Marengo (1994) highlights the trade-off between the need to promote diversity of approaches within a given organization as a source of innovative behaviour and the need to have a coherent representation of the world among the individuals that compose the organization. For this purpose, the development of a set of rules, codes and languages shared by the members of the organization – a 'corporate culture' following Crémer (1990) – plays a fundamental role. On this issue see also Dosi and Marengo (1994).

16 For instance Lundvall and Johnson (1994) distinguish four categories: (a) know-what (that is, knowledge about facts); (b) know-why (knowledge about natural, human, and social principles and laws); (c) know-how (the capabilities of doing something well); and (d) know-who (knowing who knows what, who knows how to do what, and how to establish social relations with them).

17 See the pioneering work by Polany (1967). See also the discussion of this issue in Nelson and Winter (1982: 76–82).

18 The above mentioned distinction between 'tacit' and 'codified' knowledge largely corresponds to the one between 'procedural' and 'declarative' knowledge (see Cohen 1991; Cohen and Bacdayan 1994). The latter constitutes explicit knowledge of facts and theories; the former centres on individual and collective know-how, can be retained longer, and is quite difficult to verbalize (i.e., to be transformed into codified knowledge) and transmit.

19 In this perspective, there clearly is a correspondence between this taxonomy and the one proposed by Lundvall and Johnson (1994) and mentioned in note 16. On the one hand, know-what and know-why essentially refer to codified knowledge. On the other, know-how and know-who basically include knowledge of a more tacit nature, related to practical and social experiences, respectively.

20 A radically different view is proposed by Dasgupta and David (1994) and David and Foray (1995). These authors argue that the differences in the extent to which knowledge gets codified rather than retained in tacit form reflect the reward structure as well as the costs of codification. 'Going back to Polany's perceptual analogy, what gets brought into focus (and codified), and what remains in the background (as tacit knowledge) will be, for us, something to be explained endogenously by reference to the structure(s) of pecuniary and non-pecuniary rewards and costs facing the agents involved' (Dasgupta and David 1994: 495). Relying on such a view, they also claim that there is a long-term tendency towards increasing codification and that such a trend has been accelerated by the diffusion of information technology. First, the existence of information infrastructure suitable to transmission of codified knowledge makes it more attractive to put knowledge in such a form. Second, information technology makes available new techniques (for instance, computer simulation) which allow production of knowledge in a codified form. While I accept the argument that the degree of tacitness is influenced by the decisions of economic agents, I contend that those decisions are constrained by the intrinsic nature of different kinds of knowledge. In other words, the opportunities to codify knowledge and then the degree of tacitness are to a large extent determined exogenously. For an interesting discussion of such issues, see Lundvall (1996).

21 Simon (1978) distinguishes 'substantial rationality', that is 'the extent to which appropriate courses of actions are chosen', from 'procedural rationality', defined as 'the effectiveness, in light of human cognitive powers and limitations, of the procedures used to choose actions'.

22 According to Knight (1921), there are two forms of uncertainty: risk, that is to say

statistically measurable uncertainty, and radical uncertainty. In a world of true (i.e., non measurable) uncertainty, the outcomes of the possible courses of actions, or even the set of the available actions are not known *ex ante*; thus, uncertainty does not allow a statistical description of the relevant phenomena. Under many circumstances the main source of uncertainty resides in the limitations of the cognitive capabilities of economic agents, which cannot be improved by mere collection of additional information. 'Bayesian decision making reduces all uncertainty to mere risk. It cannot account therefore for another fundamental source of uncertainty: ignorance' (Dosi and Marengo 1994: 161). On these issues see also the discussion of procedural uncertainty as opposed to substantive uncertainty by Dosi and Egidi (1991), with the former kind of uncertainty being based on lack of information and the latter one being centred around a competencies gap, and the work by Brian Loasby (for instance Loasby 1976).

23 For a detailed analysis of such argument, see Fransmann (1994). Differences among the above mentioned bodies of literature concern both the sources of information asymmetries and the mechanisms to deal with them: for a survey see Holmström and Tirole (1989). The divergences between contractual and competence-based (see below) theories of the firm are effectively synthesized by Foss (1993).

24 This view has been rapidly gaining momentum in the strategic management literature due to the acknowledgement of the role played by a firm's unique resources in obtaining sustainable competitive advantages. See Wernerfelt (1984), Barney (1986), Dierickx and Cool (1989).

25 I will use the terms core (or distinctive) competencies and capabilities as synonyms.

26 On these and related issues see Hodgson (1994a), Langlois (1994), Langlois and Robertson (1995), Teece and Pisano (1994), Foss (1996) and Teece *et al.* (1997).

27 See the analysis of routines in Nelson and Winter (1982). For a critical review of the concept of routines and its relation to firms' distinctive capabilities, see Cohen *et al.* (1996).

28 See the related literature on organizational learning, for instance Holland (1975), Argyris and Schön (1978), Fiol and Lyles (1985) and Cohen and Sproull (1996).

29 On this issue, see Lundvall (1988). See also Chapter 9 by Bart Nooteboom (in this volume) and the references mentioned there.

30 On the determinants of the surge in collaborative arrangements see also the study by Delapierre and Mytelka in Chapter 4.

31 For a radical criticism of the assumption of efficiency underlying the transaction cost approach, see the study by Pitelis in Chapter 3.

32 Nooteboom (1992) emphasizes empirical anomalies that cannot be explained by transaction cost economics, notably the extensive recourse to outsourcing of productive inputs in spite of high specificity of the required investments and high technological and market uncertainty.

33 The distinction between learning costs and dynamic transaction costs as were defined by Langlois (Langlois 1992; Langlois and Robertson 1995), is extensively discussed in the study by Cantwell and Paniccia (Chapter 8).

34 Such activities include identifying the most promising fields for joint research, selecting partners on the basis of a sound appraisal of their own technological capabilities, and evaluating the possible implications of the results of joint R&D.

35 Some recent econometric studies have examined the influence exerted on the likelihood to co-operate by the similarity between firms' fields of technological specialization, and the impact of co-operation upon changes in alliance partners'

technological capabilities. See Mowery *et al*. (1996), Nakamura *et al*. (1996) and Mowery *et al*. (1998).

36 This is apparent if one considers the lists of the advantages a firm can obtain through alliances on the one hand and M&As on the other, which are quite popular among managers and consultants.

37 Even though Kay focuses on joint ventures, the reasoning could be also applied to other kinds of agreements.

38 In a dynamic framework, one could also interpret the above arguments as suggesting an evolutionary path according to which firms move from an initial organizational stage where the focus primarily is on the internal development of specific resources, to one where M&As prevail, to a maturity stage where the emphasis is placed on collaborative arrangements.

39 Influence costs are defined by Milgrom and Roberts (1990: 58) as 'the losses that arise from individuals within an organization seeking to influence its decision for their private benefit (and from their perhaps succeeding in doing so) and from the organization's responding to control this behaviour'.

40 This implies that a predatory view of the choice of institutional arrangements, opposed to the efficiency enhancing view shared by the transaction cost literature, cannot be entirely rejected. See the discussion of this issue by Pitelis (Chapter 3) and the references mentioned there.

41 This issue is addressed in Kay's and Cantwell and Paniccia's chapters. For an analysis of the evolution of firms' propensity towards co-operative relations along technological project entries, see Cainarca *et al*. (1992).

42 Adversarial relations are typical of the Western traditional subcontracting system, based on multiple sourcing. Bilateral and multilateral co-operative relations are rather similar to sole and parallel sourcing, as were defined by Richardson (1993), respectively.

43 The description of such practices goes beyond the purpose of the present chapter. See the references in Helper's study (Chapter 10).

References

Alchian, A. (1950) 'Uncertainty, evolution and economic theory', *Journal of Political Economy* 58: 211–22.

Alchian, A. and Demsetz, H. (1972) 'Production, information costs, and economic organization', *American Economic Review* 62: 777–95.

Argyris, C. and Schön, D. (1978) *Organizational Learning*, Reading, MA: Addison-Wesley.

Arrow, K.J. (1962) 'Economic welfare and the allocation of resources for invention', in *The Rate and Direction of Inventive Activity: Economic and Social Factors*, NBER Conference No. 13, Princeton, NJ: Princeton University Press.

Barney, J. (1986) 'Strategic factor markets: expectations, luck, and business strategy', *Management Science* 32: 1,231–41.

Brander, J.A. and Spencer, B.J. (1984) 'Strategic commitment with R&D: the symmetric case', *Bell Journal of Economics* 14: 225–35.

Bresnahan, T. and Salop, S. (1986) 'Quantifying the competitive effects of production joint ventures', *International Journal of Industrial Organization* 4: 155–75.

Cainarca, G.C., Colombo, M.G. and Mariotti, S. (1992) 'Agreements between firms and the technological life cycle model', *Research Policy* 21: 45–62.

Coase, R.H. (1937) 'The nature of the firm', *Economica* 4: 386–405.

Cohen, M.D. (1991) 'Individual learning and organizational routines', *Organization Science*, 2; repr. in M.D. Cohen and L.S. Sproull (eds) *Organizational Learning*, London: Sage, 1996.

Cohen, M.D. and Bacdayan, P. (1994) 'Organizational routines are stored as procedural memory: evidence from a laboratory study', *Organization Science* 5: 554–68.

Cohen, M.D., Burkhart, R., Dosi, G., Egidi, M., Marengo, L., Warglien, M. and Winter, S. (1996) 'Routines and other recurring action patterns of organizations: contemporary research issues', *Industrial and Corporate Change* 5: 653–98.

Cohen, M.D. and Sproull, L.S. (eds) (1996) *Organizational Learning*, London: Sage.

Cohen, W.M. and Levinthal, D.A. (1989) 'Innovation and learning: the two faces of R&D', *Economic Journal* 99: 569–96.

Colombo, M.G. (1995) 'Firm size and cooperation: the determinants of cooperative agreements in information technology industries', *International Journal of the Economics of Business* 2: 3–29.

Cournot, A. (1927) *Researches into the Mathemathical Principles of the Theory of Wealth*, New York: Macmillan (originally published in French in 1838).

Crémer, J. (1990) 'Common knowledge and the co-ordination of economic activities', in M. Aoki, B. Gustafsson and O.E. Williamson (eds) *The Firm as a Nexus of Treaties*, London: Sage.

D'Aspremont, C. and Jacquemin, A. (1988) 'Cooperative and noncooperative R&D in duopoly with spillovers', *American Economic Review* 78: 1,133–7.

Dasgupta, P. and David, P. (1994) 'Towards a new economics of science', *Research Policy* 23: 487–521.

David, P. and Foray, D. (1995) 'Accessing and expanding the science and technology knowledge-base', *STI-Review*, OECD, 16: 13–68.

De Bondt, R. (1996) 'Spillovers and innovative activities', *International Journal of Industrial Organisation*, 15: 1–28.

Dierickx, I. and Cool, K. (1989) 'Asset stock accumulation and sustainability of competitive advantage', *Management Science* 35: 1,504–11.

Dosi, G. (1982) 'Technological paradigms and technological trajectories: a suggested interpretation of the determinants and directions of technical change', *Research Policy* 11: 47–62.

—— (1988) 'Sources, procedures, and microeconomic effects of innovation', *Journal of Economic Literature* 26: 1,120–71.

Dosi, G. and Egidi, M. (1991) 'Substantive and procedural uncertainty', *Journal of Evolutionary Economics* 1: 145–68.

Dosi, G. and Marengo, L. (1994) 'Some elements of an evolutionary theory of organizational competences', in R.W. England (ed.) *Evolutionary Concepts in Contemporary Economics*, Ann Arbor, MI: Michigan University Press.

Dosi G. and Nelson R.R. (1994) 'An introduction to evolutionary theories in economics', *Journal of Evolutionary Economics* 4: 153–72.

Economides, N. (1996) 'The economics of networks', *International Journal of Industrial Organization* 14: 673–99.

Fiol, C.M. and Lyles, M.A. (1985) 'Organizational learning', *Academy of Management Review* 10: 803–13.

Foss, N.J. (1993) 'Theories of the firm: contractual and competence perspectives', *Journal of Evolutionary Economics* 3: 127–44.

—— (1996) 'Capabilities and the theory of the firm', *Revue d'Economie Industrielle* 77: 7–28.

Fransmann, M. (1994) 'Information, knowledge, vision, and the theory of the firm', *Industrial and Corporate Change* 3: 713–57.

Fusfeld, D.R. (1958) 'Joint subsidiaries in the iron and steel industry', *American Economic Review* 48: 578–87.

Grossman, S. and Hart, O. (1986) 'The costs and benefits of ownership: a theory of vertical integration', *Journal of Political Economy* 94: 691–719.

Hart, O.D. and Tirole, J. (1990) 'Vertical integration and market foreclosure', *Brookings Papers on Economic Activity: Microeconomics* 205–86.

Hodgson, G.M. (1988) *Economics and Institutions*, Oxford: Polity Press.

—— (1994a) 'Evolutionary and competence-based theories of the firm', University of Cambridge, Research Papers in Management Studies, No. 26.

—— (1994b) 'Decomposition and growth: biological metaphors in economics from the 1880s to the 1980s', University of Cambridge, Research Papers in Management Studies, No. 28.

Holland, J.H. (1975) *Adaptation in Natural and Artificial Systems*, Ann Arbor, MI: University of Michigan Press.

Holmström, B. and Tirole, J. (1989) 'The theory of the firm', in R. Schmalensee and D. Willig (eds) *Handbook of Industrial Organisation*, Amsterdam: North Holland.

Jacquemin, A. and Slade, M.E. (1989) 'Cartels, collusion, and horizontal mergers', in R. Schmalensee and D. Willig (eds) *Handbook of Industrial Organisation*, Amsterdam: North Holland.

Jensen, M. and Meckling, W. (1976) 'Theory of the firm: managerial behavior, agency costs, and ownership structure', *Journal of Financial Economics* 3: 305–60.

Katz, M.L. (1986) 'An analysis of cooperative research and development', *Rand Journal of Economics* 17: 527–43.

Katz, M.L. and Ordover, J.A. (1990) 'R&D cooperation and competition', *Brookings Papers on Economic Activity: Microeconomics* 137–203.

Katz, M. L and Shapiro, C. (1994) 'Systems competition and network effects', *Journal of Economic Perspectives* 8: 93–116.

Kamien, M.I., Muller, E. and Zang, I. (1992) 'Research joint ventures and R&D cartels', *American Economic Review* 82: 1,293–1,306.

Knight, F. (1921) *Risk, Uncertainty, and Profit*, Boston, MA: Houghton Mifflin.

Kwoka, J.E. (1992) 'The output and profit effects of horizontal joint ventures', *Journal of Industrial Economics* 40: 325–38.

Langlois, R.N. (1992) 'Transaction-cost economics in real time', *Industrial and Corporate Change* 1: 99–127.

—— (1994) 'Capabilities and the theory of the firm', paper prepared for the colloquium in honour of G.B. Richardson, St John's College, Oxford.

Langlois, R.N. and Robertson, P.L. (1995) *Firms, Markets, and Economic Change: A Dynamic Theory of Business Institutions*, London: Routledge.

Loasby, B.J. (1976) *Choice, Complexity, and Ignorance*, Cambridge: Cambridge University Press.

Lundvall, B.Å. (1988) 'Innovation as an interactive process: from user-producer interaction to the national system of innovation', in G. Dosi, C. Freeman, R.R. Nelson, G. Silverberg and L. Soete (eds) *Technical Change and Economic Theory*, London and New York: Pinter Publishers, 1990.

—— (1996) 'The Social Dimension of the Learning Economy', DRUID Working Paper, No. 96–1.

Lundvall, B.Å. and Johnson, B. (1994) 'The learning economy', *Journal of Industry Studies* 1: 23–42.

Malerba, F. (1992) 'Learning by firms and incremental change', *Economic Journal* 102: 845–59.

Marengo, L. (1994) 'Coordination and organizational learning in the firm', *Journal of Evolutionary Economics* 2: 313–26.

Milgrom, P. and Roberts, J. (1990) 'Bargaining costs, influence costs, and the organization of economic activity', in J. Alt and K. Shepsle (eds) *Perspectives on Positive Political Economy*, Cambridge: Cambridge University Press.

Mowery, D.C. and Rosenberg, N. (1989) *Technology and the Pursuit of Economic Growth*, Cambridge: Cambridge University Press.

Mowery, D.C., Oxley, J.E. and Silverman, B.S. (1996) 'Strategic alliances and interfirm knowledge transfer', *Strategic Management Journal* 17: 77–91.

—— (1998) 'Technological overlap and interfirm cooperation: implications for the resource-based view of the firm', *Research Policy*, forthcoming.

Nakamura, M., Shaver, J.M. and Yeung, B. (1996) 'An empirical investigation of joint venture dynamics: evidence from US-Japan joint ventures', *International Journal of Industrial Organization* 14: 521–41.

Nelson, R.R. (1995) 'Recent evolutionary theorizing about economic change', *Journal of Economic Literature* 33: 48–90.

Nelson, R.R. and Winter, S.G. (1977) 'In search of a useful theory of innovation', *Research Policy* 6: 37–76.

—— (1982) *An Evolutionary Theory of Economic Change*, Cambridge, MA: The Belknap Press of Harvard University Press.

Nooteboom, B. (1992) 'Towards a dynamic theory of transactions', *Journal of Evolutionary Economics* 2: 281–99.

—— (1996) 'Globalization, learning and strategy', EMOT workshop, Durham.

Pavitt, K. (1984) 'Sectoral patterns of innovation: toward a taxonomy and a theory', *Research Policy* 13: 343–75.

Penrose, E.T. (1959) *The Theory of the Growth of the Firm*, New York: Wiley.

Polanyi, M. (1967) *The Tacit Dimension*, Garden City, New York: Doubleday Anchor.

Prahalad, C.K. and Hamel, G. (1990) 'The core competence of the corporation', *Harvard Business Review* May–June: 79–91.

Reinganum, J. (1989) 'The timing of innovation: research, development, and diffusion', in R. Schmalensee and D. Willig (eds) *Handbook of Industrial Organisation*, Amsterdam: North Holland.

Reitman, D. (1994) 'Partial ownership arrangements and the potential for collusion', *Journal of Industrial Economics* 42: 313–22.

Reynolds, R. and Snapp, B. (1986) 'The competitive effects of partial equity interests and joint ventures', *International Journal of Industrial Organization* 4: 141–53.

Richardson, G.B. (1972) 'The organisation of industry', *Economic Journal* 82: 883–96.

Richardson, J. (1993) 'Parallel sourcing and supplier performance in the Japanese automobile industry', *Strategic Management Journal* 14: 339–50.

Rosenberg, N. (1976) *Perspectives on Technology*, Cambridge: Cambridge University Press.

Schumpeter, J.A. (1950) *Capitalism, Socialism, and Democracy*, New York: Harper (3rd edn).

Simon, H.A. (1959) 'Theories of decision making in economics and behavioral science', *American Economic Review* 49: 253–83.

—— (1978) 'Rationality as process and as product of thought', *American Economic Review* 68: 1–16.

Spence, A.M. (1984) 'Cost reduction, competition and industrial performance', *Econometrica* 52: 101–21.

Teece, D.J. (1986) 'Profiting from technological innovation: implications for integration, collaboration, licensing, and public policy', *Research Policy* 15: 285–305.

Teece, D.J. and Pisano, G. (1994) 'The dynamic capabilities of firms: an introduction', *Industrial and Corporate Change* 3: 537–56.

Teece, D.J., Pisano, G. and Shuen, A. (1997) 'Dynamic capabilities and strategic management', *Strategic Management Journal* 18: 509–34.

Teece, D.J., Rumelt, R., Dosi, G. and Winter, S. (1994) 'Understanding corporate coherence, Theory and evidence', *Journal of Economic Behavior and Organization* 23: 1–30.

Wernerfelt, B. (1984) 'A resource-based view of the firm', *Strategic Management Journal* 5: 171–80.

Williamson, O.E. (1975) *Markets and Hierarchies: Analysis and Antitrust Implications. A Study in the Economics of Internal Organization*, New York: Free Press.

—— (1979) 'Transaction-cost economics: the governance of contractual relations', *Journal of Law and Economics* 22: 233–61.

—— (1981) 'The modern corporation: origins, evolution, attributes', *Journal of Economic Literature* 19: 1,537–68.

—— (1985) *The Economic Institutions of Capitalism*, New York: Free Press.

Winter, S.G. (1988) 'On Coase, competence, and the corporation', *Journal of Law, Economics, and Organization* 4: 163–80.

Part I

ALLIANCE CAPITALISM?

2

REAPPRAISING THE ECLECTIC PARADIGM IN AN AGE OF ALLIANCE CAPITALISM

John H. Dunning

Introduction

Over the last decade or so, a number of events have occurred which, viewed collectively, suggest that the world economy may be entering a new phase of market-based capitalism – or, at least, changing its trajectory of the past century. These events recognize no geographical boundaries; and they range from changes in the way in which individual firms are organizing their production and transactions, to a reconfiguration of location specific assets and the globalization of many kinds of economic activity.

The pre-eminent driving force behind these events has been a series of systemic technological and political changes, of which a new generation of telecommunication advances and the demise of central planning in Eastern Europe and China are, perhaps, the most dramatic. But, no less far reaching has been the economic rejuvenation of Japan and the emergence of several new industrial powers – especially from east Asia – whose approach to market-based capitalism – both at a socio-institutional and a techno-economic level (Freeman and Perez 1988) – is very different from that long practised by Western nations.

The inter-related and cumulative effects of these phenomena have compelled scholars to re-examine some of their cherished concepts about market based capitalism – and to do so in two major respects. The first is that the growing acceptance that, by themselves, competitive market forces do not necessarily ensure an optimum innovation led growth path in a dynamic and uncertain world. This is partly because technology is an endogenous variable – not an exogenous one as assumed in the received literature – and partly because the pressures of frequent and unpredictable technological and political changes do not permit a Pareto optimal allocation of resources (Pigou

1932). With the acceleration of technological change, and a growing emphasis on institutional learning and continuous product improvement, both the concepts and the policy prescriptions of our predecessors are becoming less relevant each day.

The second revered concept which is now under scrutiny, is that the resources and competencies of wealth creating institutions are largely independent of each other; and that individual enterprises are best able to advance their economic objectives, and those of society, by competition, rather than co-operation. Unlike the first idea, this concept has only been severely challenged over the last decade, although, for more than a century, scholars have acknowledged that the behaviour of firms may be influenced by the actions of their competitors (Cournot 1851); while Alfred Marshall (1920) was one of the first economists to recognize that the spatial clustering or agglomeration of firms with related interests might yield agglomerative economies and an industrial atmosphere external to the individual firms, but internal to the cluster.

It is the purpose of this chapter to consider some of the implications of the changes now taking place in the global market-place economy for our understanding about the determinants of multinational enterprise (MNE) activity; and especially for our own framework of analysis, namely the eclectic paradigm of international production.[1] The main thrust of the chapter is to argue that, although the autonomous firm will continue to be the main unit of analysis for analysing the extent and pattern of foreign owned production, the OLI (ownership/location/internalization) configuration determining trans-border activities is being increasingly affected by the collaborative production and transactional arrangements it engages in with other firms; and that these need to be more systematically incorporated into the eclectic paradigm. But, prior to subjecting this idea to closer examination, we briefly outline the underlying assumptions of the extant theory of MNE activity in the mid-1980s.

Hierarchical capitalism

For most of the present century, the deployment of resources and capabilities in market oriented economies has been shaped by a micro-organizational system known as Fordism and a macro-institutional system known as hierarchical capitalism.[2] The essential characteristic of both these systems is that the governance of production and transactions is determined by the relative costs and benefits of using markets and firms as alternative organizational modes. In conditions of perfect competition, where exchange and co-ordination costs are zero and where there are no externalities of production or consumption, all transactions will be determined by market forces. Business entities will buy their inputs at arm's length prices from independent firms and households; and sell their outputs at arm's length prices to independent purchasers.

In practice, such a governance structure has rarely existed; to some degree, all markets contain some impurities. Such impurities are of two kinds. The first is structural market failure, which follow the actions of participants in or outside the market to distort the conditions of demand or supply. The second is endemic or natural market failure, where either, given the conditions of supply and demand, the market *qua* market is unable to organize transactions in an optimal way, *or* it is difficult to predict the behaviour of the participants. Such endemic market failure essentially reflects the presence of uncertainty, externalities, and the inability of producers to fully capture increasing returns to scale in conditions of infinite demand elasticity. It also accepts that, rather than perfect cognition and profit or utility, maximizing behaviour on the part of the transaction in the market, bounded rationality, information asymmetries and opportunism are more realistic principles governing economic conduct (Williamson 1985, 1993).

It is partly to avoid or circumvent such market imperfections, and partly to recoup the gains of a unified governance of inter-related activities, that single activity firms choose to internalize intermediate product markets and, in so doing, become diversified firms. To co-ordinate these different activities, the administrative system takes on the guise of a hierarchy; and as Alfred Chandler (1962, 1990) has well demonstrated, as US firms internalized more markets in the last quarter of the nineteenth century, so hierarchical capitalism came to replace 'arm's length' capitalism.

Throughout most of the present century, as economic activity has become increasingly specialized and more complex, and as technological advances and political forces have created more endemic market imperfections, the role of large hierarchies, relative to that of markets, as an organizational modality has intensified. At the firm level, the fully integrated production facilities of enterprises like the Ford Motor Company in the 1960s epitomized the *raison d'être* for, and the extreme form of, hierarchical capitalism;[3] hence the coining of the term 'Fordism'. At a sectoral level, the proportion of output from most industrial countries supplied by vertically integrated or horizontally diversified firms rose throughout most of the twentieth century.[4] Until the late 1970s, scholars usually considered co-operative forms of organizing economic activity as *alternatives* to hierarchies or markets, rather than as part and parcel of an organizational *system of firms*, in which inter-firm and intra-firm transactions complement each other. This, in part, reflected the fact that, in the main, economists viewed the boundary of a firm as the point at which its owners relinquished *de jure* control over resource harnessing and usage; and, to a large extent, this boundary was thought to be coincident with a loss of majority equity ownership. It is not surprising, then, that for the most part, minority joint ventures were regarded as a second best alternative to full ownership. At the same time, most contractual arrangements were considered as market transactions – even in situations in which there was some element of a continuing and information sharing relationship between the parties to the exchange.

We would mention two other important features of twentieth century hierarchical capitalism. The first is that it implicitly assumes that the prosperity
of firms depends exclusively on the way in which their management internally
organizes the resources and capabilities at their disposal. These include the
purchased inputs from other firms and the marketing and distribution of
outputs. Admittedly, the behaviour of such firms might be affected by the
strategies of other firms, e.g., oligopolistic competitors, monopolistic suppliers,
large customers and labour unions. But, with these exceptions, in hierarchical
capitalism the external transactions of firms are assumed to be *exogenous*, rather
than *endogenous*, to their portfolio of assets and skills, and to the way in which
these assets and skills are combined with each other to create further value
added advantages.

The second characteristic of hierarchical capitalism is that firms primarily
react to endemic and structural market failure by adopting 'exit', rather than
'voice' type strategies. Alfred Hirschman (1970) first introduced this concept
of exit and voice to explain the responses of firms and States to threats to their
economic sovereignty. He postulated two such responses, namely 'exit' to a
better alternative, and 'voice', which he defined as any attempt at all to
change, rather than escape from, an objectionable state of affairs (Hirschman
1970: 30). Borrowing from Hirschman's terminology, we might identify two
reactions of firms to the presence of market failure. These are:

1   to 'exit', where the response is to replace the market by internal adminis-
    trative fiat, and
2   to 'voice', where the response is to work with the market (in this case the
    buyers of its products or the sellers of its purchases) to reduce or eliminate
    market failure.

Our reading of the *raison d'être* for hierarchical capitalism, particularly its
US brand, is that it was (and still is) an 'exit' type reaction to market failure.[5]
To a limited extent, 'voice' strategies are evident in joint equity ventures and
contractual agreements and in compensatory institutional instruments – e.g.,
futures and insurance markets. But, in general, collaborative production,
marketing or innovatory projects or problem solving are eschewed. Contract
disputes are usually resolved by litigation procedures rather than by propiti-
ating attempts to remove the cause of the disputes. Competition and
adversarial relations, rather than co-operation and synergistic affinities, are the
hallmarks of hierarchical capitalism; and this is evident in the conduct of both
inter-firm and intra-firm co-ordination procedures and transactions.
Hierarchical capitalism rarely interprets the roles of firms and governments as
being complementary to each other (World Bank 1992).

It is beyond the scope of this chapter either to trace the factors which led to
hierarchical capitalism and the scale system of production, or to describe its
characteristics in any detail. Suffice to mention that, between the mid-1870s

and the early 1970s, a series of technological, organizational and financial events occurred which helped reduce the transaction and co-ordination costs of multiactivity hierarchies relative to those of arm's length intermediate product markets. Moreover, in contrast to the craft system of production which preceded it, the main impact of the mass production system was felt in the fabricating or assembling, rather than in the processing sectors. And, it was in the former sectors where – in order to better co-ordinate the stages of production, to reduce the risks of supply irregularities, and to ensure quality control over down-stream operations – firms began to internalize intermediate product markets and to engage in vertical integration and horizontal diversification in order to capture the economies of scope and scale.

We have already asserted that mainstream economic and organizational theorists paid only scant attention to this phenomena until the post-Second World War period,[6] and that much of the credit for such work as was done must go to scholars interested in the explanation of the growth of MNEs.[7] In the 1950s, both Edith Penrose (1956) and Maurice Bye (1958) sought to explain the extension of a firm's territorial boundaries in terms of the perceived gains to be derived from vertical and horizontal integration. Later, Penrose formulated a more general theory of the growth of firms (Penrose 1959); but, her penetrating insights into the advantages of internalized markets (although she never used this term)[8] had to wait many years before they were adequately acknowledged.[9]

Since the mid-1970s, there have been a plethora of academic papers and monographs which have tried to interpret the existence and growth of MNEs in terms of the benefits which such firms are perceived to derive from internalizing cross-border intermediate product markets.[10] Although several scholars have considered co-operative arrangements as alternatives to fully owned affiliates, and as forms of quasi internalization,[11] for the most part, they have been accommodated in a market/hierarchies transaction costs model; with such arrangements being perceived as a point on the continuum between arm's length markets and complete hierarchies.

The eclectic paradigm, first put forward by the present author at a Nobel Symposium in 1976, is different from internalization theory in that it treats the competitive (so called O specific) advantages of MNEs, apart from those which arise from the act of cross-border internalization, as *endogenous* rather than as *exogenous* variables.[12] This means that the paradigm is not just concerned with answering the question of why firms engage in FDI, in preference to other modes of cross-border transactions. It is also concerned with why these firms possess unique resources and competencies – relative to their competitors of other nationalities – and why they choose to use at least some of these advantages jointly with a portfolio of foreign based immobile assets.

At the same time, as so far enunciated, the eclectic paradigm is embedded within a socio-institutional framework of hierarchical capitalism, which, as stated earlier, presumes that the wealth creating and efficiency enhancing properties of a MNE are contained within the jurisdiction of its ownership. Thus, using the OLI nomenclature, except where they are acquired by mergers and acquisitions (M&As), the O advantages of firms are presumed to be created and organized quite independently of its dealings with other firms; the L advantages of countries are assumed to reflect the scope and character of their unconnected immobile assets, and the way in which hierarchies and markets determine their use; and, the propensity of firms to internalize intermediate product markets is based primarily on the presumption that most kinds of market failure faced by firms are generally regarded by them as immutable, i.e., exogenous.[13] Currently, the eclectic paradigm only peripherally embraces the ways in which the participation of firms in collaborative arrangements, or in networks of economic activity, affect the configuration of the OLI variables facing firms at a given moment of time, or on how this configuration may change over time. Partly, one suspects, this is because the value of such arrangements is difficult to quantify; and, partly because inter-firm transactions have been perceived to be of only marginal significance to the techno-economic production system of Fordism and to the socio-institutional paradigm of hierarchical capitalism.

Alliance capitalism

As suggested in the introduction, a series of events over the last two decades has led several scholars to suggest that the world is moving to embrace a new trajectory of market capitalism. This has been variously described as alliance, relational, collective, associate and the 'new' capitalism.[14] A critical feature of this new trajectory – which is essentially the outcome of a series of landmark technological advances and of the globalization of many kinds of value added activity – is that it portrays the organization of production and transactions as involving both co-operation and competition between the leading wealth creating agents.[15] This view is in marked contrast to that which has dominated the thinking of economists since Adam Smith, whereby collaboration among firms is viewed as a symptom of *structural* market failure,[16] rather than as a means of reducing *endemic* market failure. And, it would be a bold scholar who would argue that most agreements concluded between firms over the last 100 years have been aimed at facilitating rather than inhibiting competition.

But, our reading of the literature suggests that, both the *raison d'être* for concluding inter-firm alliances, and their consequences for economic welfare, have significantly changed over the last two decades. We would at least hypothesize that a powerful contemporary motive for concluding such arrangements is to reduce the transaction and co-ordinating costs of arm's length market transactions; and to leverage the assets, skills and experiences of partner firms. Another motive is to create or extend hierarchical control, which may also prompt firms to engage in M&As. However, co-operative arrangements differ from M&As in three respects: First the former usually involve only a part – and sometimes a minor part – of the collaborating firms' activities. Second, they may involve no change in the ownership structure of the participating firms; and third, whereas the hierarchical solution implies an 'exiting' by firms from the dictates of the market-place, the alliance solution implies a 'voice' strategy of working within these dictates to maximize the benefits of the joint internalization of inter-related activities.

The choice between a hierarchical and alliance modality as a means of lessening arm's length market failure, clearly depends on their respective costs and benefits. The literature on the rationale for joint ventures and non-equity transactions – *vis à vis* markets and hierarchies – is extensive and well-known, and will not be repeated here[17] It is, however, generally accepted that the choice rests on a trade-off between the perceived benefits of sharing risks and capital outlays on the one hand, and the costs of a loss of control associated with a reduced (or no) ownership on the other. Partly, the outcome will be influenced by the success of the 'voice' between the participants – as illustrated, for example, by the exchange of information, the division of managerial and financial responsibility, and the distribution of profits. But, in the main, most scholars view the choice as being determined by the most cost effective way of organizing a portfolio of resources and capabilities.

Another reason for collaborative arrangements, however, has less to do with reducing the co-ordinating and transaction costs of alternative organizational modalities, and more to do with protecting existing – or gaining new – proprietary, or O specific, advantages. Cooperative alliances have a parallel with strategic asset-acquiring foreign direct investment (FDI): and, according to several researchers, over the past decade, the principal incentives for alliance formation has been to lower transaction costs, develop new skills and to overcome or create barriers to entry in national or international markets.[18] Sometimes, these alliances take the form of shared ownership, i.e., the merging of firms, or the setting up of greenfield joint ventures. But, since the early 1980s, the great majority of inter-firm associations have tended to be less formal in structure and more specific in scope and purpose. According to research undertaken at MERIT (Hagedoorn 1993a), the goals of most strategic alliances have been to gain access to new and complementary technology, to speed up the innovatory or learning process and to upgrade the efficiency of particular activities – e.g., research and development (R&D), marketing and distribution, manufacturing methods, etc. – rather than to enhance the overall prosperity of the participating firm.

It is, perhaps, worth rehearsing some of the reasons for the spectacular growth of competitiveness-enhancing alliances since 1980. Essentially, these reduce to the impact that technological advances and the globalization of the market economy have had on the organization of economic activity. The consequences of the former – a supply-side phenomenon – have been five-fold; first, to increase the fixed – and particularly the learning and innovatory – costs of a wide range of manufacturing and service activities; second, to increase the interdependence between distinctive technologies which may need to be used jointly to supply a particular product;[19] third, to increase the significance of multipurpose, or core, technologies, such as robotization, informatics and biotechnology; fourth, to truncate – and sometimes dramatically so – the product life cycle of a particular product;[20] and fifth – which is partly a consequence of the other four characteristics, and partly a result of the changing needs of consumers – to focus on the upgrading of core competencies of firms, and on the way these are organized as a means of enhancing their global competitive advantages.

One of the main consequences of the globalization of economic activity earlier described has been to force firms to be more dynamically competitive. This is particularly the case of firms from advanced industrial countries, and it is demonstrated in two main ways, namely, first a more determined effort to raise the efficiency with which they produce their existing products, and second, to successfully innovate new products and to upgrade the assets and skills throughout their value chains.

This combination of global supply and demand pressures on competitiveness has caused firms – and particularly large hierarchies – to reconsider both the scope and organization of their value added activities. In particular, the 1980s and early 1990s have seen three major responses. First, there has been a fairly general movement by firms towards the shedding or disinternalization of activities both along and between value chains; and a movement towards the specialization on those activities which require resources and capabilities in which firms already have (or can acquire) a perceived competitive advantage. This is a 'concentrate on critical competency' response. At the same time, because of the interdependence of technological advances, e.g., computer aided design and manufacturing techniques, firms find that they need to assure access to the products over which they have now relinquished control. Firms may also wish to exercise some influence over the quality and price of those products, and over the innovation of new products. This means that disinternalization is frequently replaced, not by arm's length transactions, but by some kind of controlled inter-firm co-operative arrangements. Such agreements are particularly noticeable between firms and their subcontractors in the more technologically advanced and information intensive sectors (Hagedoorn 1993b).[21]

Second, because of competitive pressures, the huge and rising costs of R&D and speedier rates of obsolescence, firms – particularly in high technology sectors – have been increasingly induced to engage in cross-border alliances. Freeman and Hagedoorn traced 4,192 of these alliances between 1980 and 1989. They found that 42 per cent were organized through R&D pacts; that 90 per cent were between companies from the Triad; and that 63 per cent were formed during the second half of the 1980s. The majority of the alliances involved large firms competing as oligopolies in global markets.[22] The need, on the one hand, for operational participation and, on the other, for complementarity, shared learning and an encapsulation of the innovation time span has combined to make the 'voice' strategy of co-operative ventures a particularly suitable mode for sustaining and advancing competitive advantage.[23] At the same time, to be successful, an 'asset-seeking alliance response' does have implications for governance structures, a point which we will take up later in this paper.

The third response of firms to recent events has been to try to widen the markets for their core products, so as to benefit fully from the economies of scale. This is, itself, a cost-reducing strategy. It serves to explain much of market-seeking and strategic asset-acquiring FDI – especially between firms servicing the largest industrial markets – as well as those of minority owned foreign joint ventures and non-equity arrangements which are intended to gain speedy entry into uncharted and unfamiliar territories. Thus, of the 4,192 alliances identified by Freeman and Hagedoorn, 32 per cent were geared towards improving access to markets. As might be expected, such alliances were particularly numerous among firms with Japanese partners. Such a 'voice' strategy might be termed a 'market-positioning alliance response'.

Each of the three responses identified has widened the sphere of influence of the firms participating in external partnerships. Such actions have also caused a heightened degree of dependence on firm co-partners for their own prosperity. Thus, the resources and capabilities of companies like Philips, IBM and Toyota – each of which has several hundred inter-firm alliances – cannot be considered in isolation. Gomes-Casseres and Leonard-Barton (1994) have identified some eighty recently established learning, supply, and positioning partnerships in the personal digital assistants (PDA) sector alone.[24] One must also consider the impact which these alliances have had on their internally generated O specific advantages. The design and performance of the next generation of autos, micro chips and computers critically depend, not only on the advances in innovatory and manufacturing capabilities of the leading assembling companies, but also on the way these capabilities interact with those of their suppliers. Boeing's competitive advantages in producing the next breed of large passenger aircraft are likely to rest as much on the interaction it has with its suppliers and its customers – e.g., the airlines – as it does on its own technological and commercial strengths. Siemens – a leading producer of main-frame computers – relies heavily on cutting-edge technology supplied by Fujitsu. In its venture to explore the seabed, Kenecott's mining consortium brings together a large number of firms supplying very different, but inter-related, technologies from many different sectors. Lorenzoni and Baden Fuller (1995) give several examples of organizations which view their subcontractors as partners in innovation and skill development.[25]

Of course, inter-firm co-operation is not a new phenomenon. What is, perhaps, new is its relative significance as an organizational form, whereby the success of the firms involved is being increasingly judged by each party's ability to generate innovation-led growth; by the range, depth and closeness of the interaction between themselves and their alliance or networking parties; and by the effect which such alliances are having on overall industrial performance. It is the combination of these factors, taken together with the twin forces of the disinternalization of hierarchical activities and the impressive growth of M&As to gain access to complementary assets,[26] which lead us to suggest – along with Michael Gerlach (1992) – that the term *alliance* capitalism might be a more appropriate description of the features of innovation-led capitalism now spreading through the globalizing economy than the term *hierarchical* capitalism.

A distinctive feature of alliance capitalism is its governance structure. Within a hierarchy, decisions rest on a pyramid of delegated authority. In establishing and strengthening relationships with other firms, customers and labour unions, success is usually judged by the extent to which the hierarchy is able to obtain its inputs at the least possible cost, and to sell its output at the most profitable price. Relationships between firms and within firms are normally delineated by a written contract.

In alliance capitalism, decisions are more likely to rest on a consensus of agreement between the participating parties; and, there is rarely any formal structure of authority. Such an agreement is based upon a commitment, on the part of each party, to advance the interests of the alliance; and upon mutual trust, reciprocity and forbearance between the partners. In the modern factory – practising flexible manufacturing or Toyota-like production methods – labour is not thought of as a cog in the wheel, as it is in traditional Fordism, but as a partner in the wealth-producing process. Suppliers are not just expected to produce goods to agreed specifications, but to actively work with the purchasing firms to continually upgrade the quality and/or lower the price of their outputs. Even within the hierarchical firm, technological and organizational imperatives are requiring each function, activity or stage of production to be closely integrated with the other. Thus, for example, the purchasing and R&D departments may be expected to work with the manufacturing departments over the design and development of new products and production methods. The personnel, finance and production departments each need to be involved in the introduction of new working procedures and incentive arrangements. At the same time, industrial customers and large wholesale and retail outlets may be expected to play an increasingly significant role in determining the direction and pattern of product improvement.

The growing significance of inter-firm co-operative transaction arrangements would suggest that 'voice', relative to 'exit', strategies are becoming more cost effective. This, of course, could be either due to the 'push' factor of the increasing net costs of hierarchical control, or to the 'pull' factor of the reduced costs of alliances. It is likely that both factors have been at work in recent years; but, it can surely be no accident that the thrust towards alliance capitalism first originated in Japan, whose culture especially values such qualities as team work, trust, consensus, shared responsibility, loyalty and commitment, which are the essential ingredients of any successful partnership. These qualities – together with the recognition that, by improving quality control throughout the value chain, and cutting inventories to the minimum – essentially enabled Japanese producers – particularly in the fabricating sectors, to break into their competitors' markets, and to adopt the production strategies and working practices that conformed to the resource and institutional advantages of their home countries. Indeed, most researchers are agreed that the two most significant competitive advantages of Japanese firms that evolved during the post-Second World War period were, first, the way they restructured their production and intra-firm transactions, and second, the way they managed and organized their vertical and horizontal relationships with other firms.[27]

Before considering the implications of the new trajectory of market-based capitalism for our theorizing about MNE activity, we would mention three other trends in economic organization which are also favouring more, rather than less, inter-firm co-operation. The first of these trends concerns the renewed importance of small and medium size firms in the global economy.[28] This has led some commentators, notably Naisbitt (1994), to assert that yesterday's commercial behemoths are tomorrow's dinosaurs. The reasoning behind this assertion that 'small is beautiful' is that modern production methods, accelerating technological advances, more demanding consumers and the growing importance of services, are all eroding the advantages of large sized plants, based on a continuous scale-friendly and relatively inflexible production system.

While accepting that there is some evidence for this contention – for example, much of the growth in employment now taking place in the advanced industrial countries is in small to medium size firms – we, like Bennett Harrison (1994), are not convinced that the strategic influence of large firms is diminishing. We would prefer to argue that any restructuring of the activity of large firms reflects their preferences for replacing hierarchical for alliance relationships; and, that an increasing number of small firms are, in fact, part of *keiretsu*-like networks, which are, more often than not, dominated by large, lead or flagship firms, or as Lorenzoni and Baden Fuller (1995) put it 'strategic centers' (D'Cruz and Rugman 1992, 1993). Many small firms, too, are either spin-offs of large firms; or owe their prosperity to the fact that the latter are frequently their main clients and suppliers of critical assets. The kinds of examples one has in mind are the hundreds of second or third tier suppliers to the large Japanese automobile companies;[29] the intricate web of horizontal relationships between the various associated companies of the Japanese 'soga shosa'; the extensive outsourcing of both hardware and software development by the Japanese video game producer Nintendo; the network of knitwear firms in the Modena region of northern Italy; the many hundreds of Asian subcontractors to the giant footwear and apparel firms, e.g., Nike and

Benetton.[30] The competitive advantages of the firms in these and similar groups are closely dependent on the exchange of skills, learning experiences, knowledge, and finance between the firms in the network; and on the example and lead given by the flagship firms.

The second trend is related to the first. It is the growth of spatial clusters of economic activities which offer external or agglomerative economies to firms located within the cluster. The idea, of course, is not new. Alfred Marshall paid much attention to it in his study of UK industry in the early twentieth century (Marshall 1920). Recently, it has been given a new lease of life by Michael Porter (1990), who considers the presence of related industries as one of the four key determinants of a country's competitive assets; and, by Paul Krugman (1991) who believes that such economies largely explain the geographical specialization of value added activity. While the evidence on the sub-national spatial concentration of particular activities is still fragmentary, such as we have suggests that, in the technology and information intensive sectors, not only are MNEs creating multiple strategic centres for specialized activities, but these clusters of such activity are becoming an increasingly important component of competitiveness (Enright 1994). The form and extent of the clusters may differ.[31] Sometimes, they relate to a range of pre-competitive innovatory activities, e.g., science parks; sometimes to very specific sectors, e.g., auto-assemblers and component suppliers[32]; and, some-times, to entrepreneurial or start up firms, and co-operative research organizations, e.g., SEMITECH. Sometimes the local networks are contained in a very small geographical area, e.g., financial districts in London and New York; sometimes they spread over a whole, e.g., the cluster of textile firms in north Italy.

The third trend is the growth of industrial networks. Inter-firm alliances can, in fact, range from being simple dyadic relationships to being part of complex, and often overlapping, networks consisting of tens, if not hundreds, of firms. The literature on industrial networks is extensive;[33] but, up to now, the subject has been mainly approached primarily from a marketing or an organizational – rather than an economic – perspective. This is, perhaps, one reason why internalization theory and the eclectic paradigm of international production have sometimes been portrayed as alternative approaches to network analysis. But to the economist, a network is simply a web of interde-pendent dyadic relationships. To be admitted, this makes theorizing about the behaviour of the participants very difficult – but no more so than theorizing about the behaviour of oligopolists. It is also true that the economist is primarily concerned with the firm as a unit of analysis; but, this in no way should inhibit him (or her) from considering the implications for the firm when it is a part of a network of related firms.

What is clear, however, is that, as networks of alliances become more important, the composition and behaviour of the group of firms becomes a more important determinant of the foreign production of the individual firms comprising the network. Nowhere is this more clearly seen than in the role played by the keiretsu in influencing both the competitive advantages of member firms, and in the way in which these advantages are created, upgraded and used.

⸱Reappraising the eclectic paradigm

We now turn to consider the implications of alliance capitalism for our theorizing about the determinants of MNE activity; and, more particularly, for the eclectic paradigm. In brief, the implications are three-fold. First, the concept of the competitive – or O specific – advantages of firms, as traditionally perceived, needs to be broadened to take *explicit* account of the costs and benefits derived from inter-firm relationships and transactions (both at home and abroad) – and particularly those that arise from strategic alliances and networks. Second, the concept of location (or L) advantages of countries, as traditionally perceived, needs to give more weight to the following factors: (i) the territorial embeddedness of interdependent immobile assets in particular geographical areas;[34] (ii) the increasing need for the spatial integration of complex and rapidly changing economic activities; (iii) the conditions under which inter-firm competitive enhancing alliances may flourish; and, (iv) the role of national and regional authorities in influencing the extent and structure of localized centres of excellence.

Third, the idea that firms internalize intermediate markets, primarily to reduce the transaction and co-ordination costs of markets, needs to be widened to encompass other – and, more particularly, dynamic competitive enhancing – goals, the attainment of which may be affected by micro-governance structures. The incorporation of external alliances into the theory of internalization presents no real problems, other than a semantic one. Either one treats a non-equity alliance as an extension of intra-firm transactions, and accepts that the theory is concerned less with a *de jure* concept of hierarchical control and ownership, and more with the *de facto* ways in which interdependent tangible and intangible assets are harnessed and leveraged; or, one treats the inter-firm alliance as a distinctive organizational mode, and more specifically one which is complementary to, rather than substitute for, a hierarchy. Partly, of course, the choice will depend on the unit of analysis being used. Is it the alliance or the network, *per se*, in which case the idea of 'group internalization', may be a relevant one? Or, is the unit of analysis the individual enterprises which comprise the alliance or network? For our purposes, we shall take the individual enterprise as the unit of analysis.[35]

Let us now be more specific about the modifications which alliance capitalism seems to require of the eclectic paradigm. We consider each of its components in turn. On the left-hand side of Table 2.1, we set out some of the more important OLI variables which scholars have traditionally hypothesized to influence the level and structure of MNE activity. Research has shown that the composition and significance of these determinants will differ according to the value of four contextual variables, namely (i) the kind of MNE activity being considered (is it *market, resource, efficiency* or *strategic asset* seeking?), (ii) the portfolio of location bound assets of the countries from which the FDI originates, and to which it is being directed, (iii) the technological *et al.* attributes of the sectors in which it is being directed, and (iv) the specific characteristics (including the production, innovatory and ownership strategies) of the firms undertaking the investment.

The variables identified in Table 2.1 are more than a check list. They are chosen because a trilogy of extant economic and behavioural theories – namely *the theory of industrial organization and market entry*, *the theory of location*,[36] and *the theory of the firm*[37] – suggests that they offer robust explanations of the ownership structure of firms, the location of their activities, and the ways in which they govern the deployment of resources and capabilities within their control or influence. However, until very recently, none of these theories have paid much attention to the role of co-operative agreements in influencing MNE activity.

On the right-hand side of Table 2.1, we identify some additional OLI variables, which we believe, in the evolving era of alliance capitalism, need to be incorporated into our theorizing about MNE activity. The Table shows that not all of the OLI variables listed require modification. Thus, of the Oa specific variables, we would not expect the formation of strategic partnerships to greatly influence the internal work processes of the participating firms – although technological advances, and the need for continuous product improvement, is likely to demand a closer interaction between related value adding activities, and may well enhance the contribution of shopfloor labour to enhancing process productivity. Nor would we expect the proprietary rights of brand ownership, a favoured access to suppliers or the financial control procedures of firms, to be much affected by co-operative agreements.

By contrast, Oa advantages stemming from a firm's ability to create and organize new knowledge, to maintain and upgrade product quality, to seek out and forge productive linkages with suppliers and customers, especially – in unfamiliar markets – to externalize risk, to successfully manage a complex portfolio of core assets and value creating disciplines, and to internalize the skills and learning experiences of other organizations – may be strongly influenced by some kinds of co-operative arrangements. And, each of these advantages may better enable a firm both to engage in transborder activities, and to seek out appropriate agreements to strengthen and consolidate its competitive competencies.

The literature identifies two groups of competitive (Ot) advantages arising from the way in which a firm combines its own resources and capabilities with those of other firms. The first are those which a firm gains from being a multi-activity enterprise, independently of where these activities are located. Such economies of common governance may enable an established firm of one

Table 2.1 A reconfiguration of the eclectic paradigm of international production*

1 *Ownership specific advantages (of enterprise of one nationality (or affiliates of same) over those of another)*	
Hierarchical-related advantages	*Alliance or network-related advantages*

a Property right and/or intangible asset advantages (Oa)

   Product innovations, production management, organizational and marketing systems, innovatory capacity, non-codifiable knowledge: 'bank' of human capital experience; marketing, finance, know-how, etc.

a Vertical alliances

  (i) Backward access to R&D, design engineering and training facilities of suppliers. Regular input by them on problem solving and product innovation on the consequences of projected new production processes for component design and manufacturing. New insights into, and monitoring of, developments in materials, and how they might impact on existing products and production processes

  (ii) Forward access to industrial customers, new markets, marketing techniques and distribution channels, particularly in unfamiliar locations or where products need to be adapted to meet local supply capabilities and markets. Advice by customers on product design and performance. Help in strategic market positioning.

b Advantages of common governance, i.e. of organizing Oa with complementary assets (Ot)

b Horizontal alliances
Access to complementary technologies and innovatory capacity. Access to additional capabilities to captive benefits technology fusion, and to identify new uses for related technologies. Encapsulation of learning and development time. Such inter-firm interaction often generates its own knowledge feedback mechanisms and path dependencies

(i) Those that branch plants of established enterprises may enjoy over *de novo* firms. Those due mainly to size, product diversity and learning experiences of enterprise, e.g. economies of scope and specialization. Exclusive or favoured access to inputs, e.g. labour, natural resources, finance, information. Ability to obtain inputs on favoured terms (due, e.g. to size or monopsonistic influence). Ability of parent company to conclude productive and cooperative inter-firm relationships e.g., as between Japanese auto-assemblers and their suppliers. Exclusive or favoured access to product markets. Access to resources of parent company at marginal cost. Synergistic economies (not only in production, but in purchasing, marketing, finance, etc., arrangements)

c Networks

(i) of similar firms
Reduced transaction and co-ordination costs arising from better dissemination and interpretation of knowledge and information, and from mutual support and cooperation between members of network. Improved knowledge about process and product development and markets. Multiple, yet complementary, inputs into innovatory developments and exploitation of new markets. Access to embedded knowledge of members of networks. Opportunities to develop niche R&D strategies; shared learning and training experiences, e.g. as in the case of cooperative research associations. Networks may also help promote uniform product standards and other collective advantages

ii) Which specifically arise because of multinationality. Multinationality enhances operational flexibility by offering wider opportunities for arbitraging, production shifting and global sourcing of inputs. More favoured access to and/or better knowledge about international markets, e.g., for information, finance, labour, etc. Ability to take advantage of geographic differences in factor endowments, government intervention, markets, etc. Ability to diversify or reduce risks, e.g., in different currency areas and creation of options and/or political and cultural scenarios. Ability to learn from societal differences in organizational and managerial processes and systems. Balancing economies of integration with ability to respond to differences in country specific needs and advantages.

(ii) business districts
As per (i) plus spatial agglomerative economies, e.g. labour market pooling. Access to clusters of specialized intermediate inputs, and linkages with knowledge-based institutions, e.g. universities, technological spillovers.

43

2 *Internalization incentive advantages (i.e. to circumvent or exploit market failure*	
Hierarchical-related advantages	*Alliance or network-related advantages*
Avoidance of search and negotiating costs	While, in some cases, time limited inter-firm co-operative
To avoid costs of moral hazard, information asymmetries	relationships may be a substitute for FDI; in others, they
and adverse selection; and to protect reputation of	may add to the I incentive advantages of the participating
internalizing firm	hierarchies, R&D alliances and networking which may help
To avoid cost of broken contracts and ensuing litigation	strengthen the overall hierarchical advantages of the
Buyer uncertainty (about nature and value of inputs (e.g.	participating firms. Moreover, the growing structural
technology) being sold)	integration of the world economy is requiring firms to go
When market does not permit price discrimination	outside their immediate boundaries to capture the complex
Need of seller to protect quality of intermediate or final	realities of know-how trading and knowledge exchange in
products	innovation, particularly where intangible assets are tacit and
To compensate for absence of future markets	need to speedily adapt competitive enhancing strategies to
	structural change
To avoid or exploit government intervention (e.g. quotas,	Alliances or network related advantages are those which
tariffs, price controls, tax differences, etc.)	prompt a 'voice' rather than an 'exit' response to market
To control supplies and conditions of sale of inputs	failure; they also allow many of the advantages of
(including technology)	internalization without the inflexibility, bureaucratic or risk
To control market outlets (including those which might be	related costs associated with it. Such quasi-internalization is
used by competitors)	likely to be most successful in cultures in which trust,
To be able to engage in practices, e.g. cross-subsidization,	forbearances, reciprocity and consensus politics are at a
predatory pricing, leads and lags, transfer pricing, etc. as a	premium. It suggests that firms are more appropriately
competitive (or anti-competitive) strategy	likened to archipelagos linked by causeways rather than
	self-contained 'islands' or conscious powers. At the same
	time, flagship or lead MNEs, by orchestrating use of mobile
	O advantages and immobile advantages, enhance their role
	as arbitrageurs of complementary cross border value-added
	activities

3 *Location specific variables (these may favour home or host countries)*	
Hierarchical-related advantages	*Alliance or network-related advantages*
Spatial distribution of natural and created resource	The L specific advantages of alliances arise essentially from
endowments and markets	the presence of a portfolio of immobile local complementary
Input prices, quality and productivity, e.g. labour, energy,	assets, which when organized within a framework of
materials, components, semi-finished goods	alliances and networks produce a stimulating and
International transport and communication costs	productive industrial atmosphere. The extent and type of
Investment incentives and disincentives (including	business districts, industrial or science parks and the
performance requirements, etc.)	external economies they offer participating firms are
Artificial barriers (e.g. import controls) to trade in goods	examples of these advantages which, over time, the presence
and services	of foreign owned firms might expect cross-border alliance or
Societal and infrastructure provisions (commercial, legal,	network relationships may also allow foreign firms to better
educational, transport and communication)	tap into, and exploit, the comparative technological and
Cross-country ideological, language, cultural, business,	organizational advantages of host countries. Networks may
political, etc. differences	also help reduce the information asymmetries and
Economies of centralization of R&D production and	likelihood of opportunism in imperfect markets. They may
marketing	also create local institutional thickness, intelligent regions
Economic system and policies of government: the	and social embeddedness (Amin and Thrift 1994)
institutional framework for resource allocation	

Note:

These variables are culled from a variety of sources, but see especially Dunning 1993a.

nationality to penetrate a foreign market more easily than a single activity competitor of the same or of another nationality. The second type of Ot advantage arises as a direct consequence of foreign production.[38] The impact of alliance capitalism is to offer an additional avenue for firms to acquire and build up both types of advantages – and, normally, to do so with less financial outlay and risk than hierarchical capitalism might require.[39]

It is, however, the second kind of Ot advantage which is the quintessence of both the multiactivity and the multinational firm. The implication is, then, that any decline in hierarchical activity reflects a diminution in the net benefits of internalized markets – which may lead to a 'concentrate on core competency strategy'. It is also implied that other ways of obtaining the advantages are becoming more attractive (for example, as a result of a reduction of other kinds of market failure). In our present context, the switch in organizational form is a reflection of a shift in the techno-economic system of production. As we have already argued, this tends to favour a 'voice', rather than an 'exit', response to the inability of markets to cope with the externalities of interdependent activities in the first place.

It is too early to judge the extent to which the economies of synergy (and operational flexibility) are being realized in a more cost-effective way by external partnerships, rather than by hierarchical control. In any event, as we have already stated, many – indeed, perhaps, the majority of – strategic business alliances identified by scholars should not be regarded as substitutes for FDI, as they are directed to achieving very specific purposes.

Turning next to the internalization advantages (I) of MNE activities, it is perhaps here where the co-operative interaction between Japanese firms is most clearly demonstrated as a viable alternative to the full ownership and control favoured by US firms. Here, too, it is not so much that inter-firm agreements add to the internalization incentives of firms. It is rather that they may help to achieve the same objective more effectively, or spread the capital *et al.* risks of the participating firms. In other words, inter-firm agreements may provide additional avenues for circumventing or lessening market failure where the FDI route is an impractical option.

Clearly, the impact of alliance capitalism on the organization of economic activity will vary according to the type of market failure being considered; it is also likely to be highly industry and country specific. Institutional structures, learning paths, the extent of social and territorial embeddedness, cultural values and national systems of education and innovation are likely to play an especially important role. In some countries, such as Japan, there is less incentive by firms to internalize markets in order to avoid the costs of broken contracts, or to ensure the quality of subcontracted products. The reason is simply because these types of market failure are minimized by the 'voice' strategies of buyers and sellers, which are built upon mutual interest, trust and forbearance. The *keiretsu* network of inter-firm competitive interaction – sometimes between firms in the same sector and sometimes across sectors – is perhaps the best example of an alternative to hierarchical internalization. Although there is frequently some minority cross-ownership among the networking firms, the relationship is built upon objectives, values and strategies which negate the need for the internalization of some kinds of market failure. At the same time, the extent and pattern of *keiretsu* ties varies between industrial sectors. It is, for example, most pronounced in the fabricating sectors (where the number and degree of complexity of transactions are the most numerous) and the least pronounced in the processing sectors. And, it is, perhaps, not without interest that Japanese FDI in Europe – relative to its US counterpart – is concentrated in those sectors in which inter-firm, rather than intra-firm, transactions are the preferred modality of counteracting market failure in Japan (Dunning 1994b).

While it would be inappropriate to generalize from this example, it is nevertheless the case that – again due to the adoption of new and flexible production techniques – American firms in the auto and consumer electronic sectors are disinternalizing parts of their value chains. At the same time they are reducing the number of their major suppliers and delegating more design and innovatory functions to them.[40] Moreover, Japanese owned auto-assemblers in the US are replicating or modifying the *keiretsu* type relationships of their parent companies; for, more Japanese suppliers have been setting up subsidiaries, or engaging in co-operative agreements, with US firms to supply components to the assemblers (Banjerji and Sambharya 1994).

Most certainly, a 'voice' response to market failure is raising the profile of strategic partnerships in the organizational strategies of MNEs. Nevertheless, it is the case that some kinds of benefits of cross-border value added activity can only be effectively realized through a full hierarchical control over such operations. Examples include situations in which path dependency, learning experience and the global control over financial assets and key technologies and competencies bring their own O specific advantages, which, because of possible conflicts of interest, would not be realizable from inter-firm agreements. Such agreements, then, would seem to be likely to be confined to very specific areas of a firm's value added activities; and, noticeably, those which are outside its core competencies, need specialized proficiencies, can be closely monitored for quality control, and which are too costly to produce internally (Quinn and Hilmer 1994). But, to achieve and sustain many of the most valuable O specific advantages of multinational operations, hierarchical control will probably remain the principal mode of internationalization, and this applies as much to the Japanese as it does to US and European based MNEs.

We finally consider how the advent of alliance capitalism is affecting the location specific variables influencing international production. We have already indicated that the received literature generally assumes these variables to be exogenous to individual firms, at least at a given moment of time; although, over time, such firms may affect the L advantages of particular countries or regions.

There are essentially two main ways in which alliance capitalism may affect, or be affected by, the presence and structure of immobile assets. The first is that it may introduce new L specific variables, or modify the value of those traditionally considered by location theory. The second is that the

46

response of firms to economic geography may be different because of the impact which external alliances may have on their competitive strengths and global strategies.

Let us first deal with the first type of effect. Chief among the L variables affecting MNE activity – and which surveys have revealed have become more significant in the past decade – is the availability of resources and capabilities which investing firms believe are necessary to both upgrade and make best use of their core O specific advantages. In some cases, these complementary assets, or the rights to their use, can be bought on the open market (e.g., power supplies and transport and communication facilities); but, in others, and noticeably in regimes of rapid technological progress (Teece 1992), the 'continuous handshake' of an alliance relationship, rather than the 'invisible hand' of the market is required (Gerlach 1992). Since, frequently, a foreign direct investment requires the establishment of several of these bilateral relationships, it follows that the positioning of a constellation of related partners becomes a prime locational factor. Where part or all of the constellations are sited in close proximity to each other, then additional benefits may arise. These not only include the static agglomerative economies earlier identified, but also the dynamic externalities assorted with the gathering and dissemination of information, and with the cross-fertilization of ideas and learning experiences.

The attention given by governments of host countries – or of regions in host countries – to the building of a critical mass of inter-related activities, which is consistent with the perceived dynamic comparative advantage of their location bound assets, and to the use of FDI in order to create or upgrade core competencies to advance this goal, is just one illustration of the growing pulling power of the opportunities to benefit from inter-firm linkages.[41] Namely, they serve as L pull factor. Casual empiricism, both past and present, provides ample examples of how the presence of spatially related business networks attract new investors. But, recent evidence unearthed by Wheeler and Mody (1992), Harrison (1994), Lazerson (1993), Herrigel (1994), Audretsch and Feldman (1994), and Enright (1994) confirms these impressions. It also reveals that an innovation driven industrial economy, which seeks to be fully integrated into world markets, needs to focus more attention on the development of clusters of inter-firm linkages, of intelligent regions and of local institutional thickness (Amin and Thrift 1994).

The new trajectory of capitalism has other implications for the locational requirements of MNE investors. Some of these are set out in Table 2.1. As a generalization, while traditional production related variables are generally unaffected or becoming less important, those to do with minimizing transaction and co-ordination costs of markets or the dysfunctioning of hierarchies, those specific to being part of a group or cluster of related activities, and those which help protect or upgrade the global competitiveness of the investing firm, are becoming more important.[42]

47

Turning now to the second type of effect that alliance capitalism has on L advantages, we ask the following question: How far, and in what ways, are the responses of MNEs to the L advantages of countries themselves changing because of the growing pluralism in corporate organization? The answer is that such pluralism allows firms more flexibility in their locational strategies; and, that the immobile assets of countries will not only affect the extent and pattern of foreign participation, but also its organizational form. Thus, on the one hand, the opportunities for networking in a specific country may increase FDI. This is particularly the case when an MNE acquires a firm which is already part of a network. On the other hand, however, the potential to network may also reduce FDI, as it may allow a foreign firm to acquire the complementary assets it needs without making an equity stake.

Of the two scenarios, the one which is more likely to occur will, of course, depend on a host of industry, firm and country specific considerations. But, our point will have been made if it is accepted that the hypothesis of scholars about the response of firms to at least some L specific variables may need to be modified in the light of the growing significance of non-equity based co-operative arrangements, and of networks of firms with related interests. We also believe that the ways in which MNEs choose to leverage and use a port-folio of inter-related location bound assets, with those of their own O specific advantages and the complementary competencies of external partners, are increasingly a core competitive advantage of such firms.

Conclusions

This chapter has suggested that the socio-institutional structure of market-based capitalism is undergoing change. The catalyst is a new wave of multi-purpose generic technological advances and the demands of innovation led production, which are commanding more co-operation among economic agents. Though part of that co-operation is 'bought' by firms through M&A activity, the growing significance of inter-firm partnering and of networking, is demanding a re-examination of traditional approaches to our understanding of the extent and form of international business activity.

Our discussion has concentrated on only one of these approaches, namely the eclectic paradigm of international production, and has suggested that this explanatory framework needs to be modified in three main ways. First, the role of innovation in sustaining and upgrading the competitive advantages of firms and countries needs to be better recognized. It also needs to be more explicitly acknowledged that firms may engage in FDI and in cross-border alliances in order to acquire or learn about foreign technology and markets, as well as to exploit their existing competitive advantages. *Inter alia*, this suggests a strengthening of its analytical underpinnings to encompass a theory of innovation – as, for example, propounded by Nelson and Winter (1982), and Cantwell (1989, 1994) – which identifies and evaluates the role of technological accumulation and learning as O specific advantages of firms, and the role of national education and innovation policies affecting the L advantages of countries.

Second, the paradigm needs to better recognize that a 'voice' strategy for reducing some kinds of market failure – and particularly those to do with opportunism and information impactness by participants in the market – is a viable alternative to an 'exit' strategy of hierarchical capitalism; and that, like hierarchies, strategic partnerships are intended to reduce endemic market failure, and may also help to advance innovatory competitiveness rather than to inhibit it. *Inter alia*, this suggests that theories of inter-firm co-operation or collective competition, which tend to address themselves to issues of static efficiency (Buckley 1994), need to be widened to incorporate questions of dynamic efficiency, e.g., market positioning.

Third, the eclectic paradigm needs to acknowledge that the traditional assumption that the capabilities of the individual firm are limited to its ownership boundaries – and that, outside these boundaries, factors influencing the firms competitiveness are exogenous to it – is no longer acceptable whenever the quality of a firm's efficiency related decisions is significantly influenced by the collaborative agreements they have with other firms. The concept of deci sion taking has implications which go well beyond explaining FDI and international production; indeed, it calls into question some of the fundamental underpinnings of the theory of industrial organization.

Much of the thrust of this paper has been concerned with suggesting how these three evolving concepts – innovation-led growth, a 'voice' reaction to market failure, and co-operation as a competitive enhancing measure – affect the OLI configuration facing firms engaging, or wishing to engage, in crossborder transactions. In doing so, it has thrown up a number of casual hypotheses as to the kinds of O specific advantages which are most likely to be affected by inter-firm alliances and networks; and about how the opportuni ties to engage in such alliances or networks may affect, and be affected by, the portfolio of inter-related location specific assets. Our analysis has also sought to identify some of the implications of the gathering pace of innovation-led production, and of alliance capitalism, for the organization of economic activity. In doing so, we have suggested that the internalization paradigm still remains a powerful tool of analysis – as long as it is widened to incorporate strategic asset acquiring FDI and the dynamic learning activities of firms, and to more explicitly take account of the conditions under which a 'voice' strategy of inter-firm co-operation may be a preferable option to an 'exit' strategy for reducing the transaction and co-ordination costs of arm's length markets, and building inter-active learning based competitiveness.[43]

There has been some exploratory empirical testing – using both field and case study data – of the impact that alliances and networks have had on the performance of locational and organizational strategies of participating firms. Studies by Gomes-Casseres (1994, 1995) on the global computer and electronics industries; by Gomes-Casseres and Leonard-Barton on the multimedia sector; by Mowery (1991) on the commercial aircraft industry; by Brooks *et al.* (1993) on the container transport industry; by Shan and Hamilton (1991) and Whittaker and Bower (1994) on the pharmaceutical industry; by Peng (1993) on the role of network and alliance strategies in assisting the transition from a collectivist to a market-based economy; by Helper (1993) on the 'exit' and 'voice' sourcing strategies of the leading auto-assemblers; by Enright (1993), Glaismeier (1988), Henderson (1994), Lazerson (1993), Piore and Sabel (1984), Saxenian (1994) and Scott (1993) on the rationale for regional clusters and specialized industrial districts in Europe and the US; and, multiple case studies by a number of authors on the roles of *keiretsu*-based transactions and relational contracting as alternatives to hierarchies (e.g., Lincoln 1990) are just a few examples.

But, much more remains to be done. Indeed, it is possible that the basic contention of this chapter, that innovation led production systems and co-operative inter-firm agreements are emerging as the dominant form of market based capitalism, is incorrect. At the same time, it would be difficult to deny that important changes – and, for the most part, irreversible technological changes – are afoot in the global economy; and, that these changes are requiring international business scholars to re-examine at least some of the concepts and theories which have dominated the field for the last two decades or more.

Notes

1 As set out, most recently, in Dunning (1993a: Chapter 4).
2 See e.g., Dunning (1994a) and Gerlach (1992) for a more extensive analysis of this proposition.
3 Especially at River Rouge (US), where its empire included ore and coal mines, 28,350 hectares of timberland, saw mills, blast furnaces, glass works, ore and coal barges and a railway (Williamson 1985).
4 As, for example, is shown by data published in the US Census of Manufacturers and the UK Census of Production (various issues).
5 For full details, see Chandler (1962) and Dunning (1994a).
6 At the time it was published (1937), Ronald Coase's article on 'The nature of the firm' was treated as an 'aberration' by his fellow economists (Williamson 1993). As Coase himself acknowledged (1993), in the 1980s there was more discussion of his ideas than during the whole of the preceding forty years.
7 I do not know, for sure, which particular scholar first used the concept of market failure to explain the existence and growth of the MNE. I first came across the concept of internalization in the early 1970s in a chapter by J.M. McManus entitled 'The theory of the multinational firm', in an edited volume by G. Pacquet (McManus 1972).
8 It is also of some interest that Penrose did not cite Coase in any of her work.
9 There were, I think, two reasons for this. The first was that mainstream micro-economists were strongly influenced (one might almost say hidebound) by the static equilibrium models of Edward Chamberlin (1933) and Joan Robinson

(1933); and the second was that Penrose had not formalized her theory in a manner acceptable to her colleagues.

10 Among the most frequently quoted scholars are Buckley and Casson, Hennart, Rugman, and Teece. A summary of the views of the internalization school are contained in Dunning (1993a). See also Rugman (1981), Hennart (1982), Buckley and Casson (1985) and Casson (1987).

11 See, for example, the contributions to Buckley's edited volume (1993).

12 Elsewhere (Dunning 1993b), we have suggested that paradigm is a more appropriate term to apply to explain the reactions of firms to cross-border market failure.

13 Exceptions include structural market failure deliberately engineered by firms and the extent to which they may be able to influence the content and degree of market failure, e.g., by lobbying for particular government action, and by the setting up of compensating institutions, e.g., insurance and future markets, to reduce risk.

14 See especially Best (1990), Gerlach (1992), Lazonick (1991, 1992), Michalet (1991), Dunning (1994a) and Ruigrok and Van Tulder (1995).

15 Here, we think it appropriate to make the point that the expression *alliance capitalism* should be perceived partly as a socio-cultural phenomenon and partly as a techno-organizational one. The former suggests a change in the ethos and perspective towards the organization of capitalism, and, in particular, towards the relationships between the participating institutions and individuals. The latter embraces the formal structure of the organization of economic activity, including the management of resource allocation and growth. Alliance capitalism is an eclectic [*sic*] concept. It suggests both co-operation and competition *between* institutions (including public institutions) and between interested parties *within* institutions. *De facto*, it is also leading to a flattening out of the organizational structure of decision-taking of business enterprises, with a pyramidal chain of command being increasingly replaced by a more heterarchical inter-play between the main participants in decision taking. Finally, we would emphasize that we are not suggesting that alliance capitalism means the demise of hierarchies, but rather than the rationale and functions of hierarchies requires a reappraisal in the socio-economic climate of the global market-place now emerging.

16 In the words of Adam Smith (1776) 'people of the same trade seldom meet together, even for merriment and diversion, but the conversation ends in a conspiracy against the public, or in some contrivance to raise prices'.

17 See especially Buckley and Casson (1988), Contractor and Lorange (1988), Kogut (1988), Hennart (1988, 1989) and Hagedoorn (1993a and 1993b).

18 The facts are documented in various publications, e.g., Freeman and Hagedoorn (1992), Hagedoorn (1990, 1993a and b), Gomes-Casseres (1993) and UNCTAD (1993, 1994).

19 Some examples are set out in Dunning (1993a: 605ff.) 'Optoelectronics, for example, is a marriage of electronics and optics and is yielding important commercial products such as optical fibre communication systems (Kodama 1992). The latest generation of large commercial aircraft, for example, requires the combined skills of metallurgy, aeronautical engineering and aero-electronics. Current medical advances often need the technological resources of pharmacology, biotechnology, laser technology and genetic engineering for their successful commercialization. The design and construction of chemical plants involves innovatory inputs from chemical, engineering and materials sectors. New telecommunication devices embrace the latest advances in carbon materials, fibre optics, computer technology and electronic engineering. Modern industrial

building techniques need to draw upon the combined expertise of engineering, materials and production technologies. In its venture to explore the sea-bed, Kenecott's consortium brings together a large number of technical disciplines and firms from many different industrial sectors (Contractor and Lorange 1988). Since both the consumption and the production of most core technologies usually yield externalities of one kind or another, it follows that one or the other of the firms involved may be prompted to recoup these benefits by integrating the separate activities, particularly those which draw upon the same generic technology'.

20 Examples include the rapid obsolescence of successive generations of computers and the information carrying power of microchips.

21 One particularly good example is the pharmaceutical industry, where the large drug companies are increasingly internalizing the most novel and risky types of biotechnology innovations to small specialist firms. In the words of two British researchers (Whittaker and Bower 1994) 'The large pharmaceutical companies no longer view themselves as the primary innovators in the industry . . . . The biotechnology companies take on the role of supplier of innovatory activity'. The authors go on to illustrate the symbiotic supplier–buyer relationship which is developing between the two groups of firms. 'The large drug company needs technologically novel products to market and the biotechnology company needs finance, sometimes some ancillary technical expertise in later-stage process development and formulation, skill in handling regulatory agreements and marketing forces' (Whittaker and Bower 1994: 258).

22 For example, of the alliances identified by Freeman and Hagedoorn, 76.3 per cent were accounted for by twenty-one MNEs, each of whom had concluded 100 or more alliances.

23 At the same time, MNEs have increased the R&D intensity of their foreign operations, and have set up technological listening posts in the leading innovating countries.

24 The authors assert that such alliances result from the fusion of technologies from computer communications and consumer electronics; and that because no single firm had (or has) the internal capabilities or the time needed to produce a PDA, that it was necessary to form a cluster of 'matching' alliances.

25 In their words 'Competitive success requires the integration of multiple capabilities (e.g., innovation, productivity, quality, responsiveness to customers) across internal and external organizational boundaries' (Lorenzoni and Baden Fuller 1995: 151).

26 Not to mention to preclude competition from gaining such assets.

27 See, for example, several chapters in an edited volume by Encarnation and Mason (1994).

28 As shown by a variety of indices.

29 See, for example, Banjerji and Sambharya (1994).

30 For further illustrations, see Hamel (1991), Harrison (1994), Stopford (1995), Whittaker and Bower (1994) and Lorenzoni and Baden Fuller (1995).

31 For an interesting discussion of the differing nature of business districts both in the US and in other countries, see Markusen *et al.* (1991).

32 It is estimated that 70 per cent of all Toyota's suppliers are within 160 km radius of Toyota's main assembling complex in Tokyo.

33 See particularly, Forsgren and Johanson (1991), Håkansson and Johanson (1993), Johanson and Mattsson (1987, 1994) and Johanson and Vahlne (1977).

34 In the words of Amin and Thrift (1994), and in the context of the globalizing economy, 'centers of geographical agglomeration are centers of representation, interaction and innovation within global production filieres. [It is their] unique

ability to act as a pole of excellence and to offer to the wide collectivity a well consolidated network of contacts, knowledge, structures and institutions underwriting individual entrepreneurship which makes a center a magnet for economic activity' (p. 13).

35 For an examination of the alliance as a unit of analysis see Gomes-Casseres (1994).

36 Where country specific characteristics are regarded as endogenous variables, then the theory of international economics becomes relevant. This is the position of Kojima (1978, 1990), who is one of the leading exponents of a trade related theory of MNE activity.

37 In particular, the transaction cost theories of Ronald Coase and Oliver Williamson. The resource based theory of the firm (Wernerfelt 1984, Barney 1991, Peteraf 1993) is much broader and, in many respects, is closer in lineage to industrial organization theory, as it is concerned with explaining the origin of a firm's sustainable competitive advantages in terms of resource heterogeneity, limits to competition, and imperfect resource immobility.

38 It is these latter advantages which internalization economists claim *follow* from foreign owned production, rather than *precede* it; although, of course, once established, these advantages may place the MNE in a more favoured position for sequential investment.

39 Of course, in some instances, e.g., jointly funded R&D projects, the resulting economic rents may also have to be shared.

40 Stopford (1995), drawing upon the World Automotive Components supplement published by the *Financial Times* on the 12 July 1994, gives several examples of this phenomenon.

41 As is amply realized by the national governments of foreign investment agencies in their attempts to attract foreign firms to locate in their territories.

42 We accept that it may be difficult to separate the specific effect of alliance capitalism from the other forces influencing the L advantage of countries. This, indeed, is a fertile area for empirical research.

43 According to Storper (1994) those firms, sectors, regions and nations that can learn faster or better become competitive because knowledge is scarce and, therefore, cannot be imitated by new entrants or transferred by codified and formal channels to competitor firms, regions or nations.

References

Amin, A. and Thrift, N. (eds) (1994) *Globalization, Institutions and Regional Development in Europe*, Oxford: Oxford University Press.

Audretsch, D.B. and Feldman, M.P. (1994) 'External economies and spatial clustering', in P.R. Krugman and A. Venables (eds) *The Location of Economic Activity: New Theories and Evidence*, London Centre of Economic Policy Research, CPER.

Banjerji, K. and Sambharya, R.B. (1994) *Vertical Keiretsu and International Market Entry: The Case of the Japanese Automobile Industry*, Virginia, and New Jersey: West Virginia University, and Rutgers University (Camden), Mimeo.

Barney, J.B. (1991) 'Firm resources and sustained competitive advantage', *Journal of Management* 17: 99–120.

Bartness, A. and Cerny, K. (1993) 'Building competitive advantage through a global network of capabilities', *California Management Review*: 78–103.

Best, M. (1990) *The New Competition: Institutions of Restructuring*, Cambridge, MA: Harvard University Press.

Brooks, M.R., Blunder, R.G. and Bidgood, C.I. (1993) 'Strategic alliances in the global container transport industry', in R. Culpan (ed.) *Multinational Strategic Alliances*, New York and London: The Haworth Press, pp. 221–50.

Buckley, P.J. (ed.) (1993) *Cooperative Forms of TNC Activity*, UNCTC Library on Transnational Corporations, London and New York: Routledge.

—— (ed.) (1994) *Cooperative Forms of the TNC Activity*, UNCTC Library on Transnational Corporations. London: Routledge.

Buckley, P.P. and Casson, M.C. (1985) *The Economic Theory of the Multinational Enterprise*, London: Macmillan.

—— (1988) 'A theory of cooperation in international business', in F.J. Contractor and P. Lorange (eds) *Cooperative Strategies in International Business*, Lexington, MA: D.C. Heath, pp. 31–53.

Bye, M. (1958) 'Self-financed multiterritorial units and their time horizon', *International Economic Papers* 8: 147–78.

Cantwell, J.A. (1989) *Technological Innovation and Multinational Corporations*, Oxford: Basil Blackwell.

—— (ed.) (1994) *Transnational Corporations and Innovatory Activities*, United Nations Library on Transnational Corporations, London: Routledge.

Casson, M.C. (1987) *The Firm and the Market*, Oxford: Basil Blackwell.

Chamberlin, E. (1933) *The Theory of Monopolistic Competition*, Boston, MA: Harvard University Press.

Chandler, A.D. Jr (1962) *Strategy and Structure*, Boston, MA: Harvard University Press.

—— (1990) *Scale and Scope: The Dynamics of Industrial Capitalism*, Cambridge, MA: Harvard University.

Coase, R.H. (1937) 'The nature of the firm', *Economica* 4 (November): 386–405.

—— (1988) *The Firm, the Market and the Law*, Chicago, IL, and London: University of Chicago Press.

—— (1993) 'The nature of the firm: meaning and influence', in O.E. Williamson and S.G. Winter (eds) *The Nature of the Firm*, New York and Oxford: Oxford University Press, pp. 34–74.

Contractor, F.J. and Lorange, P. (1988) *Cooperative Strategies in International Business*, Lexington, MA: D.C. Heath.

Cournot, A.A. (1851) *Researches into Mathematical Principles of the Theory of Wealth*, trans. N.T. Bacon, New York: Macmillan.

D'Cruz, J.R. and Rugman, A.M. (1992) 'Business networks for international business', *Business Quarterly* 54 (Spring): 101–7.

—— (1993) 'Business networks for global competitiveness', *Business Quarterly* 57 (Summer): 93–8.

Dunning, J.H. (1977) 'Trade location of economic activity and the multinational enterprise: A search for an eclectic approach', in B. Ohlin, P.O. Hesselborn and P.M. Wikman (eds) *The International Allocation of Economic Activity*, London: Macmillan, pp. 395–418.

—— (1993a) *Multinational Enterprises and the Global Economy*, Wokingham, Berkshire: Addison-Wesley.

—— (1993b) *Globalization of Business*, London and New York: Routledge.

—— (1994a) *Globalization, Economic Restructuring and Development*, Geneva: UNCTAD, The Prebisch Lecture for 1994.

—— (1994b) 'The strategy of Japanese and US manufacturing investment in Europe', in M. Mason and D. Encarnation (eds) *Does Ownership Matter? Japanese Multinationals in Europe*, Oxford: Clarendon Press, pp. 59–86.

Encarnation, D. and Mason, M. (eds) (1944) *Does Ownership Matter?*, Oxford: Clarendon Press.

Enright, M.J. (1993) 'Organization and coordination in geographically concentrated industries', in D. Raff and N. Lamoreaux (eds) *Coordination and Information: Historical Perspectives on the Organization of Enterprise*, Chicago, IL: Chicago University Press.

—— (1994) 'Geographic concentration and firm strategy', Paper presented to Prince Bertil Symposium on *The Dynamic Firm: The Role of Regions, Technology, Strategy and Organization*, Stockholm, June.

Forsgren, M. and Johanson, J. (eds) (1991) *Managing Networks in International Business*, Philadelphia, PA: Gordon and Breach.

Freeman, C. (1991) 'Networks of innovators: a synthesis of research issues', *Research Policy* 20: 499–514.

Freeman, C. and Hagedoorn, J. (1992) *Globalization of Technology*, Maastricht Research Institute on Innovation and Technology (MERIT), Maastricht: Working Paper 92.013.

Freeman, C. and Perez, C. (1988) 'Structural crises of adjustment, business cycles, and investment behavior', in G. Dosi, C. Freeman, R. Nelson, G. Silverberg and L. Soete (eds) *Technical Change and Economic Theory*, London: Pinter Publishers.

Gerlach, M.L. (1992) *Alliance Capitalism: The Social Organization of Japanese Business*, Oxford: Oxford University Press.

Glaismeier, A. (1988) 'Factors governing the development of high tech industry agglomeratives: a tale of three cities', *Regional Studies* 22: 287.

Gomes-Casseres, B. (1993) 'Computers, alliances and industry evolution', in D.B. Yoffie, *Beyond Free Trade: Firms, Governments and Global Competition*, Boston, MA: Harvard Business School Press.

—— (1994) 'Group versus group: how alliance networks compete', *Harvard Business Review*, July–August.

—— (1995) *Collective Competition: International Alliances in High Technology*, Boston, MA: Harvard University Press.

Gomes-Casseres, B. and Leonard-Barton, D. (1994) *Alliance Clusters in Multimedia: Safety Net or Entanglement?*, Boston, MA: Harvard Business School, Mimeo.

Hagedoorn, J. (1990) 'Organizational modes of inter-firm cooperation and technology transfer', *Technovation* 10, 1: 17–30.

—— (1993a) 'Understanding the rationale of strategic technology partnering: inter-organizational modes of cooperation and sectoral differences', *Strategic Management Journal* 14: 371–85.

—— (1993b) 'Strategic technology alliance of cooperation in high technology industries', in G. Grabher (ed.) *The Embedded Firm*, London and New York: Routledge, pp. 116–137.

Hagedoorn, J. and Schakenraad, J. (1993) 'Strategic technology partnering and international corporate strategies', in K.S. Hughes (ed.) *European Competitiveness*, Cambridge: Cambridge University Press, pp. 60–86.

Håkansson, H. and Johanson, J. (1993) 'The network as a governance structure', in G. Grabher (ed.) *The Embedded Firm*, London and New York: Routledge, pp. 35–51.

Hamel, G. (1991) 'Competition for competence and inter-partner learning with international strategic alliances', *Strategic Management Journal* 12: 82–103.

Harrison, B. (1994) *Lean and Mean: The Changing Landscape of Power in the Age of Flexibility*, New York: Basic Books.

Helper, S. (1993) 'An exit-voice analysis of supplier relations: the case of the US automobile industry', in G. Grabher (ed.) *The Embedded Firm*, London and New York: Routledge, pp. 141–60.

Henderson, V. (1994) 'Externalities and industrial development', in P. Krugman and A. Venables (eds) *The Location of Economic Activity: New Theories and Evidence*, London: Centre of Economic Policy Research (CPER).

Hennart, J.-F. (1982) *A Theory of the Multinational Enterprise*, Ann Arbor, MI: University of Michigan Press.

—— (1988) 'A transaction costs theory of equity joint ventures', *Strategic Management Journal* 9: 361–74.

—— (1989) 'Can the new forms of investment substitute for the old forms: a transaction costs perspective', *Journal of International Business Studies* XX: 211–33.

Herrigel, G.B. (1994) 'Power and the redefinition of industrial districts: the case of Baden Württemberg', in G. Grabher (ed.) *The Embedded Firm*, London and New York: Routledge, pp. 227–52.

Hirschman, A.O. (1970) *Exit, Voice and Loyalty*, Boston, MA: Harvard University Press.

Johanson, J. and Mattsson, L.G. (1987) 'Internationalization in industrial systems – network approach', in H. Hood and J.-E. Vahlne (eds) *Strategies in Global Competition*, Chichester and New York: John Wiley

—— (1994) 'The markets-as-networks tradition in Sweden', in G. Laurent, G.L. Lilien and B. Pras (eds) *Research Traditions in Marketing*, Dordrecht and Boston, MA: Kluwer Academy Publishers, pp. 321–46.

Johanson, J. and Vahlne, J.-E. (1977) 'The internationalization process of the firm – a model of knowledge development and increasing foreign market commitments', *Journal of International Business Studies* 8 (Spring/Summer): 23–32.

Kobrin, S.J. (1993) *Beyond Geography: Inter-Firm Networks and the Structural Integration of the World Economy*, Centre for International Management Studies Working Paper 93–10, Philadelphia, PA: William H. Wuntek.

Kodama, F. (1992) 'Japan's unique capability to innovate: technology, fusion and its international implications', in T.S. Arrison, C.F. Bergsten and M. Harris (eds) *Japan's Growing Technological Capability: Implications for the US Economy*, Washington, DC: National Academy Press.

Kogut, B. (1988) 'Joint ventures: theoretical and empirical perspectives', *Strategic Management Journal*: 319–22.

Kogut, B., Shan, W. and Walker, G. (1993) 'Knowledge in the network and the network as knowledge', in G. Grabher (ed.) *The Embedded Firm*, London and New York: Routledge, 67–94.

Kogut, B. and Chang Sea Jin (1991) 'Technological capabilities and Japanese direct investment in the United States', *Review of Economics and Statistics* LXXIII, 3: 401–13.

Kojima, K. (1978) *Direct Foreign Investment: A Japanese Model of Multinational Business Operations*, London: Croom Helm.

—— (1990) *Japanese Direct Investment Abroad*, Social Science Research Institute Monograph Series 1, Mitaka, Tokyo: International Christian University.

Krugman, P.R. (1991) *Geography and Trade*, Leuven: Leuven University Press, and Cambridge, MA: MIT Press.

Lazerson, M. (1993) 'Factory or putting out? Knitting networks in Modena', in G. Grabher (ed.) *The Embedded Firm*, London and New York: Routledge.

Lazonick, W. (1991) *Business Organization and the Myth of the Market Economy*, Cambridge: Cambridge University Press.

—— (1992) 'Business organization and competitive advantage: capitalist transformation in the twentieth century', in G. Dosi, R. Giannelti and P.A. Toninelli (eds) *Technology and Enterprise in a Historical Perspective*, Oxford: Clarendon Press, pp. 119–63.

Lincoln, J. (1990) 'Japanese organization and organizational theory', *Research and Organizational Behavior* 12: 255–94.

Lorenzoni, G. and Baden Fuller, C. (1995) 'Creating a strategic center to manage a web of partners', *California Management Review* 37, 3: 146–63.

Malecki, E.J. (1985) 'Industrial location and corporate organization in high technology industries', *Economic Geography* 61, 4: 345–69.

Markusen, A., Hall, P., Deitrick, S. and Campbell, S. (1991) *The Rise of the Gunbelt: The Military Remapping of Industrial America*, New York and Oxford: Oxford University Press.

Marshall, A. (1920) *Principles of Economies*, London: Macmillan.

McManus, J.C. (1972) 'The theory of the multinational firm', in G. Paquet (ed.) *The Multinational Firm and the Nation State*, Toronto: Collier Macmillan.

Michalet, C.-A. (1991) 'Strategic partnerships and the changing international process', in L.K. Mytelka (ed.) *Strategic Partnerships: States, Firms and International Competition*, London: Pinter Publishers.

Mody, A. (1993) 'Learning through alliances', *Journal of Economic Behavior and Organization* 20: 151–70.

Mowery, D.C. and Teece, D.J. (1993) 'Japan's growing capabilities in industrial technology: implication for US managers and policy makers', *California Management Review* (Winter): 9–34.

Mytelka, L.K. (ed.) (1991) *Strategic Partnerships: States, Firms, and International Competition*, London: Pinter Publishers.

Naisbitt, J. (1994) *Global Paradox: The Bigger the World Economy, the More Political its Smallest Players*, New York: William Morrow.

Nelson, R.R. and Winter, S.G. (1982) *An Evolutionary Theory of Economic Change*, Cambridge, MA: Harvard University Press.

Peng, M.W. (1993) *Blurring Boundaries: The Growth of the Firm in Planned Economies in Transition*, Washington Center for International Business Education and Research, University of Washington, Mimeo.

Penrose, E.T. (1956) 'Foreign investment and growth of the firm', *Economic Journal* 60: 220–35.

—— (1959) *The Theory of the Growth of the Firm*, Oxford: Basil Blackwell.

Perez, C. (1983) 'Structural changes and the assimilation of new technologies on the economic and social system', *Futures* 15: 357–75.

Peteraf, M. (1993) 'The cornerstones of competitive advantage: a resource based view', *Strategic Management Journal* 14: 179–91.

Pigou, A.C. (1932) *The Economics of Welfare*, 4th edn, London: Macmillan.

Piore, M.J. and Sabel, C.F. (1984) *The Second Industrial Divide: Possibilities for Prosperity*, New York: Basic Books.

Porter, M. (1990) *The Competitive Advantage of Nations*, New York: Free Press.

Powell, W.W. (1990) 'Neither market nor hierarchy: network firms of organization', *Research in Organizational Behavior* 12: 245–336.

Quinn, J.B. and Hilmer, F.G. (1994) 'Strategic outsourcing', *Sloan Management Review* (Summer): 43–55.

Robinson, J. (1933) *The Economics of Imperfect Competition*, London: Macmillan.

Ruigrok, W. and Van Tulder, R. (1995) *The Logic of International Restructuring*, London and New York: Routledge.

Rugman, A.M. (1981) *Inside the Multinationals: The Economics of Internal Markets*, London: Croom Helm.

Saxenian, A.L. (1991) 'The origins and dynamics of production networks', in *Silicon Valley Research Policy* 20: 423–37.

—— (1994) *Regional Advantage: Culture and Competition in Silicon Valley and Route 128*, Cambridge, MA: Harvard University Press.

Scott, A.J. (1993) *Technologies: High-Technology Industry and Regional Development in Southern California*, Berkeley and Los Angeles, CA: University of California Press.

—— (1994) 'The geographic foundations of industrial performance', Paper presented to the Prince Bertil Symposium on *The Dynamic Firm, the Role of Regions, Technology Strategy and Organization*, Stockholm, June.

Shan, W. and Hamilton, W. (1991) 'Country-specific advantage and international cooperation', *Strategic Management Journal* 12, 6: 419–32.

Smith, A. (1776) *An Inquiry into the Nature and Clauses of the Wealth of Nations*, Vol. 1 (1947 edition published by J.M. Dent and Sons, London).

Stopford, J.M. (1995) *Competing Globally to Create and Control Resources*, London: London Business School, Mimeo.

Storper, M. (1944) *Institutions of a Learning Economy*, Los Angeles School of Public Policy and Social Research, UCLA.

Teece, D.J. (1992) 'Competition, cooperation and innovation', *Journal of Economic Behavior and Organization* 18: 1–25

UNCTAD (1993). *World Investment Report*, Geneva: UNCTAD Program on Transnational Corporations.

—— (1994) *World Investment Report*, Geneva: UNCTAD Program on Transnational Corporations.

Weiermar, K. (1991) 'Globalization and new forms of industrial organization', in I.H. Rima (ed.) *The Political Economy of Global Restructuring*, Vol. II, Aldershot, England and Brookfield, Vermont: Edward Elgar, pp. 159–171.

Wernerfelt, B. (1984) 'A resource-based view of the firm', *Strategic Management Journal* 5, 2: 171–80.

Wheeler, K. and Mody, A. (1992) 'International investment and location decisions: the case of US firms', *Journal of International Economics* 33: 57–76.

Whittaker, E. and Bower, D.J. (1994) 'A shift to external alliances for product development in the pharmaceutical industry', *R&D Management* 24, 3: 249–60.

Williamson, O.E. (1985) *The Economic Institutions of Capitalism*, New York: Free Press.
—— (1993) 'The logic of economic organization', in O.E. Williamson and S.E. Winter (eds) *The Nature of the Firm*, New York and Oxford: Oxford University Press.
World Bank (1992) *The World Development Report*, New York and Oxford: Oxford University Press.

3

ON KNOWLEDGE AND POWER IN THE THEORY OF THE FIRM[†]

Christos Pitelis

Introduction

The notions of 'knowledge' and 'power' represent threats to mainstream neo-classical economics.[1] In general equilibrium theory (GET) *market* power is absent while information is free and knowledge perfect. Monopoly and oligopoly power are seen as structural market failures, which may be corrected through state intervention. This requires state neutrality towards agents (e.g., monopolies) which, however, presupposes the absence of market (and other types of) power! Knowledge is in the form of information and it is treated just as a commodity. For its acquisition, rational agents will spend just enough time to offset the costs of search by acquired benefits. If as a result, information asymmetries appear, and (thus) market failures, the state can solve them, or these can be prevented through internalization of markets by firms.

The possibility that differential power can emerge from differential knowledge (that 'knowledge is power') is, however, appealing enough to have found its way in the transaction costs, markets and hierarchies (TCMH) perspective and the theory of 'managerial capitalism'. There are many other instances where knowledge and/or power ideas creep in mainstream economic theory, some mentioned in this chapter. However, our concern here is the theory of the firm and, more specifically, its aspects mentioned above. The following sections critically assess the debates on knowledge and power in the emergence of the firm and the 'managerial revolution', and then pick on critiques arising, to provide alternative insights and a new perspective, paying

† Earlier versions of this paper have been presented to numerous workshops and conferences. For comments and discussion, I am grateful to Keith Cowling, Gregory Dow, Arthur Francis, Douglass North and Oliver Williamson. Errors are mine.

particular attention to the issue of inter-firm organization. Remarks and policy implications conclude.

Knowledge, power, and the theory of the firm

Coase (1937) addressed the question why firms arise from markets. He observed that if markets (which rely on voluntary transactions) were perfect, hierarchies, e.g. firms (which rely on entrepreneurial direction) should not exist (efficient allocation of resources would take place through perfect markets). Since firms exist, their existence should be attributed to market failures. Such failures were due to costs intrinsic in the market ('marketing costs') such as costs of information relating to finding relevant prices and costs of contracting. Coase's claim was that such costs could be reduced if entrepreneurial authority, in the form of a hierarchy (the firm) replaced the market. Notably, this would happen in the case of labour, where spot contracts could be replaced by a single long-term contract, which would reduce the number (thus *ceteris paribus* the costs) of transactions. As a result, internalization of markets by hierarchies (firms) would 'correct' market failure, and increase efficiency in resource allocation.

Oliver Williamson extended the Coasean approach by elaborating on the types of 'marketing' costs, on the nature of market failure, and by accounting for issues other than the 'employment contract', notably vertical integration, the multidivisional (M-form) firm, conglomerate diversification and (to a lesser extent) the transnational corporation, e.g. Williamson (1975, 1981), Williamson and Winter (1991). Concerning 'marketing costs', the term 'transaction costs' has been adopted and these have been taken to also include costs of bargaining and policing and enforcing agreements.[2] Transaction costs has been attributed to bounded rationality (limits to acquiring and processing information), opportunism (self-interest seeking with guile) and asset specificity (investments in assets specific to use or user, which existence implies sunk costs, therefore locks agents into transactions). The coexistence of these factors creates organizational (in particular market) failures by rendering the costs of transacting in markets excessive. Hierarchies can perform a transaction more economically, by reducing the number of transactions, but also by virtue of the development of a community of interest between agents in the firm, and the ability of management to end prolonged disputes through the use of *fiat*. This reinforces the conclusion that hierarchy can be efficiency enhancing.

There have been extensive criticisms of the TCMH perspective, see for example Pitelis (1993) and Groenewegen (1996) for readings. Here we focus on the issue of knowledge and power which has received little attention. In the TCMH perspective, power relations are introduced through the existence of entrepreneurial authority. Moreover, in Williamson there is a link between knowledge (in the form of information) and (market) power. In his 1975 'organizational failures' version of TCMH, Williamson links bounded rationality and opportunism to generate 'information impactedness' (asymmetries in information) which in turn are said to lead to 'small numbers', for example (bilateral) monopolies, therefore to organizational (notably market) failures. In this scenario, (market) power through asymmetric information (knowledge) leads to market failures which are attenuated through the emergence of entrepreneurial authority (power?) within the firm.[3]

While the TCMH scenario does not ignore (knowledge and) power, it asserts that one form of power can prevent the emergence of another so as to increase efficiency. Relatedly, it implies that the process of the emergence of hierarchy is contractual (not predatory). The validity of this assertion is necessary for the claim that authority in firms is aimed at economizing transaction costs to be true. If instead it is claimed that such power is imposed by one group over another, the process ceases to be (Pareto) efficient.

Coase tried to address this problem by observing the 'paradox' that while most people would be expected to choose being their own 'masters', they relinquish their autonomy and work for others *voluntarily*. Coase's reason for this was the efficiency properties of the firm. This, however, is tantamount to asserting a (Pareto) efficient distribution of the benefits. This need not be true, see e.g. Francis (1983), Dow (1993). Even if it is, it ignores the possible existence of 'psychic' costs of the employees-to-be (see McGuinness 1987; Pitelis 1991).

In conclusion, the TCMH perspective asserts that authority in firms serves the higher aim of overall efficiency and that all actors involved share this objective, in that they have voluntarily accepted their roles. Both claims are questionable.

The best known alternative to the TCMH perspective is that of Marglin (1974). For Marglin the emergence of the 'factory system', from the putting-out system, was due to the increased control and power that the former gave to employers (capitalists) over labour (employees). In the putting-out system raw materials were 'put out' to quasi-independent producers who were required to produce commodities, often by using their own tools/machinery (capital) and at their own place and (up to a point) pace. Instead, in the factory system employees were placed under the direct control of the supervisor. This increased control over (thus productivity of) labour, and profits for capitalists. This was the very motivation of the factory system. Given that employees lost their opportunity to be opportunistic (Francis 1983), Marglin presumed that the process was not (Pareto) efficient.[4]

In responding to Marglin's views, Williamson accepted the idea that power explanations have merit, but claimed that Marglin's view is consistent with the idea that hierarchy may serve efficiency objectives. These he attributed to the widely observed (by Marglin 1974; Stone 1974; Landes 1966; and others) efficiency (productivity) gains of the factory system and concluded that 'the efficiency hypothesis (or a combined efficiency-power hypothesis) cannot be rejected' (Williamson 1985: 236).

A most interesting ally to the Marglinian thesis is Douglass North's (see e.g., North 1981, 1991). Having first adopted an efficiency perspective, Douglass North has moved to a potentially predatory view of institutional change (that 'principals' objectives are the driving force behind the emergence of institutions and institutional change). This, after what is arguably the most detailed yet analysis of the historical evidence on these issues.

A possible problem with the Marglinian perspective is this: if the factory system (and like institutional changes) are driven by sectional interests, why did cottage labourers not remain just that, i.e. (quasi-independent) cottage labourers? Relatedly, why did cottage labourers not become capitalists themselves? This question is fundamental in political economy as it relates to the very origin of the capitalist system. The marxian answer, for example, is that feudal farmers and cottage labourers became 'proletariats' through coercion (e.g. farm enclosures) by the emerging capitalist state, acting in concert with the emerging capitalist class (see Hymer 1979: 30). Once, moreover, the factory system consolidated itself, the 'capital barrier' (the need to raise capital in order to become a capitalist) helped maintain a relative lack of mobility among classes.[5]

Marglin focused on the issue of the 'capital barrier'. He observed that for cottage labourers, the capital barrier was not a legitimate explanatory factor of them accepting the capitalist employment relation. As they owned their own capital, they had the choice to become capitalists. For Marglin (1983), they did not, because (the emerging) capitalists had access to 'organizational knowledge' which they tried to protect through secrecy (Marglin mentions historical cases where semi-idiotic persons were employed so that organizational knowledge remained the property of the few). As (organizational) knowledge is power, for Marglin, cottage labourers could not become capitalists because they did not have the knowledge, and because they were prevented from obtaining it. In this sense, the factory system was (Pareto) inefficient.

Marglin's perspective fails to address the question how organizational knowledge has been derived to start with; through coercion (as stressed by Marx) or through merit, as stressed by Marshall (see Hymer 1979). If merit is the answer, the efficiency view might still follow. However, even so, the question would remain why one form of power (authority) is required to prevent the emergence of another form (market power).[6]

To summarize the arguments so far, differential possession of knowledge can lead to market failure (which however could be prevented through the internalization of markets by hierarchies) or it can lead to capitalist imposition of potentially (Pareto) inefficient forms of organization (the factory system) on cottage labourers, which can then be used to enhance the power and control over employees (labour) by employers (capitalists). In the former case power (through knowledge) is offset by contractually derived authority-type power, in the latter power through knowledge can lead to cumulative power in a self-sustaining and enhancing predatory process, which is not (Pareto) efficient and need not enhance overall efficiency![7]

Departing now from the issue of the *raison d'être* of the firm, firms exist and have experienced a dramatic increase in their size since the industrial revolution, 'so persistent that it might almost be formulated as a general law of capital accumulation' (Hymer 1979: 42).

Hymer distinguished four stages in the growth of firms; the owner-managed and controlled typically small firm, the 'national' corporation, typically joint stock and vertically integrated, the multidivisional (M-form) firm (division-based with a separation of strategic from operational decisions) and the multinational (or transnational corporation, TNC) with firms controlling production activities in countries outside that of their origin.[8] Our interest here is in the second phase, the emergence of the joint stock, or 'public limited' corporation.

The two major characteristics of such firms is that their ownership is dispersed among often very numerous shareholders. By virtue of their sheer number, it is not possible for all these to be involved in management. Accordingly, there exists a separation of ownership from management, with an often highly specialized group of managers now managing the firms. The 'separation of ownership from management' concept has a long history, going at least as far back as in Karl Marx. More recently the idea has been extended to the assertion of a separation of ownership from *control*. Managers do not just manage, but have effective control of the joint-stock companies. This is tantamount to a 'managerial revolution'. A reason for this is the differential knowledge that managers possess over owners by virtue of the fact that they are insiders, see Herman (1979).

Managers can make strategic use of their inside information/knowledge, so they can pursue their own objectives.[9] In this sense, knowledge once again becomes power for managers who now control the corporations. An interesting twist in this argument is provided by the dramatic growth in many industrialized countries in the post-Second World War period, of funded occupational pension funds. Such funds consist of contributions by employees (mostly a condition of employment) to a fund, which is managed by the company concerned (in-house management) or by financial institutions, namely is invested in shares, property, etc., at home or abroad, with an eye to financing employees' retirement, see Pitelis (1987). By virtue of their participation on pension schemes, employees become *indirectly* shareholders. However, such indirect shareholders know next to nothing about the whereabouts of their money, or even whether they are shareholders at all! In this extreme version of asymmetric information/knowledge, the idea of management control becomes apparently more plausible.[10] It follows that, in this view, asymmetric knowledge may help a group impose its will on others. This is consistent with Marglin's analysis, but applied to a different set of actors!

To summarize, the concepts of (knowledge and) power creep in mainstream economic analysis to explain market failure in the TCMH framework and the alleged 'managerial revolution'. Authority (*fiat*) in firms is also seen as a contractually-derived, efficiency-enhancing process (but as a predatory capitalist control enhancing process in the Marglinian alternative).

A critique and proposed alternative

Once authority is accepted as being at least one characteristic of the private hierarchy (the firm) the treatment of (knowledge and) power in the TCMH perspective and in the notion of a 'managerial revolution' becomes suspect.

Let us first consider the idea that 'information impactedness' leads to market failures of the (bilateral) monopoly type and that firms can prevent the emergence of market failures through internalization. This is a problematic assertion. For one, economizing in market transaction costs can itself be a factor that confers market power to firms, let alone prevents its appearance.

If market power can emerge through either organizational failures of the Williamson type, or through the removal of such failure by hierarchies, then we are back to the assertion that the state can be the means of removing such market (power) failures. This, however, ignores the very nature and role of the state in capitalism. It is not our purpose here to pursue such an analysis, but an obvious remark can be made. In the neo-classical theory of welfare economics (and its political science counterpart, the 'pluralist theory' of the state) the idea of a neutral state is predicated upon the idea of the absence of economic (including market) power to start with (Pitelis 1991).[11] Unless this is accepted, it can no longer be assumed that a neutral state will 'correct' market failures. The opposite is more likely, that the state will tend to favour sectional interests of the stronger groups, such as capitalists as the marxists assert, or big industrialists, trade unions and other organized groups as the 'New Right' theorists believe (see Green 1987 for a survey, and North 1990). Unless perfect competition and/or more generally the absence of (market) power is assumed to start with (either from the firm or from the state) it does not necessarily follow that firms or the state will tend to remove (market) power. Instead, it is possible that (market) power will be cumulative, e.g. through its impact on the state.

The other problem of the TCMH scenario is its assertion that hierarchies are the result of a contractual process. Besides this being inconsistent (acceptance of power considerations in the case of information impactedness on the one hand, rejection of its potential predatory nature within the firm-hierarchy) it is also subject to the critique that it is an assertion to be shown true; the opposite assertion by Marglin, for example, could be argued to be equally plausible. As already noted, this is supported by Douglass North's adoption of the predatory perspective after having first expounded (and then rejected) a contractual view (see North 1981, 1990).

Coming to the 'managerial revolution', the claim that managers control because they are insiders begs the question how did they become insiders to start with? For example, if one observes that historically owners were the insiders to start with (Hilferding 1910) then one has to explain how and why owners lost their insider status.

The last observation raises the important issue that history and evolution are not just 'optional extras' in the theory of the firm, but the *sine qua non* of the analysis. Neo-classical economics can be criticized for ignoring these. Relatedly they can be criticized for being static, and (thus) for failing to provide a unified integrative framework explaining the existence, evolution and (nature of) (knowledge and) (power in) (the theory of) the firm. An attempt in this direction is made in Pitelis (1991). Here we limit our attention to some of the conceptual critical elements of that approach.

Accepting that in capitalist economies there exist employers and employees and that the former seek to further their interests, including the pursuit of profit (ideas widely shared in mainstream theory), important repercussions follow. First, that employers seek profits implies that any source of such profits (reduced costs of production, of transactions, increased power over markets, thus prices, increased power over governments, etc.) will be considered. Accordingly, one cannot separate efficiency from power; in fact, it is through efficiency improvements that power is often attained. Second, if capitalist production is about employers increasing their realized capital, then the concepts of why firms exist and what their controllers do are not separable. Firms exist to realize the objectives of their controllers. Existence and objectives are inseparable. This also casts doubt on the concept of managers being the insiders. Historically, it is the owners who are the insiders. If firm's growth itself is part and parcel of the (original) owners' objective to increase their (market) power and profits (through obtaining finance for expansion by issuing shares) then it should also be assumed that they do not allow control to pass from them to managers, for example by simply retaining sufficient shares-knowledge to allow them to retain control (which, if lost, may defeat the whole purpose of the original decision to expand anyway) (see Pitelis and Sugden 1986).

The knowledge equals power approach of Marglin needs to be seen in the context of history. Historically, the emerging capitalist class consisted primarily of merchant-manufacturers whose early experience of capitalist-type production was the putting-out system. This *explains* (rather than asserts) Marglin's claim that capitalists possessed organizational knowledge. Such knowledge was obtained by merchant-manufacturers (capitalists-to-be) in the very process of them being such.

The above suffices to support our point that knowledge and (as) power pose serious threats to mainstream economic theories of the firm. One way out of this appears to be the assertion that market (and economic) power do not exist. However, we are now aware of no-one prepared to defend this.[12] This leaves the mainstream economic theory of the firm in need of a theory of (knowledge and) power, both consistent and fully integrated with its emphasis on efficiency.[13]

Whether this is possible is very much an open question. In this author's view, it would require building a theory of the firm which integrates no less than insights from Hayek (1978), Schumpeter (1942), Chandler (1986), Hymer (1979) and Penrose (1959). This would appear at the very least to require abandoning the concepts of Pareto efficiency and absolute (as opposed to relative) efficiency, and the use of comparative static analysis. Whether the effect could still be mainstream (neo-classical) is an open question too.[14] This is beyond the scope of this chapter, where instead we pursue the implications of our approach for some recent developments in industrial organization concerning in particular inter-firm relationships.

A number of most important (relatively) recent developments in industry organization can be helpfully examined within a knowledge equals power perspective. These include outsourcing and subcontracting, networks, joint ventures and strategic alliances.

A major obstacle in outsourcing and subcontracting arrangements has been the possibility of subcontractors obtaining and making use of know-how provided to them by the subcontracting company. Potentially, this could turn them into competitors. By investing heavily however in intangibles and knowledge-related attributes of the business operation, the risk is highly alleviated. The importance of the brand name, organizational and managerial knowledge, knowledge of markets and control of distribution, allows firms to subcontract the 'hardware' while keeping overall control through knowledge and intangibles.

Networks of primarily small and medium sized enterprises (SMEs) can also be seen within this context. External economies obtained through shared information and culture is seen as a major explanatory factor for the success of industrial districts (see Best 1990). Involved here, in effect, is sharing knowledge with an eye to strengthening the position of industrial firms and the networks as a whole in (inter)national markets.

Joint ventures and strategic alliances can be seen as responses to a 'trade-off'. The need to obtain knowledge of 'rivals' on the one hand, and the need to outcompete them on the other. Firms can enter joint ventures and/or strategic alliances with an eye to increasing their knowledge-power over rivals other than their partners, but also their partners themselves if they can make better use of knowledge obtained. In part, this could explain the fragility of such ventures.

The cases mentioned above serve different tactical objectives. In the first case, we have knowledge for power over subcontractors and rivals. In the second case, we have co-operation for knowledge which provides power primarily *vis-à-vis* outsiders. The case is similar to joint ventures and strategic alliances, albeit the latter are less spontaneous and less reliant on external economies. In all cases however, knowledge for power seems to be the driving force.

The above account is rather rudimentary and just aiming to make the point that knowledge is power. This does matter, and it may well have something to offer in explaining inter-firm relationships and potentially far more. The knowledge equals power thesis appears like a promising avenue for future research.

Concluding remarks and policy implications

Unlike in traditional GET, which denies the existence of market power and/or knowledge asymmetries, modern approaches explicitly recognize issues of (knowledge and) power. In this paper we focused on the TCMH perspective and the 'managerial' theory of the firm. In both cases it was found that the introduction of knowledge and power into these theories is *ad hoc* and assertive. An alternative perspective provides new insights (inseparability of existence and objectives, and of power and efficiency). It also questions the 'inside' status of managers and provides a reason for Marglin's assertion about capitalist possession of organizational knowledge.

All these lack history and evolution (thus) an integrative coherent (approach to the) theory of the firm. Coase himself recently (Coase 1991) admits that we are only just starting now! In this 'start', we believe, history, evolution and the issues of (knowledge and) power should be essential ingredients, not optional extras.

Despite its scholastic nature, our analysis has important implications for policy, public and business. It questions the policy implications of the TCMH perspective, which emphasis on efficiency suggests minimal intervention of governments in the economy due to the alleged ability of markets and firms to 'correct' each others' 'failures', or lead to an 'optimal' institutional mix which minimizes transaction costs. Our perspective points to a less sanguine view of firms' motives and role. Concerning firm strategies, our analysis implies that it is premature to reject some of the traditional beliefs of industrial economists who used to view firm strategies as, in part at least, the result of (market) power seeking motives. Indeed, we suggest here that firm strategy should be extended to allow for power motives more general than *market* power, including influence over government, labour and other firms. Recent trends in industrial organization, notably outsourcing, networks, joint ventures and strategic alliances, can in part be seen within this framework.

Notes

1 We define 'power' as the ability of one (group of) agent(s) to impose their will on other(s), despite resistance, see Zeitlin (1974) for a similar definition of control. However, the existence of power need not be predicated on the existence of resistance, see Clegg (1989) for a detailed discussion of different notions of power. For the meaning and role of power in alternative economic perspectives, see Young (1994).

2 North (1981, 1990) also includes measurement costs, see also Eggertson (1991).

3 Indeed, entrepreneurial authority is the *differentia specifica* of the firm *vis-à-vis* the market. That this authority is somehow separable from 'power' and/or does not lead to it, is, in this author's view, a contentious point in the TCMH framework, see below.

4 This will be true even if, from a pecuniary point of view, cottage labourers are better off in the factory system, provided they did not want the change, to start with, and that these 'psychic' costs are taken into consideration in the definition of (Pareto) efficiency.

5 Mobility between classes does exist, as 'evidenced' by dozens of folklore stories of newspaper boys turned tycoons. Our claim is not that this does not happen, rather that for whatever reason in most industrialized countries, those employed by others (including the state) are a staggering 80–90 per cent of the working population!

6 A way out of this puzzle is to suggest that Coase and Williamson were wrong to start with, in that firms do not involve authority at all, but rather a symmetrical relationship between employers and employees. This view has been expounded by Alchian and Demsetz for whom 'Telling an employee to type this letter rather than to file that document is like my telling a grocer to sell me this brand of tuna rather than that brand of bread' (Alchian and Demsetz 1972: 120). However, even Alchian and Demsetz have more recently accepted that direction (thus authority?) is involved in the firm, see Williamson and Winter (1991). Moreover, Demsetz (1988) has even accepted earlier critiques to the effect that team production need not involve efficiency gains. This leaves little, if at all, from the original construct which now Demsetz regards as a potential explanation of the firm's inner organization, not its existence (which he believes is also true of transaction costs explanations).

'Abating the costs of shirking helps explain the firm's inner organization but provides no rationale for the firm's existence' (Demsetz 1988: 154). He goes on to observe that a more general theory of the firm should focus on the acquisition and use of knowledge, see also Hayek (1978), Kay (1984).

7 To complicate the issues further, Williamson normally accepts the existence of 'market power', but doubts the existence and/or significance of Marglin-type power, especially in explaining long-term organizational performance and change, in part due to the non-operationizability of power, see Williamson (1996) and Pitelis (1996) for a critique.

8 In Hymer's perspective, firms obtain 'monopolistic advantages' in the very process of them growing. These monopolistic advantages allow them to become TNCs. Among others, 'monopolistic advantages' include know-how. Accordingly knowledge here is a source of market power. Similar considerations apply for Chandper (1986) and Penrose (1959). Penrose views the firm as a bundle of resources which can develop firm specific competences by virtue of its very existence. All these are definitionally knowledge related. In the Penrosian perspective, these competences allow firms to grow, and in so doing to often obtain market power, see Penrose (1956). Here again, knowledge leads to (market) power.

9 Such could include things other than profits which could question the neo-classical focus on profit maximization. This assertion has also been made and theories have emerged where managers maximize sales revenues (Baumol 1959) discretionary expenditures (Williamson 1963) and the balanced rate of growth of the firm (Marris 1967). Numerous criticisms have also emerged, questioning whether a managerial revolution implies non-profit maximization but also importantly, whether a managerial revolution has ever existed to start with, see Pitelis (1987) for example, for a critical survey.

10 The concept of propertyless managers who control the firms has been questioned on theoretical and empirical grounds, see e.g. Baran and Sweezy (1966), Francis (1983), Pitelis and Sugden (1986). All these claim that for a multitude of reasons it is more likely that the controlling group of corporations would comprise a subset of large owners and top managers often with sizeable shareholdings of the corporation, see Scott (1986) for a survey.
11 While market power is only part of economic and/or political power, the two are widely recognized to be related. For example, marxists and neo-liberals (e.g., Friedman 1962) alike point to the ability of monopolies to 'capture' the state, thus transforming market power to political power.
12 Even proponents of the contestable markets idea, e.g. Baumol (1982) (namely that potential competition obliges even monopolies to behave as perfect competitors) admit that the concept is not intended as more than a benchmark (see Baumol 1991).
13 Worth noting is that economics is rather lonely in failing to acknowledge the link between knowledge and power. In stark contrast to this, for example, Foucault claims that 'power produces knowledge . . . that power and knowledge directly imply one another; that there is no power relation without the correlative constitution of a field of knowledge, nor any knowledge that does not presuppose and constitute at the same time power relations' (in Heracleous 1996: 27).
14 For a fascinating (and entertaining) discussion of more general problems to the mainstream which arise from knowledge-related issues, see Kay (1984).

References

Alchian, A. and Demsetz, H. (1972) 'Production, information costs and economic organization', *American Economic Review* 62, 5: 777–95.
Baran, P. and Sweezy, P. (1966) *Monopoly Capital*, Harmondsworth: Pelican.
Baumol, W (1959) *Business Behaviour, Value and Growth*, New York: Macmillan.
—— (1982) 'Contestable markets: an uprising in the theory of industry structure', *American Economic Review* 72, 1: 1–15.
—— (1991) *Perfect Markets and Easy Virtue*, Oxford: Blackwell.
Best, M. (1990) *The New Competition: Institutions for Industrial Restructuring*, Oxford: Polity Press.
Chandler, A.D. (1986) 'Technological and organisational underpinnings of modern industrial multinational enterprise: the dynamics of competitive advantage', in A. Teichova, M. Levy-Leboyer and H. Nussmaum (eds) *Multinational Enterprise in Historical Perspective*, Cambridge: Cambridge University Press, pp. 30–54.
Coase, R. (1937) 'The nature of the firm', *Economica* 4 (November): 386–405.
—— (1991) 'The nature of the firm: meaning and the nature of the firm: influence', in O.E. Williamson and S.G. Winter (eds) *The Nature of the Firm: Origins, Evolution and Development*, Oxford: Oxford University Press.
Clegg, S.R. (1989) *Frameworks of Power*, London: Sage.
Cowling, K. and Sugden, R. (1987) *Transnational Monopoly Capitalism*, Brighton: Wheatsheaf.
Demsetz, H. (1988) 'The theory of the firm revisited', in *Ownership, Control and the Firm: The Organization of Economic Activity Vol 1*, Oxford: Basil Blackwell.
Dow, G. (1993) 'The appropriability critique of transaction cost economics', in C. Pitelis (ed.) *Transaction Costs, Markets and Hierarchies*, Oxford: Blackwell.

Eggertson, Y. (1990) *Economic Behaviour and Institutions*, Cambridge: Cambridge University Press.

Francis, A. (1983) 'Markets and hierarchies: efficiency or domination?', in A. Francis *et al.* (eds) *Power, Efficiency and Institutions*, London: Heinemann.

Friedman, M. (1962) *Capitalism and Freedom*, Chicago, IL: University of Chicago Press.

Green, D. (1987) *The New Right*, Brighton: Wheatsheaf.

Groenewegen, J. (ed.) (1996) *Transaction Costs Economics and Beyond*, Dordrecht: Kluwer.

Hayek, F.A. (1978) *New Studies in Philosophy, Politics and the History of Ideas*, London: Routledge and Kegan Paul.

Heracleous, L. (1996) 'On Foucault's Discourse', Research Paper in Management Studies, Cambridge: Judge Institute, University of Cambridge.

Herman, E.S. (1979) *Corporate Control, Corporate Power*, Cambridge: Cambridge University Press.

Hilferding, R. (1910) *Finance Capital*, London: Routledge and Kegan.

Hymer, S.H. (1979) in Cohen *et al.*, *The Multinational Corporation: A Radical Approach. Papers by Stephen Herbert Hymer*, Cambridge: Cambridge University Press.

Kay, N. (1984) *The Emergent Firm: Knowledge, Ignorance and Surprise in Economic Organization*, London: Macmillan.

Landes, D.S. (1966) *The Rise of Capitalism*, New York: Macmillan.

Marris, R. (1967) *The Economic Theory of Managerial Capitalism*, London: Macmillan.

Marglin, S.A. (1974) 'What do bosses do? The origins and functions of hierarchy in capitalist production', *Review of Radical Political Economics* 6 (Winter): 60–112.

—— (1983) 'Knowledge and power', in F.H. Stephen (ed.) *Firms Organisations and Labour: Approaches to the Economics of Work Organisation*, London: Macmillan.

McGuinness, T. (1987) 'Markets and managerial hierarchies', in R. Clarke and T. McGuinness (eds) *The Economics of the Firm*, Oxford: Basil Blackwell.

North, D. (1981) *Structure and Change in Economic History*, New York: Norton.

—— (1990) *Institutions, Institutional Change and Economic Performance*, Cambridge: Cambridge University Press.

—— (1991) 'Institutions', *Journal of Economic Perspectives* 5, 1.

Penrose E (1956) 'Foreign investment and the growth of the firm', *Economic Journal* 66: 220–35.

—— (1959) *The Theory of the Growth of the Firm*, Oxford, Blackwell.

Pitelis, C.N. (1987) *Corporate Capital*, Cambridge: Cambridge University Press.

—— (1991) *Market and Non-Market Hierarchies*, Oxford: Basil Blackwell.

—— (1993) (ed.) *Transaction Costs, Markets and Hierarchies*, Oxford: Blackwell.

Pitelis, C.N. and Sugden, R. (1986) 'The separation of ownership from control in the theory of the firm: a reappraisal', *International Journal of Industrial Organization* 4, 69–86.

Schumpeter, J. (1942) *Capitalism, Socialism and Democracy*, London: Unwin.

Scott, J. (1986) *Capitalist Property and Financial Power*, Brighton: Wheatsheaf.

Stone, K. (1974) 'The origins of job structures in the steel industry', *Review of Radical Political Economics* 6: 61–97.

Williamson, O.E. (1963) Managerial discretion and business behaviour, *American Economic Review* 53: 1,032–57.

—— (1975) *Markets and Hierarchies*, New York: Free Press.

—— (1981) 'The modern corporation: origins, evolution, attributes', *Journal of Economic Literature* 19, 4: 1,537–68.

—— (1985) *The Economic Institutions of Capitalism*, New York: Free Press.

—— (1996) 'Efficiency, power, authority and economic organization', in J. Groenewegen (ed.) *Transaction Costs Economics and Beyond*, Dordrecht: Kluwer.

Williamson, O.E. and Winter, S.G. (eds) (1991) *The Nature of the Firm: Origins, Evolution and Development*, Oxford: Oxford University Press.

Young, D. (1994) 'The meaning and role of "power" in economic theories', in J. Groenewegen, C. Pitelis and S.-E. Sjostrand (eds) *On Economic Institutes:Theory and Applications*, Aldershot: Edward Elgar.

Zeitlin, M. (1974) 'Corporate ownership and control: the large corporation and the capitalist class', *American Journal of Sociology* 79: 1,073–118.

4

BLURRING BOUNDARIES: NEW INTER-FIRM RELATIONSHIPS AND THE EMERGENCE OF NETWORKED, KNOWLEDGE-BASED OLIGOPOLIES

Michel Delapierre and Lynn Krieger Mytelka

Introduction

This chapter looks at strategic partnerships and the way in which they restructure industries, redefining boundaries and creating new barriers to entry. The analysis proceeds in three steps. We briefly discuss the emergence of a knowledge based mode of competition and its globalization. We emphasize the way in which these changes have eroded the basis for the formation of traditional oligopolies. Then mapping the growth of inter-firm collaboration and its relationship to decentralization within the firm, we examine one of the most interesting and potentially most important of the changes in longer-term firm strategy – the emergence of new forms of global competition based on networked, knowledge-based oligopolies,[1] and illustrate this with examples from electronics and biotechnology.

Changes in the mode of competition

For much of its history, modern industrial capitalism has been characterized by oligopolistic market competition in which entry barriers are created and destroyed (Ernst and O'Connor 1992: 21) and competition for market shares is pursued via a cost reduction strategy based on a continuous process of innovation. The latter, Alfred Chandler Jr (1990) pointed out, requires massive investment aimed not only at the exploitation of economies of scale and scope but also at the creation of marketing networks.[2] Since the last quarter of the nineteenth century when the mass production model came into its own, exploiting fully the scale economies of new technologies, maximizing throughput and operating at full capacity has brought with it a vulnerability to fluctuations in demand and to variations in the price and supply of inputs.[3] Vertical integration, trust-building, patent pooling and a variety of market sharing arrangements historically have been the strategies pursued by large firms in their attempt to smooth out variations in price and throughput.

The growth of knowledge-based competition

During the 1970s and 1980s a number of changes made the use of these traditional strategies less effective. The semiconductor industry is particularly illustrative here, but the impact of these changes has been equally felt in industries as diverse as automobiles, telecommunications, biotechnology, textiles and clothing and new materials.

First, traditional barriers to entry resulting from scale economies, already a major factor in many of these industries at the unit level, became even more constraining, particularly where the cost of each new generation rose dramatically and the generations succeeded each other with increasing rapidity. Access to capital for investment and the high sunk costs that this investment represented became especially strong disincentives to those attempting a catch-up strategy, for example, in the semiconductor industry as was the case in Europe in the 1980s or in moving beyond the frontier in the 1990s.[4] In addition, a new dimension was added to these barriers to entry: time. Catch-up was thus a continuous process and the resulting barriers to entry for newcomers became highly dynamic.

At the corporate level, large established firms with access to financial resources, however, had an advantage in overtaking front runners. Thus Flamm attributes the rapid rise of the Japanese semiconductor industry in the early 1980s, in part, to the fact that 'Japanese chip production has been dominated by large vertically-integrated systems houses' with deep pockets (Flamm 1992: 5). Similarly, the main challengers to new upstarts in the computer industry, Chandler argues, came from the established firms, who alone, had the resources to make the major investments needed in production and marketing. In the 1970s , for example, 'IBM's main-frame rivals were all, like IBM, established enterprises' GE, RCA, Philco and Sperry Rand (Chandler 1990: 611). In the 1980s the pattern persisted with Fujitsu, Hitachi and NEC moving into second, third and fourth place (*Datamation* 15 June 1992: 26). In personal computers, Apple was the pioneer in 1978 when it introduced its Apple II, but by 1984 IBM held 37 per cent of the market in microcomputers (*Datamation* 1 June 1984). Although a window of opportunity opened in the early 1980s, European firms in the information technology industry were individually too small and disintegrated to undertake the volume of investment in R&D, production and marketing required by a catch-up strategy such as that pursued earlier by their Japanese competitors.

The slow rate of growth, falling rates of national savings and rising real interest rates in the European Community, especially in France, Italy and the UK in this period (CEP II 1992: 105–16), placed them at an added disadvantage by making it more difficult to match the pace of investment by their Japanese and American competitors.[5] In biopharmaceuticals, upstarts such as Genentech and Chiron fell prey to large established pharmaceutical firms, Hoffman-La Roche and Ciba-Geigy, despite their early access to venture capital. Barriers to entry, therefore, are not only built on economies of scale at the plant level but at the level of the group as a whole. Here the financial power made possible by the pooling of resources across multiple product lines, along with the oligopolistic rents derived from a large share of existing markets, gave to the large diversified group the capacity to penetrate new markets or contribute to the emergence of entirely new ones.

Second, barriers to entry broadened and competition increasingly centred on the newer intangible investments in R&D, management and marketing (Mytelka 1984, 1987; OECD 1992: 113–34). This was reflected, *inter alia*, in the increasing design intensity of production for 'commodities' such as DRAMs which have since evolved into a differentiated product with multiple design configurations for 'standard' memory chips (Ernst and O'Connor 1992: 27). Similarly, in microprocessors, by 1992 Intel was making nearly thirty new variants of its leading-edge 486 chip (*Business Week* 1 January 1992: 87).

Learning economies in production also became more complex and their mastery has emerged as an ever more important part of the competitiveness story. Although, some learning passes with greater or lesser rapidity into the public domain, much of it, consists in what Teece, discussing 'the technology generated by R&D activities' has called 'tacit' knowledge (Teece 1988: 264). For the most part, this is firm specific learning and it provides one basis upon which a firm can build competitive advantages especially when it is cumulative and transferable to other products (Nelson and Winter 1982: 255–6).

In the information technology industry, learning economies of this sort have been particularly important in semiconductor manufacture where DRAMs have been the traditional 'technology driver' in the industry (Ernst and O'Connor 1992: 89). It is here, however, that the barriers to entry posed by the growing complexity of learning economies are increasingly more apparent. Thus, as competition in the DRAM market shifted from an exclusive focus on price to product differentiation, chip manufacturers who, through close ties to users were able to incorporate system design requirements early on into the development of a new DRAM generation gained an important competitive advantage. This increased the need to develop 'new institutional arrangements for improving knowledge about user requirements' (Ernst and O'Connor 1992: 27) and it heightened the importance of learning to manage these relationships. These included new forms of supplier–client relationships as well as horizontal linkages with competitors and a variety of ties to public research organizations. As these relationships developed and deepened they became the basis for creating network barriers to entry.

Third, uncertainty and unpredictability have grown as a result of the rapid pace of technological change. The latter is reflected in the radical shortening of product life cycles and the emergence of discontinuities in technological trajectories.[6] Word processing is a case in point. The antecedents of the computer-as-word processor are numerous and discontinuous. The first was the mechanical typewriter which captured and held the market for twenty-five years before being displaced by the electromechanical typewriter. The latter survived only fifteen years before being replaced by the wholly electric typewriter which, however, held sway for only seven years before, in a major rupture, the first microprocessor-based machines for word processing became available. Five years later, these were replaced by the micro-computer whose successive product generations average barely eighteen months.[7]

Even in seemingly traditional industries, the pace of technological change has accelerated. The clothing industry, for example, is now based on four seasons whereas previously collections were prepared only twice a year. Today, moreover, each collection includes as many as 200 different items as compared with the fifty or so that were presented only a decade or so ago (Mytelka 1987).

The 1970s and 1980s thus marked the passage from an era in which technological change was mainly incremental and time was available to amortize heavy tangible and intangible investments, to one in which competition is based on an accelerated pace of technological change that involves a shifting combination of generic technologies and the systematic commercialization of technological competencies over as wide a range of applications as possible, or what elsewhere we have called a 'technology bunching' strategy (GEST 1986). As firms extend their competencies to new domains,[8] traditional patterns of vertical integration within the firm that linked markets, products and technology in linear fashion are undermined, industry hierarchies are destabilized and static, product-based oligopolies are weakened.

The new technological opportunities also stimulated the emergence of start-up companies on the fringes of established industries. By their very size and specialization, these firms were insulated from takeover by larger firms, initially, unable to produce in small batches as efficiently. Many such firms and products disappeared before the market attained sufficient size for the product to emerge as a close substitute. However, personal computers and workstations, being new concepts opening applications which were not exactly covered by existing products, appeared as spring boards for new entrants. The choice of innovation over cost competition insulated these firms from the barriers based on scale. But the potential for direct competition was always there, as Apple's introduction of the personal computer and IBM's delayed response to this challenge revealed.

Combined, the erosion of frontiers between industries and the discontinuities in technological change have created difficulties for firms identifying their competitors.[9] This limits the role that traditional oligopolies can play in sustaining profits and market shares. In response, firms have put a premium on technology scanning and flexibility, thus, giving impetus to the formation of strategic partnerships in R&D, production and marketing.[10] As we shall argue below, these alliances have since come to form the basis of networked, knowledge-based oligopolies.

The globalization of competition

The growth of strategic alliances was also stimulated by the globalization of competition. As traditional markets matured and sometimes stagnated and new competitors emerged from other industries and from the newly industrialized economies of Asia, cross-investments among the Triad countries (Julius 1990) and investment in the Triad countries by firms from Korea and Taiwan rose dramatically in the 1980s (Pottier 1994). Through a combination of exports, direct investments and technology transfers, all industrial sectors became theatres of intense innovation-based competition (OECD 1992) and all firms today, whether multi-national or mono-national, large or small, face competition from rivals around the world.

Within the national space, firms whose mode of competition differed dramatically, now confronted each other directly for the first time. More specialized American firms which tend to spend heavily on R&D with the aim of achieving a technological breakthrough and exploit their advantages primarily through direct foreign investment were challenged by the organization of production and attention to quality which characterized the Japanese conglomerate and drove its earlier export success.[11] As the European market opened, European firms, which differed as much amongst themselves (Delapierre and Zimmermann 1991; Taddei and Coriat 1993) as with their American and Japanese rivals, faced an upward competitive struggle.

Several consequences flowed from the globalization of competition. First, competition intensified as the number of competitors within national markets increased. Second, the dominance of traditional modes of competition within the national space gave way to a coexistence of multiple modes of competition thereby reinforcing the uncertainties generated by discontinuous technological change and the emergence of new competitors from other sectors and countries. Third, coupled with the growing importance of knowledge-based competition, the globalization of competition has led to the rapid erosion of static comparative advantage. Thus Japanese semiconductor manufacturers took the lead in computer memories during the 1980s, but the Japanese-American product-based oligopoly put in place by the Semiconductor Trade Agreement in the mid-1980s, was shortly challenged by Korean DRAM producers. Similarly, Malaysian companies emerged as world leaders in the rubber industry after taking over a major R&D centre in the UK and replaced Nigerian firms as major exporters of palm oil, although their plantations were based on Nigerian species. In sum, globalization is not limited to the internationalization of firms and markets. It also consists in a new mode of competition that is both systemic and dynamic (Humbert 1993).

As the above examples illustrate, firms can no longer cling to old specializations and practices nor can they hunker down behind seemingly invincible national barriers of cost, culture, organization or taste. Traditional product-based oligopolies are also less effective in these changed circumstances. Product differentiation strategies practised in traditional oligopolistic markets which made leader–follower behaviour possible in the past, are no guarantee that firms can gradually move up the pecking order today. New competitive strategies are in large part responsible for this.

Under the pressure of accelerated and discontinuous technological change and a globalization of knowledge-based competition, market leaders have began to internalize industry change in order to maintain their competitive advantage. By turning themselves into moving targets they create new barriers to challengers attempting to leapfrog over existing products in their effort to forge ahead. The old product cycle approach is thus being superseded by a process of continuous innovation as front runners no longer wait for older products to reach maturity before introducing new products onto the market. Nevens *et al.* (1990), for example, show that firms which became market leaders in their industries, commercialized two to three times as many new products or processes, incorporated more technologies into their products, introduced new products on the market in half the time and had twice the product range and geographical reach as their competitors of the same size.

In the past, as products became obsolete, divisions could be closed down and entire firms replaced by newcomers. Table 4.1 illustrates this process for the electronic components industry. Under current competitive conditions, however, it is rare for a firm, like IBM, to be able to establish itself in a durable fashion at the top of an industry hierarchy from whence it can orient and define the technological trajectory of its industry. The continuous entry of newcomers, with new solutions, applications or products, engenders a perennial process of reclassification at the top of industry hierarchies. Along with the absence of clear cut reference models and modes of competition, there is thus a continuous jockeying for position at the top amongst a cluster of firms seeking to maintain their place within the group of front runners. Creating new, more flexible barriers to entry by latecomers has thus become a critical means for firms at the top to reduce the costs of staying ahead, window on the myriad of technological advances which someday might challenge their primacy and hedge against the uncertainties and unpredictabilities inherent in knowledge-based, globalized competition.

Table 4.1 Ranking of the main electronics components producers

	1955	1960		1965	1977	1987	1993	1995
	Tubes	*Transistors*		Integrated circuits				
1	RCA	Hughes	Texas Inst.	Texas Inst.	Texas Inst.	NEC	Intel	Intel
2	Sylvania	Transitron	Transitron	Motorola	Fairchild	Toshiba	NEC	NEC
3	GE	Philco	Philco	Fairchild	Philips	Hitachi	Motorola	Toshiba
4	Raytheon	Sylvania	GE	GE	Nat. Semi.	Motorola	Toshiba	Hitachi
5	Westinghouse	Texas	RCA	Gen. Instr.	Intel	Texas Inst.	Hitachi	Motorola
6	Amperex	GE	Motorola	RCA	Motorola	Fujitsu	Texas Inst.	Samsung
7	Nat. Vid.	RCA	Clevite	Sprague	NEC	Philips	Samsung	Texas Inst.
8	Ranland	Westinghouse	Fairchild	Philco	Gen.Instr.	Intel	Fujitsu	Fujitsu
9	Eimac	Motorola	Hughes	Transitron	RCA	Mitsubishi	Mitsubishi	Mitsubishi
10	Londsdale	Clevite	Sylvania	Raytheon	Rockwell	Matsushita	IBM	Hyundai

Sources: 'Rapport sur l'état de la technique', CPE/Sciences et Techniques 1983; *Computerworld* (11 July 1988) and *Dataquest* quoted by *Usine Nouvelle* (10 November 1994) in M. Delapierre and J.B. Zimmermann, 'La globalisation, une remise en perspective des structures techniques de l'industrie', *Terminal*, hiver 1994, No. 66 and *Dataquest* in the *Financial Times* (28 June 1996).

Strategic partnering activity

There is considerable confusion in the literature between traditional joint ventures, licensing and subcontracting relationships and newer forms of part-nering activity. Of paramount importance in the latter is their structure as a 'two-way' rather than a hierarchical relationship and their focus on knowledge production and sharing as opposed to the one-way transfer of technology.[12] Strategic partnerships tend therefore to be contractual in nature and while they may include both equity and cross-equity investments, evolve into a joint venture or result in a merger or acquisition, the equity involvement is not a defining feature of the relationship. Lastly, they are part of the longer term planning activity of the firm rather than simply an opportunistic response to short-term financial gains. Strategic partnerships are thus not about the statics of allocative choices but about the dynamics of innovation and competition.

The growth of strategic partnering

During the 1980s, strategic partnering activity rose dramatically in impor-tance. Data from the MERIT-CATI database, for example, show that the number of inter-firm technology collaboration agreements in biotechnology, information technology and new materials rose from an annual average of sixty-three per year in the 1975–9 period, to 300 per year in 1980–4 and reached 536 per year in the 1986–9 period (Hagedoorn and Schakenraad 1990: Tables 1, 2 and 3). Data on strategic partnering activity from the CEREM database at the Université de Paris-X similarly shows a rise in inter-firm agreements in R&D as well as marketing and production for cases in which at least one European firm is a partner. These data are illustrated in Figure 4.1.

This upward trend has continued into the 1990s. Between 1988 and 1992 the total number of strategic alliances involving major Japanese electronics corporations rose from 400 to 1,700 (Kotaka 1993).[13] In the United States 38 per cent of the 750 electronics firms responding to a survey conducted by *Electronic Business* magazine in 1990 reported having concluded R&D partnership agreements in that year and 43 per cent expected to do so over the 1990–5 period (*Electronic Business* 1990 (March): 58). Two years later, a similar survey revealed that 77 per cent of the firms expected to increase joint product development activity and 58 per cent, research partnerships over the next five years (*Electronic Business* 1992: 39).

In biotechnology, the number of alliances involving twenty of the world's largest firms rose from a total of eighty-three in the pre-1983 period to 102 in 1984–7 and 161 in 1988–91.[14] In the first two periods, moreover, the number of companies participating in these alliances remained steady at fifty-nine but in the last period, it shot up to 119 (Barbanti *et al.* 1992).

Data from the INSEAD database which includes alliances in fourteen industrial sectors show a doubling in the number of alliances in the information and biopharmaceutical sectors over the period 1979–85 and 1986–93. Their data

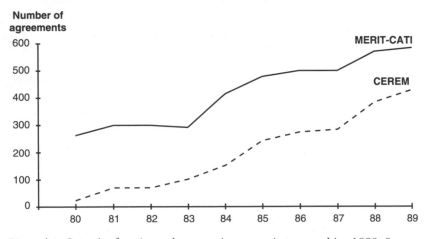

Figure 4.1 Growth of equity and non-equity strategic partnerships 1980–9

Sources: CEREM, Université de Paris-X: database (1992); and Hagedoom and Schakenraad (1992).

also illustrate the extensiveness of partnering activity which also rose dramatically over this period in the aerospace, automotive and service sectors (CEC 1995).

If we add to these private, and for the most part bilateral partnerships, the large number of state promoted R&D consortia initiated during the 1980s and early 1990s, there is no doubt that the growth of strategic partnering activity has remained robust.

Strategic partnering activity has been accompanied by an acceleration in mergers and acquisitions world-wide. Within Europe, as movement towards a single market progressed, companies sought to consolidate their positions within national markets and then to create beachheads in other major markets throughout the European Union. This took the form of an acceleration in M&As within member countries, followed by a steep increase in intra-EC mergers and acquisitions. Figure 4.2 illustrates this process. In other instances, mergers and acquisitions were complements to strategic partnerships. In 1993, for example, Rhone-Poulenc-Rorer acquired 37 per cent of Applied Immune Sciences and created a network of fourteen French and American firms and research institutions with the objective of jointly developing nine biotech-based therapeutic products (Jemain 1994).

Strategic alliances have not replaced traditional strategies of vertical

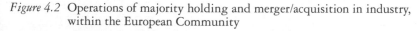

Figure 4.2 Operations of majority holding and merger/acquisition in industry, within the European Community

Source: Based on *Rapport sur la politique de concurrence*, various years.

integration but are complementary to them. Through networks that encompass players from diverse industrial segments, firms attempt to shape changes in their environment, particularly those resulting from the dynamics of innovation. Through traditional strategies of merger and acquisition firms try to reinforce their position on selected markets, refocusing on their core business where size and market share are critical.

Corporate restructuring and strategic partnering activity

Within the firm, two distinct principals of organization have thus emerged. One is based on a high degree of specialization and differentiation of tasks integrated through hierarchical structures, while the other involves a rotation of tasks with integration taking place through co-ordination and a sharing of knowledge. Proponents of the latter stress its greater flexibility in periods of high uncertainty.[15] Without entering into the details of this debate, our own research shows a growing decentralization of activities within precisely those firms that appear to engage more intensively in strategic partnering activity. Consider the restructuring undertaken at Siemens in 1988.

From seven operational divisions, Siemens was reorganized into fifteen divisions, two autonomous groups and two subsidiaries, all with highly focused activities. A large part of the central services at Siemens, involving some 9,000 people, in the areas of finance, sales, personnel and R&D were redistributed amongst the new operational divisions. Ninety per cent of the R&D at Siemens is now done in the division with only 10 per cent, mainly basic research, undertaken in a central laboratory. An intermediary level within the managerial hierarchy was eliminated and the size of the management staff was reduced.[16] Two main explanations were offered by Siemens for these changes. First, they brought the company closer to its clients. Second, they prepared the group for strategic partnerships (*Usine Nouvelle* 24 November 1988, 31 October 1990). In this sense, Siemens has come to partially replicate the horizontal segmentation that characterizes parts of the industry more generally.

Alcatel has pursued a similar strategy with regard to R&D. In the early 1970s, Alcatel built up its R&D capacity working jointly with CNET in the development of the E10 digital switch. When it took over Thomson Télécommunications in 1983, Alcatel stopped production of its electromechanical and semi-electronic switching systems and rationalized its R&D closing down a number of R&D centres. With the absorption of ITT beginning in 1986, however, Alcatel acquired several large R&D laboratories, notably those of Standard Electric Lorenz in Germany and of Bell in Belgium. Between 1986 and 1990 Alcatel's R&D capabilities grew still further through the acquisition of several large firms in Brazil. In 1990, Alcatel took over Télettra, the telecommunications subsidiary of Fiat, thereby acquiring R&D activities in Italy as well. Whereas, from the 1970s through to the early 1980s

Alcatel centralized its R&D activities, more recently it moved to a decentral-ized R&D structure and currently manages over twenty R&D centres world-wide. Instead of merging these laboratories and subjecting them to a hierarchical structure, co-ordination through networking and direct contact between R&D units, production and potential clients is the rule.

The new organizational logic has since, influenced the structure of R&D projects within European programmes such as ESPRIT and RACE, where it is no longer unusual to see participants from two or three R&D units belonging to the same company collaborating. Three subsidiaries of Alcatel, Alcatel Espace (France), Alcatel SEL (Germany) and Alcatel Siette (Italy), for example, are collaborating along with other firms in the Telemid Project within the RACE programme. Ericsson Eurolab Deutschland and Ericsson Telecommunicatie BV (Netherlands) are partners in another RACE project dealing with the management of personnel communications (CEC 1992). Within the frame-work of ESPRIT, Thomson CSF/RCC and Syseca, a wholly owned subsidiary of Thomson, collaborate on the development of real time expert systems, while Philips Lep, situated in France is a partner of Philips Research Laboratories (UK) in a project working on digital coding of video images (CEC 1990).

As with other phenomena on the margin, interpretation of these new part-nering relationships is delicate. Nevertheless, from an analysis of past participation in European projects by these firms (Mytelka 1991, 1994), we would argue that this change does not constitute an attempt by Thomson, Alcatel, Ericsson or Philips to control a project or to capture a greater share of EU R&D funds. Rather it results directly from the development of new networked structures within the firm and between firms that constitute one response to the changing competitive conditions discussed above.

The emergence of networked, knowledge-based oligopolies

In addition to reducing the investment costs needed to achieve optimal production size and R&D and the risks facing firms under contemporary conditions of uncertainty, strategic partnering activity in the information and biotechnology sectors, is also serving as the basis for a new form of regulation within the industry. It thus replaces the role that was previously assumed by a stable leader. As it does, industrial organization itself changes from one struc-tured almost exclusively by large integrated groups whose growth is predicated on an expansion of existing establishments, the acquisition of smaller firms and some greenfield investment, to one in which growth takes place through a shifting pattern of alliances between firms, many of which remain competitors. These alliances also cut across market segments and the configuration of different segments at different points in time redefines indus-trial boundaries.[17] As a result, industries can no longer easily be described in terms of particular products nor can their principal producers be ranked in a stable hierarchy. Indeed, not only do those firms which cluster at the top inter-change their positions with some frequency but the list of front runners changes from year to year, rendering classification schemes somewhat illusory.

As traditional oligopolies come under pressure, one might expect that contestability would open markets further to competition. Instead, we argue that these knowledge-based networked industrial structures constitute new entry barriers (Mytelka and Delapierre 1987; Delapierre and Mytelka 1988; Mytelka 1994) setting industry standards, rules and competitive practices that enable participating firms to control the evolution of technology, reduce the shocks of radical change and maintain their position within these shifting hierarchies.

The HDTV saga illustrates this point. By the 1980s the US had largely abandoned the manufacture of television sets.[18] The Japanese were in the fore-front with European firms holding a strong position in Europe and a toehold in the US market. This was the conjuncture within which several major Japanese electronics firms, such as NEC and Hitachi, with the strong backing of the Ministry of PTT (*International Herald Tribune* 24 February 1994) launched the first stage of their development of high resolution television – the analog based Hi-Vision. Neither Hi-Vision, nor its eventual digital successor would be downward compatible. By the end of 1993 nearly $3 billion had been invested in this project. A few years after their Japanese rivals, a European consortium composed of Philips, Thomson, Bosch and Thorn EMI began a similar two stage process with the adoption of the D2-MAC standard whose advantage was its downward compatibility. Working within the EUREKA 95 project, an analog version of a HDTV system was developed. The combined budget of the European and the various national programmes supporting HDTV totalled $1 billion as of February 1993 (*International Herald Tribune* 20–1 February 1994). In choosing to work first with analog technology these consortia built upon what they knew best and each sought to minimize risks through strong state support both financial and in terms of TV programming. The Japanese and European standards were mutually incompatible and both required global markets and world-wide acceptance of their standard. To that end, they each sought to capture the US market.

Catalysed, in part, by the US government which had come to recognize the wide scope of application for such technology in the telecommunications and computer industries, American firms embarked on the development of their own HDTV technology. Since it was clear that the future was digital by the time General Instrument, AT&T, Zenith and MIT started their consortium, an opportunity for the Americans to leapfrog Japanese and European firms presented itself. By abandoning the two stage process, moreover, the rules of the game were changed, making possible the re-entry of American firms into a new global oligopoly centred on what they would later call the information super highway.

The US firms, however, would not have the field entirely to themselves, for unlike their Japanese competitors, European firms, over the 1980s, had learned to window on alternative technologies. In parallel with the analog-based Eureka consortium, Europe's top television manufacturers formed a strategic alliance with US partners to develop the new digital technology. Among those associated with Philips and Thomson in the US-EU consortium were NBC and Compression Laboratories. When the US government called for technical trials, the all-US team thus found itself confronting an equally digitalized US-European team.

Clearly the digital techniques were superior to the Japanese, and the earlier D2-MAC European, analog technologies and both were eliminated once the United States decided to adopt a digital standard. To establish that standard, joint development work was to be undertaken by the all-US and the US-EU consortia. Shortly thereafter the D2-MAC standard was abandoned in Europe and a new Eureka Consortium in Advanced Digital Television Technologies was put in place (*Les Echos* 17 June 1994). Facing the inevitable, the Japanese government, despite the harsh reaction from industry, shut down its domestic Hi-Vision programme.[19] A cluster of firms tied together by the development of common technical specifications was thus put into a position from which they could shape the direction of technological change in an emerging sector. Gone were the days when a single dominant firm, could, through its own R&D efforts set the rules for an industry.

Transformations in the computer industry illustrate a second path towards the formation of a networked, knowledge-based global oligopoly. Until the early 1980s the computer industry was characterized by large vertically integrated firms which, using their own proprietary technology, offered complete main-frame systems. IBM, Burroughs, NCR, Digital Equipment (DEC) and Fujitsu were typical. These systems were non-compatible.

With the advent of the personal computer, microprocessors, operating systems and applications software could now become the bases for separate industry segments. These were occupied by firms such as Intel, Motorola, Texas Instruments and NEC in microprocessors, Microsoft and AT&T in operating systems and Lotus, Borland and Microsoft in applications software. Many of the new actors were emerging firms which have enjoyed a very strong rate of growth. Competition increased bearing simultaneously a very rapid path of innovations and a fast decrease in prices. The main firms, once a large market had been built started to search for ways to regulate the dynamics of the industry. One can see from Table 4.1, that, each new generation of components – tubes to transistors to integrated circuits – produced a major change in industry leaders with considerable instability throughout the 1970s and 1980s amongst leaders in the production of integrated circuits. By the 1990s, however, the rate of turnover amongst the top ten had considerably declined. Although there was some reshuffling between the leaders, there was relative stability among the main actors. The two newcomers in this period, Samsung and Hyundai, moreover, both entered the market through traditional strategies of building volume production rather than through innovation.

Computer firms now purchase components for the new PCs from these suppliers and work closely within them in a two-way collaborative development process.[20] The use of standardized components, reduces the barriers to entry based on proprietary technology which had been the bulwark of computer firms against their potential rivals. Instead of strengthening IBM's hold over the PC market, the very success of its PCs thus spawned a host of clone manufacturers who could buy components from the same sources. This further strengthened the front runners in each of the horizontal segments enabling them to consolidate their position of power *vis-à-vis* their customers. Soon Intel and Microsoft became giants in their own right and challengers to the hegemony of IBM.[21]

Figure 4.3 shows one set of reactions by the older members of the computer oligopoly to the new role of firms in the component segment of their industry. It illustrates how the formerly integrated core companies – IBM, AT&T, DEC and Fujitsu – have been obliged to form alliances with other computer firms which they would have eschewed in the past and to collaborate on the development of key components. The IBM–Motorola–Apple alliance, for example, has led to the development of a RISC microprocessor, the Power-PC, which directly competes with Intel's new Pentium chip.[22] Since the 4 megabit DRAM, each new generation of DRAMs has involved principal players in rival alliances that collectively constitute a global DRAM oligopoly. Development of 256 megabit DRAMs was undertaken in three alliances; a network of four firms including IBM, Siemens, Toshiba and Motorola, an alliance between Hitachi and Texas Instruments and a three-way partnership involving NEC, AT&T and newcomer, Samsung. Alliances allow participating firms to regulate the industry, in particular by shaping the emergence of new segments. The main objective is not to freeze the features of the industry, but rather to manage turbulence by mastering its evolution. To further strengthen their position in the evolving information technologies industry, these firms are absorbing the data processing activities of former rivals. Fujitsu's takeover of ICL and Nokia's data processing business, Siemen's takeover of Nixdorf and ATT's of NCR are cases in point.

Alliances between the four principal nodes then cement the oligopoly on a global scale while allowing the flexibility for new, but subordinate members, to be drawn in as technology and patterns of competition change. Moreover, the relationship between the nodes is more complex and flexible than earlier vertical integration strategies had been. Hitachi, for instance, supplies computers to DEC but printers to DEC's rival, IBM, which, in turn provides notebooks to Hitachi, which the latter sells under its own brand name. Firms who are cut off from these networks now face high barriers to entry as the technological frontier continues to advance

In the early 1990s biotechnology showed a somewhat different pattern. Like information technology, biotechnology is highly knowledge-intensive.

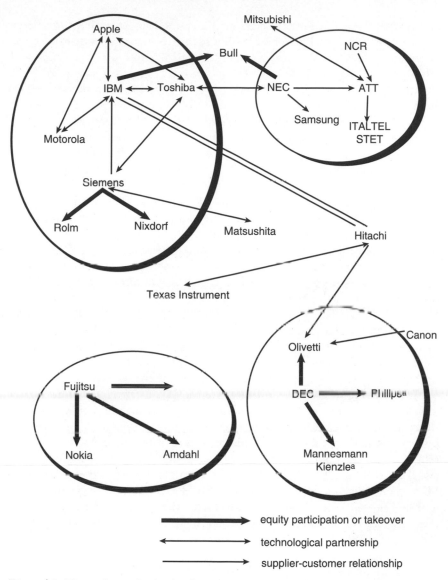

Figure 4.3 The main modes in the data processing networked oligopoly in 1993

Note:

[a]   Data processing activities

On average, $240 million is required to bring a new drug to market. Also like information technology, biotechnology has wide applicability across many industries. However, in contrast to information technology, these applications markets are still quite distinct and different kinds of biotechnology processes and products are taken up by seed companies, new materials firms and the pharmaceutical industry. Biotechnology firms are newer than the star performers in the semiconductor industry and are still too small and specialized to emerge as dominant players on horizontal market segments such as already exist in the information technology area. Genentech and Chiron are not Intel and Motorola.

Moreover, like the earlier information technology industry, hierarchies are not yet stable and firms have appeared and disappeared in rapid succession amongst the top ten. Between 1982 to 1989: Bristol-Myers moved from tenth to second place after its acquisition of Squibb, Glaxo moved from nineteenth to third place, Bayer drops from second to sixth place, Ciba-Geigy from fifth to eighth, and Pfizer from sixth to eleventh. Between 1989 and 1992, however, this process started to slow down as only two of the top ten firms changed: American Home Products dropped from the list and Hoffman-La Roche moved from sixteenth to ninth. Amongst the top five, Ciba-Geigy replaced SmithKline Beecham in fifth place.

Looking within the pharmaceutical industry, there is some evidence that a networked, knowledge-based oligopoly is emergency. Over the 1980s biotechnology inputs came to play an increasingly important role in the pharmaceutical industry, especially in diagnostics.[23] Figure 4.3, based on the MERIT-CATI database provides a sketch of the emerging oligopolistic structure in the new biotech-based pharmaceutical industry.[24] There we can see that each of the clusters involves one or more small biotech firms. This is similar to the structure of clusters in the information technology oligopoly, each of which contains a semiconductor manufacturer.

However, Figure 4.4 also reveals that the biotech-based pharmaceutical industry is not yet a global oligopoly. Unlike the information technology domain where Japanese firms now contribute technological advances, in biotechnology the technology still mainly comes from American firms. This is reflected in several of the clusters in Figure 4.4, giving them a more international flavour. In the period 1985–9, for example, Genentech was linked to Mitsubishi, Daiichi and Monsanto. Similarly, Biogen was linked to SmithKline and Cetus to Hoffman-La Roche. But a closer look at these clusters suggests that networking remains principally intra-national, as in the Japanese cluster composed of Greencross, Sumitomo, Kyowa and Toray and the more intensive linkages amongst American firms. Some cross-national alliances such as the multiple linkages between Merck and Ciba-Geigy and Bristol-Myers and Bayer, however, have developed. Alliance formation, moreover, has intensified and this emerges more clearly if we take a dynamic perspective. Thus, in the early 1980s few of the big pharmaceutical companies had formed R&D partnerships with each other.[25] For top ranking Hoechst, second place Bayer and eighth ranking Hoffman-La Roche alliances were marginal. For firms like Ciba-Geigy (fifth) and Eli Lilly (seventh) alliances were mainly with small US biotechnology firms and American universities, only ninth ranking Sandoz had formed R&D partnerships with smaller pharmaceutical firms (Barbanti *et al.* 1992). In the mid-1980s several large pharmaceutical companies became involved in technology partnerships but principally the linkages between them were in marketing. Their R&D ties were to the specialized biotechnology firms, while their earlier links to universities began to decline. By the end of the decade, as Figure 4.4 reveals, alliances among the large pharmaceutical firms had intensified and all of the largest pharmaceutical companies were now involved in technology partnerships either with other pharmaceutical companies or with biotechnology firms.

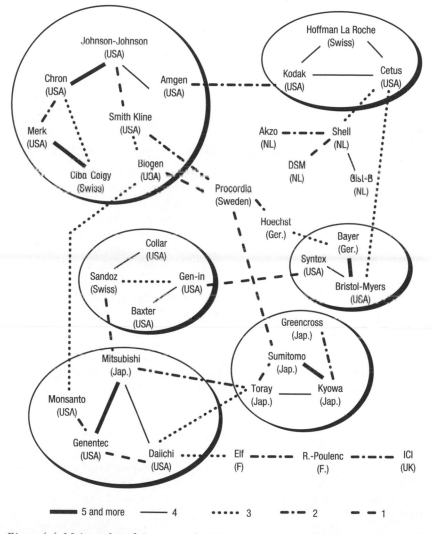

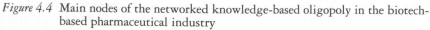

Figure 4.4 Main nodes of the networked knowledge-based oligopoly in the biotech-based pharmaceutical industry

Note:
Based on technology co-operation agreements established between 1985 and 1989.

Conclusion

For the analysis of firm behaviour and for public policy a number of critical issues emerge from this analysis. The first has to do with the boundaries of existing industries. As the strategic use of industry segments by innovative firms in the information technology and biopharmaceutical 'industries' reveals, an industry is composed of a collection of segments defined as such by its members. Rivalry occurs both within and across segments. As ruptures in technology, competitive strategies and government policies play a major role in the emergence of segments, what constitutes the contours of an industry and even its name is thus likely to change over time. Governments must thus pay closer attention to the way public policy shapes the possibilities for the creation of new industrial segments and the socio-economic consequences to which this gives rise. Access issues are particularly salient here, as current debates over the information highway and health care illustrate.

The second concerns the rise of new forms of oligopoly. The basis of new oligopoly formation is knowledge, that is, collaboration in the generation of, use of or control over the evolution of new knowledge. As a result, the new knowledge-based oligopolies are dynamic in nature, seeking to organize, manage and monitor change as opposed to rigidifying the *status quo*. In terms of their organization, the new, knowledge-based networked oligopolies can form within or across industry segments and sometimes do both at the same time. Although strategic alliances thus appear to be marginal phenomena when set against the volume of mergers and acquisitions or the value of international trade, they are increasingly important elements in shaping industry structures and technological trajectories. Through networked, knowledge-based alliances, clusters of key players are building new barriers to entry based on learning and innovation and laying the basis for global oligopolies within the shifting boundaries of traditional industries as they merge into those of the future. This requires governments to rethink the scope of competition policy and suggests a new role for international institutions such as the European Union, OECD, UNCTAD and the World Trade Organization in this process.

Notes

1 The notion of networked, knowledge-based oligopolies was first introduced in Mytelka 1984, and developed in Mytelka and Delapierre 1987, Delapierre and Mytelka 1988 and Mytelka 1994.

2 The point of capturing economies of scale as Rosenberg and Birdzell (1986: 291) emphasize, is to reduce unit costs so that the firm is able to sell at prices lower than those 'at which, competitors must sell in order to continue in business Economies of scope, in contrast, are those resulting from the use of processes within a single operating unit to produce or distribute more than one product' (Chandler 1990: 17). Economies of scope reduce changeover costs and enable the firm to differentiate products more cheaply.

3 See the work of the 'regulation' school (Boyer 1988) and the excellent discussion of the new institutional mechanisms developed in the US to ensure the profitability of investment in mass production equipment through the stabilization of markets in Chapters 3 and 4 of Piore and Sabel (1984).

4 In the semiconductor industry, as more circuitry was packed onto memory chips, capital costs of a fabrication line

> 'rose from about 15 per cent of the total fabrication cost in the mid-1970s to about half of cost by the mid-1980s, and was projected to pass 60 per cent of total cost by the early 1990s. Since much of this equipment was highly specialised – had little or no scrap value outside of the semiconductor business – and, due to the continuing rapid pace of technological change, had a relatively short economic life span, [t]he increasing share of such sunk costs in total manufacturing cost made entry and exit from the industry more expensive and difficult'.
>
> (Flamm 1992: 5)

5 The period 1982–5 was thus marked by a far more rapid rise in the number of strategic partnerships involving European firms and a far slower increase in the number of acquisitions by European firms (Delapierre 1991: 148).

6 For example, in the introduction of personal computers, Walkmen or compact discs.

7 Nevens *et al.* (1990).

8 Sony, a manufacturer of consumer electronic goods, for example, moved into the computer industry. This move does not constitute a classic case of diversification nor an opportunistic response to financial gain but an exploitation of existing technological competencies in other domains.

9 The emergence of mecatronics, the links between computers and telecommunications and the emergence of biotechnology in seed companies, petrochemical and petroleum firms and pharmaceutical companies are among the areas where this is taking place.

10 These points are discussed more fully in Mytelka and Delapierre (1987), Mytelka (1991a) and Mytelka (1994).

11 There is evidence, however, that this is changing and a recent study by Duong and Planty-Cornubert (1994) suggests that as Japanese conglomerates invest abroad they will have greater difficulty in maintaining the kinds of organizational structures that underlay their competitivity in the 1970s and 1980s.

12 The knowledge component of strategic partnerships, moreover, may involve the development of new products, new production processes or new routines within the firm or in its ability to manage inter-firm contractual relationships (Mytelka 1991).

13 These data covering alliances by NEC, Fujitsu, Matsushita, Toshiba, Hitachi, Mitsubishi, Sharp and Oki were collected by Yasukuni Kotaka when he was Vice President at NEC Corporation.

14 The survey included eighteen of the world's largest pharmaceutical firms – Merck, Sharp and Dome, Ely Lilly, Pfizer, Bristol Meyers-Squibb, Ciba-Geigy and Sandoz (now Novartis), Hoffman-La Roche, Rhone-Poulenc, Sanofi, Bayer, Hoechts, ICI, Glaxo, Novo, Yamanouchi, Sankyo, Takeda, Daiichi and two of the major biotechnology companies Genentech and Amgen.

15 For a lengthier discussion of these distinctions see Aoki 1988.

16 By way of example, the Board went from thirty-two to twenty members.

17 This is the subject of our forthcoming paper 'Technological Oligopolies and the Reconfiguration of Industries'.

18 There is only one small domestic TV set manufacturer left, Zenith. The market today is shared by the European groups Philips and Thomson who have acquired the national producers, and imports from Japan (Pottier 1994).

19 'Tokyo admits it backed wrong horse', *Financial Times* 23 February 1994.

20 In 1981 IBM signed its first agreement with Intel for the supply of microprocessors. Similarly, the largest car manufacturers are increasing their joint development of core components in a move to reclaim their autonomy and strengthen their bargaining power *vis-à-vis* specialized manufacturers, subcontractors turned partners (Duong and Planty-Cornubert 1993).

21 By 1992 Intel provided 33 per cent of the world's microprocessors and 72 per cent of the 32 bit high performance chips (*Financial Times* 26 August 1993).

22 The competition in RISC technology for workstations is another anti-Intel strategy putting into play four clusters around SUN, MIPs, IBM and HP to develop RISC components. For details see Gomes-Casseres 1994.

23 On the technological convergence between biotechnology and pharmaceuticals, see V. Griffith 'Hand in hand', *Financial Times* 6 September 1994.

24 Readers should be aware that the data used to construct Figure 4.2 on information technologies includes mergers and acquisition, supplier–customer relationships as well as technological partnerships whereas Figure 4.3 on biotechnology is based exclusively on technology agreements.

25 Rankings for 1982 are from US, Department of Commerce *A Competitive Assessment of the US Pharmaceutical Industry* (1984). For 1989 see Sharp (1991: 215) and for 1992 see *Financial Times* of 10 March 1994.

References

Aoki, M. (1988), *Information, Incentives and Bargaining in the Japanese Economy*, Cambridge, MA: Cambridge University Press.

Barbanti, P., Gambardella, A. and Orsenigo, L. (1992) 'The evolution of the forms of collaboration in biotechnologies', paper presented at the conference on *Les Accords de Coopération pour la Recherche et le Développement en biotechnologie*, Grenoble.

Boyer, R. (1988), 'Technical change and the theory of regulation', in G. Dosi, C. Freeman, R. Nelson, G. Silverberg and L. Soete (eds) *Technical Change and Economic Performance*, Cambridge: Cambridge University Press.

CEP II (1992) *Economie Mondiale 1990–2000: L'Imperatif de Croissance*, Paris: Economica.

CEREM (1992) *Les Stratégies d'Accord des Groupes Européens*, Etude pour le Commissariat Général au Plan, Paris, Mimeo.

Chandler, A. Jr (1990) *Scale and Scope, The Dynamics of Industrial Capitalism*, Cambridge, MA: The Belknap Press and Harvard University Press.

Commission of the European Communities (CEC)(1990) *Esprit Progress and Results*, Brussels, DG XIII.

—— (1995) *A European Approach to Strategic Alliances*, prepared by Braxton Associates, Horack Adler and Associates, Professor Deigan Morris, Brussels, DG III/A/3.

—— (1994) *Research and Technology Development in Advanced Telecommunications Technologies in Europe, RACE 1994*, Brussels, DG XIII.

Delapierre, M. (1991) 'Les accords inter-entreprises, partage ou partenariat? Les stratégies des groupes Européens du traitement de l'information', *Revue d'Economie Industrielle*, No. 55, ler trimestre.

Delapierre, M. and Milelli, C. (1994) 'Concurrence et transferts de technologie dans l'industrie informatique mondiale', in F. Shachwald, (ed.) *Les Défis de la Mondialisation. Innovation et Concurrence*, Paris: Masson.

Delapierre, M. and Mytelka, L.K. (1988) 'Décomposition, recomposition des oligopoles', *Cahiers de l'ISMEA, Economie et Société*, No. 11–12.

Delapierre, M. and Zimmermann, J.B. (1991) *La globalisation de l'Industrie des ordinateurs*, CEE, Bruxelles, Fast/Monitor, FOP 283, 153p.

Duong, B. and Planty-Cornubert, M. (1992) 'Le système automobile', in CEREM (1992).

Ernst, D. and O'Connor, P. (1992) *Competing in the Electronics Industry*, Paris: OECD.

Flamm, K. (1992) 'Strategic aspects of international competition in semiconductors: Europe's choices', in Humbert, M. (1993).

Foray, D. and Mowery, D.C. (1990) 'L'integration de la R&D industrielle: Nouvelles propositions d'analyse', *Revue d'Economie Industrielle*, No. 3.

GEST (1986) *Grappes Technologiques. Les Nouvelles Stratégies d'Entreprise*, Col. Stratégie et Management, Paris: McGraw-Hill.

Gomes Casseres, R. (1994), 'Group vs. group: how alliance networks compete', *Harvard Business Review*, July–August: 62–74.

Hagedoorn, J. and Shakenraad, J. (1990) *Leading Companies and the Structure of Strategic Alliances in Core Technologies*, Limburg, University of Limburg: MERIT

Humbert, M. (1993) *European Firms and Industries Coping with Globalization*, London: Pinter.

Jemain, A. (1994) 'Nouvelle donne dans les biotechnologies', *Usine Nouvelle*, No. 2482, (8 December): 20–2.

Julius, D. (1990) *Global Companies and Public Policy*, London: Pinter.

Kotaka, Y. (1993) 'Evolving pattern of innovation in a global economy', paper presented to a conference on *Strategic Alliances and Techno-Security*, Honolulu, Pacific Forum: CSIS, 26–8 July.

Morin, F. and Dupuy (1993) *Le Coeur Financier Européen*, Paris: Economica.

Mytelka, L.K. (1984) 'La gestion de la connaissance dans les entreprises multinationales', *Economie Prospective Internationale*, No. 20.

—— (1987) 'Knowledge-intensive production and the changing internationalization strategies of multinational firms', in J. Caporaso (ed.) *A Changing International Division of Labor*, Boulder, CO: Lynne Reiner, pp. 43–70.

—— (1991) *Strategic Partnerships and the World Economy*, London: Pinter.

—— (1994) 'Dancing with wolves: global oligopolies and strategic partnerships', in J. Haagedorn (ed.) *Technical Change and the World Economy/Convergence and Divergence in Technological Strategies*, Aldershot: Elgar.

Mytelka, L.K. and Delapierre, M. (1987) 'The alliance strategies of European firms and the role of ESPRIT', *Journal of Common Market Studies* XXVI, 2.

Nelson, R. and Winter, S. (1982) *An Evolutionary Theory of Economic Change*, Cambridge, MA: Harvard University Press.

Nevens, T.M., Summer, G.L. and Uttal, B. (1990) 'Commercializing technology: what the best companies do', *Harvard Business Review*, May–June: 154–63.

OECD (1992) *Technology and the Economy: The Key Relationships*, Paris: OECD.

Piore, M.J. and Sabel, C.F. (1984) *The Second Industrial Divide: Possibilities for Prosperity*, New York: Basic Books.

Pottier, C. (1994) *L'Europe Face à la Mondialisation des Firmes. Le Cas de l'Industrie Vidéo*, Recherche pour le compte de l'IRES, Paris, Mimeo.

Rosenberg, N. and Birdzell L.E. Jr (1985) *How the West Grew Rich. The Economic Transformation of the Industrial World*, New York: Basic Books.

Sharp, M. and Galimberti, I. (1993) 'Coherence and diversity: Europe's chemical giants and the assimilation of biotechnology', *STEEP Discussion Paper No. 5*, Brighton, SPRU, July.

Sharp, M., Thomas, S. and Martin, P. (1994) 'Transferts de technologie et politique de l'innovation: le cas des biotechnologies', in F. Sachwald (ed.) *Les défis de la Mondialisation: Innovation et Concurrence*, Paris: Masson.

Taddei, D. and Coriat, B. (1993) *Made in France. L'Industrie Française dans la Competition Mondiale*, Paris: Le Livre de Poche.

Teece, D. (1988) 'Technological change and the nature of the firm', in G. Dosi, C. Freeman, R. Nelson, G. Silverberg and L. Soete (eds) *Technical Change and Economic Performance*, Cambridge: Cambridge University Press.

United Nations (1992) *Transnational Corporations as Engines of Growth*, ST/CTC/130, New York: UN.

Part II

JOINT VENTURES, ALLIANCES AND HIERARCHICAL INTEGRATION

5

THE EVOLUTION OF COLLABORATIVE ACTIVITY IN THE FIRM

Neil M. Kay

Introduction

In this chapter we shall analyse the evolution of collaborative activity in the modern corporation, with special reference to joint venture arrangements. The focus will be on attempting to develop an efficiency rationale for the evolution of joint venture activity and the analysis here builds on earlier work by Kay *et al.* (1987), Kay (1992), Hennart (1988) and Buckley and Casson (1988). The basic problem here can be easily summarized; joint venture consistently appears to be a costly option compared to single firm alternatives such as those obtained through merger. Suppose we have a firm with a particular technical competence and a firm with a particular competence in marketing and distribution. They agree that a profitable opportunity may be exploited by drawing on their respective expertise to form a new venture, and that joint venture and merger represent alternative modes of organization that permit appropriate pooling and integration of resources. However, joint ventures can entail contractual agreements that are expensive to set up and police, can involve complex and cumbersome hierarchical arrangements, and may introduce the threat of leakage of sensitive corporate know-how to the other party. When compared to the relative simplicity of merger, it is not obvious why a firm would willingly enter into joint venture arrangements.

This chapter pursues the possibility that an efficiency rationale for joint venture activity can be developed that still recognizes the contractual and administrative problems involved in joint venture activity. The solution suggested here depends on distinguishing between costs incurred at business level and costs incurred at corporate level. Most analyses of co-operative activity fail to make such a distinction. Joint venture may well be an expensive solution when compared to merger alternatives at the level of the new *venture*, but it may have the virtue of avoiding the need for merger of diversified firms and a quantum leap in managerial diseconomies at the level of the *firm*. It is

97

suggested later in the paper that this point helps explain a variety of phenomena related to the evolution of collaborative activity.

In this chapter, a comparative analysis of joint venture is carried out in relation to major alternatives, and it is shown that, at the level of business strategy, joint venture appears to be clearly a more costly and inefficient solution compared to simpler alternatives. Joint venture and alternatives are then set into the corporate strategy framework of diversified corporations and I develop arguments that show that joint venture is a logical and natural phenomenon that tends to appear at advanced later stages in industrial and corporate evolution. Then this analysis is related to actual evidence attributed to patterns of industrial and corporate evolution, before the chapter winds up with a short summary.

The evolution of collaborative activity

The use of checklists in analysis of competitive strategy often obscures an important point; options such as merger, acquisition, and various forms of collaborative activity, are alternative means to achieve similar ends. Exhaustive checklists have been constructed in the strategic management literature to identify the objectives of alternative modes such as joint ventures, licensing, strategic alliances, merger and acquisition. However, the checklists for the various alternatives typically turn out to bear a strong family resemblance to each other, which is not surprising since these options are really alternative ways of doing similar things, not alternative ways of doing different things. Also, when the individual sources of potential gains are inspected in the respective checklists, they tend to fall into two main categories; supply side gains from sharing resources, and demand side gains from reducing competition. In short, combining aspects of businesses can generate competitive advantage by reducing costs and influencing demand, and there are a variety of modes of organization that enable businesses to be combined. In this paper we pursue this issue by concentrating on the choice between merger and joint venture.

The role of complementary assets has been recognized as a major stimulus to collaborative activity (Teece 1986). Teece notes that in order to bring complex projects to fruition, various assets may be required, not all of which may be possessed to the requisite degree of quality by one firm. Collaborative activity between firms providing different but complementary assets is one way that resources can be combined to produce efficiency enhancing behaviour. It follows from the discussion above that we would expect similar arguments could be made concerning the potential gains from merger. Now, suppose we have two single-business firms, Alpha and Beta. The two firms possess different bundles of skills and the management of the respective firms perceive that they could provide complementary assets or resources to pursue a new value-enhancing business opportunity ('B' in Figure 5.1). One firm would provide marketing resources in sales, distribution, advertising and/or reputation. The other firm would provide technological resources such as technical know-how and/or shared plant, equipment and work force. The firms are deciding to exploit economies from combining complementary assets through either merger or joint venture. The merger option here will create a three-division multidivisional or M-form corporation (Williamson 1975) formed out of the two existing businesses of the respective firms, and the new business opportunity. The joint venture option leads to the new business opportunity B becoming jointly owned by the two parents Alpha and Beta. As Figure 5.1 indicates, the merger option leads to the creation of a single unified hierarchy, while the joint venture solution allows both Alpha and Beta to retain their independence.

We can now consider the efficiency and cost implications of mergers versus joint ventures by looking at the associated hierarchical and contractual issues. Both merger and joint venture involve hierarchical solutions to co-ordinate complementary assets, while the joint venture solution also involves continuing contractual arrangements. We shall start by considering why a hierarchical option may be preferred to a contractual solution in the first place, and then assess the relative efficiency implications of joint venture versus the merger alternative.

Why are hierarchical solutions adopted in the first place?

Both merger and joint venture solutions involve the introduction of hierarchical control aspects into resource allocation. In the case of merger, the hierarchical arrangement is fairly conventional with the three businesses now constituting divisions within an M-form structure. Headquarters can monitor the performance of each of the divisions and can take a strategic overview of the performance and prospects of each of the divisions. Headquarters can also treat each of the three divisions as elements in an internal capital market, and

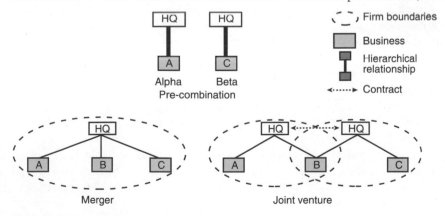

Figure 5.1 Merger versus joint venture

cross-subsidize potentially high yield areas from internal sources (Williamson 1975). The line of authority in the merger option is clear and unambiguous. The hierarchical solution in the joint venture case is more complicated, with the jointly owned subsidiary being the servant of two masters. Although both firms have full and direct control over their respective wholly-owned divisions, shared control of the jointly owned subsidiary creates a more complex hierarchical solution compared to merger.

However, why should a hierarchical solution be adopted in the first place? In principle, a contractual solution could be arranged to permit firms to combine complementary assets in a new business opportunity. Assets can be rented, licensed, leased, provided on a fee basis, etc. Either or both firms could provide physical, human or informational resources to the new business opportunity and share the potential rents with the recipient. Why should firm boundaries and hierarchical arrangements substitute contractual alternatives in cases such as new business opportunities?

The substitution of hierarchy for market reflects the differing comparative advantage of these alternative means for organizing resource allocation. Contract is appropriate for routine, standardized situations in which the asset and the services it generates can be closely specified. However, in situations characterized by novelty and uncertainty, contractual arrangements may be associated with substantial transaction costs (Williamson 1975, 1985).[1] Transaction costs may be substantial given the inherent difficulties involved in specifying rights and obligations and monitoring and policing activities in the face of uncertain outcomes, especially where incomplete information gives the other party opportunities to indulge in opportunistic behaviour (Williamson 1975, 1985). The setting up of an innovative business opportunity is likely to be characterized by considerable marketing and technological uncertainty, situations in which contractual solutions to combine complementary assets may encounter considerable levels of transaction costs. In some cases it may be impossible or impractical to write a contract for the complementary asset in question without making provision for further intervention and adjustment in the future. In such circumstances, hierarchical or in-house solutions become more attractive alternatives. Hierarchical solutions allow decision-makers to quickly respond to changing circumstances and unfold information without the need to go back and renegotiate the contract. It also can provide more effective protection of intellectual property rights than might be the case with contractual solutions such as licensing.

The differing comparative advantage of hierarchical and market solutions can best be seen by considering extreme cases. There are well established markets for commodities such as wheat and crude oil. In such cases, commodity standardization allows contracts to be established with few transaction costs. Once price, quantity and delivery time have been agreed, the respective parties have a fairly complete idea of what is expected and required from the contract. There are usually clear procedures that can be followed in the failure of either party to adhere to the terms and conditions of the contract, including legal redress if necessary in most cases. However, such conditions are unlikely to hold in innovative situations involving the allocation of resources to new areas, say the search for a new type of plastic. In these circumstances, hierarchical solutions may be preferred, for example a firm may employ a team of R&D scientists and engineers to search for the new plastic rather than put the task out to contract. Hierarchy and contract are tools for performing work, and like most tools one may be suitable for one set of circumstances, the other for a different set.

Joint venture arrangements to co-ordinate complementary assets

The previous section suggests that hierarchy may have a comparative advantage over contractual solutions in situations involving novel, non-routine decision-making in which important elements of the problem are inadequately specified at present. However, Figure 5.1 illustrates *two* alternative solutions involving hierarchical resource allocation; merger and joint venture. Since they represent alternative devices for the combination of complementary assets, the question of which organizational option should be adopted is reducible to questions of relative efficiency. There are three relevant issues here: (1) single versus dual control of the business opportunity, (2) contractual aspects of merger versus joint venture operation, (3) appropriability problems. We shall discuss each in turn.

(1) *Single versus dual control*; The control of division B resides at HQ level in the merger case, a simple and unambiguous arrangement. However, in the alternative case in Figure 5.1, division B is jointly owned and administered by two parent companies and two HQs. Even if both parents are paragons of goodwill and co-operative intent, the dual control system may create problems of conflicting objectives and imperfect co-ordination. If the parties to the joint venture are inclined to behave opportunistically (Williamson 1975), the control problems multiply. Just as ships tend to have one captain, so the simplest and most efficient way to run a business is to have one HQ in charge. The dual control system involved in joint venture will typically be more costly than single control systems involved in merger alternatives.

(2) *Contractual aspects*; Both merger and joint venture solutions involve transaction costs of search for suitable partners, and may involve significant costs in negotiating and concluding the agreement. However, while the transaction costs involved in the merger option in Figure 5.1 are effectively concluded with consummation of the merger,[2] the contractual costs associated with the joint venture (and incurred by each party) will have to anticipate contingencies and possible opportunistic behaviour throughout the life of the joint venture, and possibly beyond. While a merger contract is essentially about a once-and-for-all purchase, the joint venture contract is about continuing behaviour and may involve substantial set-up and policing costs.

(3) *Appropriability problems*; A firm that co-operates with a joint venture partner may face additional problems compared to one that goes it alone. The intimacy of joint venture relations may expose individual firms to the danger that their partner may be able to appropriate further gains than those set out in the joint venture agreement. For example, the Japanese post-war economic miracle was partly based on Japanese firms being able to obtain access to US technical and managerial know-how in earlier co-operative ventures. Firms may be reluctant to enter into joint ventures for fear of losing some or all of their competitive advantage to current partners who could turn out to be future rivals. In principle this could be regarded as potentially a zero-sum game situation that simply redistributes potential gains, but since the potential gainers may not properly compensate the losers,[3] it is more likely to represent a barrier to joint venture formation. These three issues – dual control, contractual aspects, and overlapping ownership (appropriability problems) – are inter-related and partially interchangeable in normal conditions. For example, joint venture partners may commit a great deal of resources to establishing and policing the contract in attempts to mitigate possible dual control and appropriability problems. Correspondingly, firms may skimp on contract costs and trade them off for possible dual control and appropriability problems.

The overall conclusion this leads to is that control, contractual and appropriability problems all suggest that joint venture is likely to be a less efficient method for co-ordinating complementary assets than is single firm operation as in the case of merger. Joint venture appears to have no obvious efficiency advantages, which raises the obvious question; why should firms ever wish to enter into joint venture agreements when merger appears to offer unambiguous cost advantages? Seen in this light, the argument that firms may wish to retain independence is essentially a monopoly argument,[4] since it appears the standard price of independence would be increased cost of operation, and only firms with monopoly leverage would be able to exert such discretion. It suggests that firms operating in competitive environments would be unable to indulge in the high-cost luxury of independence that joint venture helps perpetuate. It also seems to be the case that the control, contractual and appropriability issues identified here do not appear to be occasional or unusual problems, but are in fact commmonly observed in joint venture agreements (e.g. Hennart 1991).

One reason why firms may choose a mode of organization which appears to have such undesirable cost attributes is Hobson's choice; they may have no choice in the matter if they wish to pursue a particular strategy (such as access to a particular foreign market). This has been a traditional stimulus to joint venture agreements between foreign and host country firms in many developing countries. Access to host markets may be conditional on entering into joint venture arrangements with a local company. This is certainly consistent with the joint venture problems discussed above, and indeed the incentive behind host government policies on joint ventures is frequently a desire to exploit foreign firm appropriability problems and enable host country collaborators to gain access to foreign firm managerial and technical know-how. However, while this may help explain some historic patterns of joint venture activity, it does not explain the proliferation of joint venture activity between developed country firms in recent years.[5] It is an issue that we focus on now.

The evolution of joint venture activity

In so far as it goes, our analysis in the previous section is reasonable and defensible. It parallels much of the conventional treatment in the literature by focusing on the domain directly affected by the joint venture agreement. However, there are important limitations to this perspective. What Figure 5.1 illustrates is the local impact of co-ordinating complementary assets over the regions of the respective firms directly affected, effectively the business strategy domain of corporate activity relating to decisions made at the level of individual business units. However, for the diversified firm there will also be global or firm level implications that Figure 5.1 does not deal with, or issues at the level of corporate strategy. These issues are developed with the aid of Figure 5.2.

Product-market influences and specific strategies at business unit level are suppressed here by continuing to assume that individual business units have similar characteristics in terms of profitability, growth and scale.

There are two other simplifying assumptions in Figure 5.2. First, it is assumed that firms are pursuing growth motives through merger rather than internal expansion. Second, it is assumed a unit can always find a partner unit to share technology and another partner to share marketing and distribution resources, but transaction costs or the need to create hierarchy for future decision making mean that co-ordination is most efficiently achieved through internalization within a hierarchical arrangement rather than through contractual alternatives. This means that expansion takes the form of related linked diversification (Rumelt 1986) with a series of short market and technological links running through the corporate strategy, as in the Stage 3 and Stage 4 cases illustrated in Figure 5.2. Such an assumption is not essential, and our conclusions would be unaffected by diversification which exploited only a single major market or technological link.

We look at three different scenarios in Figure 5.2, each of which differ from the others in terms of at what stage in corporate evolution a completely new business opportunity appears. Each new business opportunity is presumed to be capable of exploiting complementary assets provided by two other units, as in Figure 5.2. In Scenario 1, the top case in Figure 5.2, the new business opportunity appears fairly early on in corporate evolution. Two independent firms (the grey spheres in Scenario 1 and Stage 1) see the possibility of combining their respective marketing and technological strengths in a new

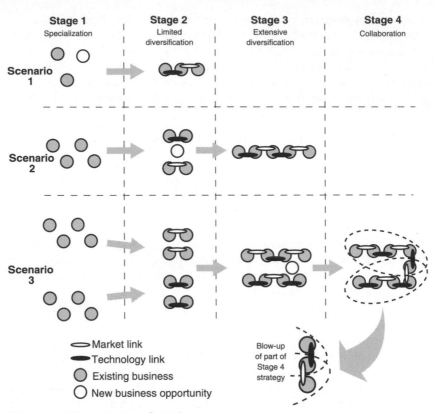

Figure 5.2 The evolution of collaboration

venture that would constitute a significant proportion of their revenues and profits. They merge to form a three-unit Stage 2 firm in which the new business opportunity forms the middle unit in the case illustrated, showing market and technological linkages with its neighbouring units. This closely parallels the example discussed in Figure 5.1: given that transaction costs mean a hierarchical solution is called for, our discussion in the previous section suggests that a single firm (merger) solution should be preferred over joint venture options in such a case.

In Scenario 2 (the middle series in Figure 5.2) some limited diversification has taken place before the new business opportunity appears. Four independent Stage 1 firms have undergone limited merger to form a pair of two-unit Stage 2 firms, one pair exploiting a technology link, the other a marketing link. The new business opportunity here can exploit a marketing link with one of the units in the technology based firm, and a technology link with one of the units in the marketing based firm. If the two firms merge to exploit this new opportunity, it would create a fairly complex five-unit Stage 3 firm, with the new business opportunity constituting the middle division of the five.

Scenario 2 introduces new issues concerning the relative merits of single firm versus joint venture operation, issues which are illustrated even more clearly in Scenario 3, the bottom series in Figure 5.2. In Scenario 3, eight firms progressively merge to exploit linkages. Stage 2 shows four pairs of merged firms, two exploiting marketing links and two exploiting technology links. The marketing based strategies merge to exploit a technology link between two units in Stage 3, and the technology based pairs do likewise to exploit a marketing link. It is at Stage 3 in this case that the two firms jointly perceive a business opportunity that could exploit complementary assets that could be provided by two units in the respective firms.

The standard solution inherited from the previous scenarios would be to merge. However, in this case the merger solution would generate a nine-unit firm in which the gains offered by the new business opportunity would constitute a relatively small part of the new merged corporation's activities, even taking into account the economies from complementary assets. Such a solution would be tantamount to taking a sledgehammer to crack a nut (Kay *et al.* 1987). More precisely, merger to exploit the venture possibility may have serious efficiency and regulatory implications for the separate or collective operation of business units in the combined firm that go well beyond the business strategy implications of co-ordinating complementary assets for the new business opportunity. Similar points have been made separately by Hennart (1988), Buckley and Casson (1988), and Hennart, who comments: 'Besides the obvious case when governments restrict mergers and acquisitions, joint venture will be preferred when the assets that yield the desired services are a small and inseparable part of the total assets held by both potential partners or when a merger or a total acquisition would significantly increase management costs' (1991: 99).

The most obvious implications follow from the scale of the merged firm. Against the gains from co-ordinating complementary assets with the new opportunity must be set any additional costs of bureaucracy in running a considerably enlarged enterprise. Unless these are zero, which may be taken to be a possible but unlikely situation, merger to exploit the new business opportunity will occur costs that are externalities from the perspective of the new opportunity (and consequently ignored in analyses like Figure 5.1), but which may have significant and adverse efficiency implications seen from the perspective of corporate strategy. In such circumstances, the firms may pass up exploitation of the common venture opportunity, or consider alternative forms of hierarchical control such as joint venture. Other problems may help block merger of diversified firms. The more units the respective firms operate, the more likely it is that merger may raise competition or antitrust issues. If two units that had been formerly operated separately within the respective firms are now likely to jointly control a significant portion of a market post-merger, then merger itself may be discouraged or prohibited. A possible solution could be to divest one of the offending units, but in Figure 5.2 this would entail sacrifice of the gains from complementary assets that the divestee would otherwise have exploited with neighbouring units before merger took place. Such reorganization creates further implied costs of merger to set against the local gains from exploiting complementary assets with the new business opportunity.

Thus, when the focus changes from the new *venture* to the new *firm* (and from business strategy to corporate strategy), it becomes apparent that single firm or merger solutions for exploiting complementarities may generate significant additional costs or prohibitions that are ignored if attention is paid only to the direct costs and benefits associated with the new business opportunity. This clearly paves the way for a rationale for joint venture activity based on efficiency and/or antitrust criteria. It is not necessary for merger to be more costly and less efficient than do-nothing alternatives for it to be passed up, only that it is more costly than a joint venture alternative once any antitrust prohibitions or constraints have been satisfied.

To illustrate this point, Figure 5.2 shows a joint venture solution for the Stage 3 business opportunity in which the dotted ellipses signify the boundaries of the respective firms. The overlap between the ellipses covers the domain of the joint venture. The single firm option would have had a single dotted ellipse encompassing all nine units involved in Stage 4 of Scenario 3. The region of joint venture activity is represented by a section blow-up in Figure 5.2, and corresponds to the case of complementary assets explored in Figure 5.1. It is an area of high contractual and administrative costs, but it has the virtue of restricting these costs to the locality of the joint venture. The scale of the respective firms is only slightly extended to the extent of their respective shares in the joint venture, while the continued independence of the two firms avoids the possibility that they may incur antitrust investigation from combining businesses unrelated to the new venture. Joint ventures may indeed be more costly than merger over the region of the new venture itself, but it is the system-wide implications of merger that are relevant, not just those directly associated with the new venture itself.

This also helps put arguments regarding the importance of trust in co-operative agreements into perspective. Some studies have attempted to justify joint venture on the basis that the venture itself may be low cost if trust and mutual forbearance exists between partners.[6] This may well be true, but a cheaper joint venture is still likely to be more expensive at the level of the venture than single firm options. Even if partners are paragons of virtue, it would be unreasonable to expect dual control systems (such as joint venture) to work as effectively as single firm, single control options. It is only when a distinction between business and firm level costs is made that a coherent efficiency-based rationale for joint venture activity really begins to appear. The implications of this are now explored further in the light of revealed patterns of joint venture activity.

Patterns of joint venture activity

The arguments so far suggest that joint venture activity will typically be more costly at the level of the venture than merger or single firm alternatives. If an efficiency rationale is to be developed for joint venture evolution, it is likely to be in terms of system-wide efficiency implications dominating considerations relevant only at the level of the venture itself. A situation in which such considerations may be important occurs where a new venture opportunity potentially involves large diversified firms. In such circumstances, joint venture may be accepted and adopted as an option which is high cost at the level of the venture but low cost at the level of the firm, relative to the merger option.

This reconciliation of joint venture high cost with potential system-wide efficiency advantages allows us to make sense of a variety of phenomena, and we discuss some of these here. First, Dunning (1993: 257) notes the relatively recent (post-Second World War) evolution of collaborative activity between technically sophisticated partners. The question of why such activity has only really begun to become widespread in recent years is best understood by turning it on its head and asking why, if they are such a good thing, firms did not pursue these options earlier. The solution suggested here is that the co-ordination solution provided by joint venture (and involving the implanting of hierarchy) was more easily provided by merger options in earlier decades. Pre-Second World War, even large corporations tended to be small and specialized when compared to the larger and diversified corporations that evolved later. Where firms found areas of overlapping interest, as in the case of complementary assets in Figure 5.1, merger was typically the obvious solution up to the limits provided by regulatory constraints on expansionary zeal. Systems wide effects of the type discussed in Figure 5.2's Stage 4 were likely to be non-existent or of minor importance. It was the post-war diversification boom that created the conditions associated with Stage 4 above that really stimulated the growth of joint venture activity.[7]

Second, and related to the first point, the relationship between merger and joint venture is more complicated than generally recognized. Merger is not only a substitute mode for co-ordinating new venture activity, through its role in helping create large diversified firms, it may also be a device that creates the crucial pre-conditions that stimulate subsequent joint venture activity. Scherer and Ross (1990: 92) note that merger played a very significant role in helping create the diversification of US corporations 1950–75. Thus, Figure 5.2 helps outline a partial evolutionary map for joint venture development, with earlier stages characterized by merger activity and later stages proving more receptive to joint venture solutions. These patterns tend to be consistent with the heavy emphasis on merger activity pre-Second World War, and increasing emphasis on joint venture activity post-Second World War.

Third, a number of cross-sectional analyses suggest there is a connection between size of firm and joint venture activity. These include Boyle (1968), Berg and Friedman (1978) and Colombo (1995). Since large firms tend to be more diversified, ceteris paribus, this is consistent with joint venture being triggered by earlier diversification. As suggested above, there does appear to be evidence of a causal link between earlier diversification on the part of the firm and its current joint venture activity. This is supported by Colombo's extensive field analysis of information technology industries, in which he concludes; 'large, widely diversified, highly internationalized firms show a much higher propensity towards collaborative ventures than their smaller rivals' (1995: 22).

Fourth, there are patterns of international joint venture activity that follow from the perspective developed here that have implications for public policy. For example, studies sponsored by the Commission of the European Communities to investigate the implications of completing the European internal Market (Emerson *et al.* 1988) found that the low level of joint venture formation between EC (European Communities) partners compared to joint venture formation between EC and non-EC partners was 'paradoxical'. It was suggested that the removal of some internal non-tariff business to intra-European trade could help facilitate such collaborative activity between European partners (e.g. Emerson *et al.* 1988: 175).

In fact, Kay (1991) argued that there were no grounds for such beliefs. A number of studies were cited, and patterns of EC joint venture formation investigated, to show that, rather than joint venture formation being inhibited by trade barriers, they tended to be stimulated. The direct impact of market completion on the internal market would be to open up alternative routes to internal market access for EC firms, such as exporting or wholly owned subsidiaries, and diminish recourse to costly joint venture solutions. These points are consistent with the points made above regarding governmental regulatory restraints as a contributing factor behind switches to joint venture activity. In view of the considerable financial resources being committed to support technological and industrial policies in the European Community (now European Union), it was suggested that public awareness of these relationships was highly desirable. Firms do not collaborate because the abandonment of trade barriers encourage them to do so; they collaborate because system wide effects and/or government controls force this locally high cost option on them.

There is one last issue that merits consideration here. This chapter has suggested that joint ventures tend to appear at advanced, later stages of a firm's development, while at the same time joint venture and other co-operative agreements tend to concentrate in high-tech, infant industries such as biotechnology, information technology and new materials (Hagedoorn and Schakenraad 1990) and also there is evidence that the propensity for firms to form joint venture and consortium agreements is higher in the early stages of the technological life cycle than at later stages (Cainarca *et al.* 1992). There is no necessary contradiction involved here, but the juxtaposition of mature firms and infant industry in the context of joint venture activity does invite further investigation and comment.

The first point that can be made is that the new industries with which collaborative activity has been particularly associated are also knowledge intensive with a high level of innovative activity. These are the circumstances in which we would expect to find hierarchical solutions being adopted. New ventures in these industries (especially at the early stages of the technological life cycle) are likely to have high innovative content and involve the deferral of important strategic decisions. Incomplete information will tend to militate against simple contractual solutions, leading to the instituting of hierarchy to deal with strategic decisions as and when the need for them arises. However, this still leaves the question of why collaborative solutions such as joint venture should be adopted in these infant industries rather than single firm options.

A study of the US biotechnology industry by Barley *et al.* (1992) is useful in this context. They found that the type of organizations most likely to indulge in co-operative activity with other organizations were diversified firms and the smaller dedicated biotechnology firms formed to pursue biotechnological R&D. The involvement of diversified firms in co-operative activity is consistent with our expectations. However this still leaves the question as to why smaller R&D performing firms also show a strong propensity to indulge in co-operative activity. The key here appears to be that when they co-operate, the small R&D performers tend to have multiple partners and these partners tend to be large and diversified. While it may be possible to consider merging with one of these partners (and risk alienating other partners who may be rivals of the preferred partner), clearly the small R&D performer cannot merge with all of them without indirectly creating a mammoth firm out of its various partners. Diversification again appears to be the key in explaining the evolution of co-operative activity. Co-operative solutions are more likely to be resorted to if new ventures involve large diversified firms, or if they involve a smaller firm which has a number of venture possibilities involving large diversified partners.[8] Diversification is again the pre-condition that helps to trigger collaborative activity, even if in the case of the small R&D performers it is other firms' diversification.[9]

Conclusions

The approach developed in this chapter develops a number of points and arguments to help provide an integrated framework for the evolution of collaborative activity in the modern corporation. The relevance of strategic issues operating simultaneously at different levels was demonstrated, and the role of scale and diversity in the modern corporation was argued to be a central consideration.

Collaboration at business unit level can be defined in a variety of ways, but normally includes joint venture and licensing options, both of which were discussed in this paper. An important point of the paper is that joint venture is typically unquestionably inferior to single ownership alternatives on efficiency grounds at the level of the venture activity itself. However, knock-on implications of single ownership alternatives for large diversified corporations mean that joint venture may be the more efficient arrangement when alternatives are compared at the global level of corporate strategies. The chapter argues that it is important to focus on the relative efficiency of all alternative arrangements for exploitation of complementary assets, and that focusing simply on the gains compared to simply not exploiting the venture opportunity is likely to obscure deeper reasons for the evolution of collaboration.

The chapter provides a basis for linking together a number of disparate findings in the empirical literature and helps identify consistency and pattern in the behaviour of corporations in these areas. In particular, much recent joint venture activity is seen as reflecting a natural, though advanced, stage in the development of modern corporations and industries in which joint venture does not simply substitute merger and diversification, but is also a consequence of previous corporate diversification and merger moves.

Notes

1   Williamson also argues that asset specificity (assets specialized by use or user) is generally a pre-condition for the appearance of significant transactional problems and the evolution of hierarchy. However, this neglects the role of property rights in creating transactional problems. For example, R&D is commonly performed within the boundaries of the firm because its outcome is difficult to predict and may *not* be specialized by use or user. Non-specificity in the form of appropriability problems can lead to firms protecting their R&D investments by containing them within corporate walls.

2   Of course, this does not mean that the administration of the venture is costless once the merger is concluded. Hierarchy will be used to allocate resources to the various businesses within the merged firm post-merger. However, as we have noted, even these hierarchical arrangements are likely to be simpler and cheaper than those associated with joint venture.

3   It is difficult to conceive of formal mechanisms to allow for what is after all, informal opportunistic behaviour, which may be difficult for the gainers to specify and anticipate *ex ante* and the losers to prove *ex post*.

4   See also Pitelis (1993) for a number of readings which look at the question of power in collaborative activity.

5   An issue that may be of relevance in deterring acquisition solutions is the Grossman–Hart problem (1980) in which shareholders in a target firm may have an incentive to hang on to their shareholding in the belief that the bidder, if successful, will raise the value of their shares even higher than the current bid price. If sufficient shareholders behave this way, it may create barriers to takeover and prevent the bid from being successful. There has been considerable discussion of the implications of the Grossman–Hart problem, and a number of articles in

Fairbairn and Kay (1989) discuss various implications of it. However, even if it is conceded that the Grossman–Hart problem can create barriers to merger activity, it still leaves the question of why merger tends to be preferred in some circumstances and joint venture in others.

6   See Kay 1992: 205–6.

7   Scherer and Ross (1990).

8   The importance of diversification in this context can be illustrated by considering a small R&D performing firm which has two partners which are themselves small firms. Merger could still be a viable option here and indeed this is one route through which small firms become large diversified firms. Now, replace the two partners of the small R&D performing firm with two large diversified firms, say Glaxo and ICI, or Daimler-Benz and Mitsubishi. Clearly merger with both its partners would be impractical in either case since the solution would be of a scale that considerably outstrips the scale and importance of the venture and its associated organizational problems.

9   These issues are discussed further in Kay (1997).

References

Barley, S.R., Freeman, J. and Hybels, R.C. (1992) 'Strategic alliances in commercial biotechnology', in N. Nohria and R. Eccles (eds) *Networks and Organizations*, Boston, MA: Harvard University Press, pp. 311–47

Berg, S.V. and Friedman, P. (1978) 'Joint ventures in American industry: an overview', *Mergers and Acquisitions* Summer: 28–41.

Boyle, S.E. (1968) 'An estimate of the number and size distribution of domestic joint subsidiaries', *Antitrust Law and Economic Review* Spring: 81–92.

Buckley, P. and Casson, M. (1988) 'A theory of cooperation in international business', in F. Contractor and P. Lorange (eds) *Cooperative Strategies in International Business*, Lexington, MA: Lexington Books, pp. 31–53.

Cainarca, G.C., Colombo, M.G. and Mariotti, S. (1992) 'Agreements between firms and the technological life cycle model: evidence from information technologies', *Research Policy* 21: 45–62.

Colombo, M.G. (1995) 'Firm size and cooperation: the determinants of cooperative agreements in information technology industries', *International Journal of the Economics of Business* 2: 3–29.

Cyert, R.M. and March, J.G. (1963) *A Behavioural Theory of the Firm*, Englewood Cliffs, NJ: Prentice Hall.

Dunning, J.H. (1993) *Multinational Enterprises and the Global Economy*, Washington, DC: Addison-Wesley.

Emerson, M., Aujean, M., Catinet, M., Goybet, P. and Jacquemin, A. (1988) *The Economics of 1992*, Oxford: Oxford University Press.

Fairbairn, J.A. and Kay, J.A. (eds) (1989) *Mergers and Merger Policy*, Oxford, Oxford University Press.

Grossman, S.J. and Hart, O.D. (1980) 'Takeover bids, the free-rider problem and the theory of the corporation', *Bell Journal of Economics* 11: 42–64.

Hagedoorn, J. and Schakenraad, J. (1990) 'Inter-firm partnerships and co-operative strategies in core technologies', in C. Freeman and L. Soete (eds) *New Explorations in the Economics of Technical Change*, London: Pinter, pp. 4–37.

Hennart, J-F. (1988) 'A transaction costs theory of equity joint ventures', *Strategic Management Journal* 9: 361–74.

—— (1991) 'The transaction cost theory of the multinational enterprise', in C.N. Pitelis and R. Sugden (eds) *The Nature of the Transnational Firm*, London: Routledge, pp. 81–116.

Kay, N.M. (1991) 'Industrial collaborative activity and the completion of the internal market', *Journal of Common Market Studies* 29, 347–62.

—— (1992) 'Collaborative strategies of firms: theory and evidence', in A. Del Monte (ed.) *Recent Developments in the Theory of Industrial Organisation*, London: Macmillan, pp. 201–31.

—— (1997) *Pattern in Corporate Evolution*, Oxford: Oxford University Press.

Kay, N.M., Robé, J-P., and Zagnoli, P. (1987) 'An approach to the analysis of joint venture', Florence: European University Institute.

Pitelis, C.N. (ed.) (1993) *Transaction Costs, Markets and Hierarchies*, Oxford: Blackwell.

Rumelt, R.P. (1986) *Strategy Structure and Economic Performance*, revised edn, Boston, MA: Harvard Business School.

Scherer, F.M., and Ross, D. (1990) *Industrial Market Structure and Economic Performance*, Boston, MA: Houghton-Mifflin, 3rd edn.

Teece, D. (1986) 'Profiting from technological innovation', *Research Policy* 15: 286–305.

Williamson, O.E. (1975) *Markets and Hierarchies: Analysis and Antitrust Implications*, New York: Free Press.

—— (1985) *The Economic Institutions of Capitalism*, New York: Free Press.

6

TESTING THEORIES OF JOINT VENTURES

Why Japanese investors in the United States
choose joint ventures over acquisitions

Jean-François Hennart and Sabine Reddy

Introduction

Joint ventures, as any other institutional arrangement, are likely to be successful only if certain conditions are met. In the last five years, a series of articles has increased our understanding of these conditions by exploring the comparative advantage of joint ventures *vis-à-vis* other possible forms of organizations (contracts and full acquisitions/mergers). The present chapter contributes to this research stream by looking at the choice between full acquisitions and greenfield joint ventures.

There are four possible ways to combine complementary assets held by different parties; (1) contracts; (2) full equity control through replication (greenfield investment) (3) full equity control through acquisition/merger (4) shared equity control, i.e., joint ventures, either (4a) a shared investment in a greenfield plant or (4b) a partial acquisition (Hennart 1988a). The choice between contracts (1) and equity (2, 3 and 4) has been discussed in the transaction costs theory literature in both a domestic and international context (Williamson 1979; Buckley and Casson 1976; Hennart 1982) and empirically tested by Davidson and McFetridge (1985), Globerman and Schwindt (1986), Joskow (1985), Stuckey (1983), Hennart (1988b), and Masten, *et al.* (1991) among others. The determinants of the choice between wholly-owned subsidiaries (2 and 3), and equity joint ventures (4) is a salient issue in international management and has been explored by Gatignon and Anderson (1988), Kogut and Singh (1988a, 1988b), Gomes-Casseres (1989), Hennart (1991a) and Blomstrom and Zejan (1991). Caves and Mehra (1986), Kogut and Singh (1988a), Zejan (1990), Yamawaki (1992) and Hennart and Park (1993) explore the choice between foreign greenfield entry (2) and acquisitions (3). However, except for Kogut and Singh (1988a) and Singh and Kogut (1989), there has

113

been no empirical research on the determinants of the choice between a full acquisition/merger (3) and a greenfield joint venture (4a).[1] (Henceforth the term acquisition will be used to mean acquisition as well as merger.)

The choice between acquisition and joint venture is of particular interest because it throws light on two competing theories of why joint ventures exist. Balakrishnan and Koza (1991, 1993) see joint ventures as a mechanism to reduce the transaction costs incurred when acquiring other firms. They predict that these costs will be lower when the acquirer and the target firm are based in the same industry, because both parties can more readily assess the value of the assets for sale. Hence the joint venture alternative will be preferred when the potential target and the acquirer belong to different industries. Hennart (1988a) and Kay et al. (1987), on the other hand, have argued that a firm will favour acquisitions over joint ventures when the assets it needs are not commingled with other unneeded assets within the firm that holds them, and hence can be acquired by buying the firm or a part of it. For Hennart, and Kay et al., the size and the organizational structure of the partner are the crucial determinants of the choice between joint ventures and acquisitions. While Balakrishnan and Koza are concerned with transaction costs in the market for firms, Hennart and Kay's focus is on the costs of integrating the target firm's labour force (what has been called the post-acquisition integration problem). Looking at the choice between joint ventures and acquisition hence allows us to sharpen our understanding of the strategic logic for these two forms of firm growth.

Our first task is to carefully specify the variables that affect the choice between joint ventures and acquisitions. To do so, we develop a transaction cost model of the necessary and sufficient conditions for equity joint ventures to be the preferred institutional mode. The discussion outlines all possible ways to organize the co-operation of competitors and looks sequentially at the choice between all the alternatives. The goal of the exercise is to derive logically the conditions that make joint ventures a relatively more efficient solution than acquisitions. Specific hypotheses are derived and then they are tested on a sample of Japanese manufacturing entries in the United States. The results show that joint ventures are preferred over acquisitions in four cases: (1) when the assets desired by Japanese investors and held by US firms are bundled within these firms with non-desired assets because the US firms are large and are not divisionalized; (2) when the Japanese parent has had no previous experience in the American market and presumably fears post-merger integration problems; (3) when both the US and Japanese partners have at least one common product; and (4) when the target market is growing neither very rapidly nor very slowly.

Joint ventures in a comparative institutional perspective

The literature on equity joint ventures is by now extremely large. One weakness of many studies is, however, that they often do not specify carefully the conditions that are both necessary and sufficient for joint ventures to be the preferred mode of coalescing inputs held by more than one firm.

Some authors (for example Contractor and Lorange 1988) have argued that the rise of economies of scale in R&D and in component production is behind the growth in the number of joint ventures. It has been written that an increase in the size of R&D budgets necessary to bring new products to market is responsible for the emergence of R&D consortia. Implicit in this argument is that the minimum efficient scale at the R&D level is now larger than at downstream stages, thus making it efficient for downstream producers to pool their R&D efforts. However, differences in economies of scale between stages do not necessarily lead to joint ventures: in many industries (for example in tin) the stage with the highest MES (smelting) is operated by specialist producers buying their inputs from independent small upstream producers (Hennart 1988b).

Another common argument is that joint ventures are needed to pool together complementary knowledge. Yet there are many other ways to achieve that goal, for example licensing and cross-licensing. While in 1982 US firms had 16,000 foreign joint ventures, they also licensed at least 31,000 independent foreign firms (Contractor 1990). A third way to pool knowledge is to acquire the foreign firm which holds the complementary know-how. Indeed acquisitions are the most common form of market entry, at least in the case of foreign entry into the United States: in 1988, foreigners spent more than five times acquiring US firms than what they spent establishing new plants (Graham and Krugman 1991, table 1.5).

In short, to understand why joint ventures exist, one must explain why they are superior to all their alternatives, contracts, wholly-owned subsidiaries, in-house development, and acquisitions/mergers. Recent empirical research has shed light on some of those choices. One area that has remained poorly understood is the choice between joint ventures and acquisitions. This is the goal of this chapter.

Equity joint ventures are one of many ways used to combine assets. They can be defined as residual-sharing agreements, in which the suppliers of inputs to the venture do not price their inputs or outputs, but instead agree to be paid with a share of the profits of the venture (the residual). This is in contrast to contracts, in which suppliers of inputs obtain a direct payment for their services. Hence 'collaborative alliances', 'strategic networks' and the like can be classified as either contracts (supply and marketing agreements) in which the supplier of inputs is paid a fee which does not depend on the profitability of the venture, and equity relationships (equity joint ventures, sharecropping) in which the input supplier is remunerated through a share of the residual of the venture.[2]

Consider two firms, A and B. Firm A supplies input I1 and firm B input I2. Assume that the production of P requires the combination of inputs I1 and I2. There are four possible ways by which I1 and I2 could be combined:

1   Input I1 and input I2 could be combined by contract. This could be done by a third party, firm C, which would buy I1 and I2 from firm A and firm B. Alternatively, if either inputs I1 or I2 are difficult to contract for on the market, the party with the difficult-to-sell input will contract for the other input on the market. Hence firm A could buy I2 from firm B by contract and combine it with its own I1 if the sale of I1 on the market is subject to high transaction costs (or firm B could purchase I1 from firm A by contract if the sale of its own I2 is subject to high transaction costs). In both cases the result is a venture wholly-owned by the party with the difficult-to-sell input.

2   Firm A, unable to obtain input I2 from firm B by contract, may decide to replicate in-house the assets that yield I2. The result is a wholly-owned greenfield investment. (The case for a greenfield investment by firm B is symmetrical).

3   Firm A, unable to acquire input I2 from firm B, may decide to acquire the assets yielding I2 by taking over firm B through acquisition (and vice versa for firm B).

4   Firms A and B may decide to form a joint venture, pooling inputs I1 and I2.

The conditions which are necessary and sufficient for joint ventures to be the most efficient arrangement can be identified by looking sequentially at the choice between these four alternatives. The argument of this section is summarized in Figure 6.1. First, we compare equity relationships (equity joint venture and wholly-owned subsidiaries) with contracts. Within the category of equity relationships, we contrast exclusive equity relationships with shared equity relationships (equity joint ventures). We then discuss why equity joint ventures may be preferred to internal development, and more importantly, to acquisition. Thus, at the end of this section, we will be able to carefully specify the conditions under which joint ventures may be preferred to acquisitions.

Contracts versus equity relationships

Equity joint ventures are shared-equity relationships. Hence the first point to address if one is to understand why joint ventures exist is why equity would be chosen over contracts.

As mentioned earlier, a crucial difference between an equity and a contractual relationship is the fact that, while in a contractual relationship the suppliers of inputs to the venture are paid a fixed amount, in an equity relationship they are rewarded through a share of the residual. Paying an input supplier through a share of the residual makes sense when the inputs contributed to the venture are difficult to define and price *ex ante*, and when enforcement of the contract for their supply would be difficult. In that case,

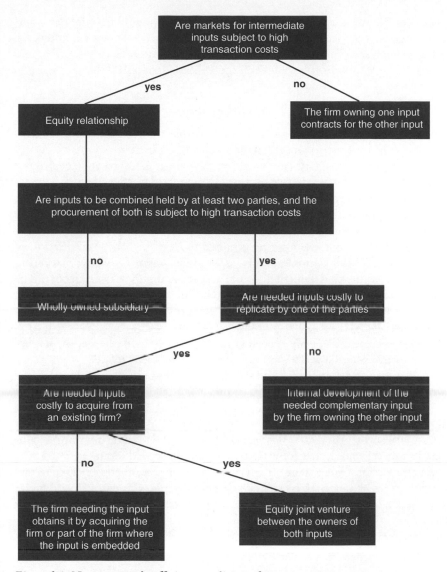

Figure 6.1 Necessary and sufficient conditions for equity joint ventures

this arrangement reduces the probability that the suppliers of inputs to the venture will behave opportunistically, because, since they are paid from the profits of the venture, they would bear some or all of the cost of their cheating in the form of reduced profits from the venture (this incentive is, of course, directly proportional to their equity stake).

There is by now an abundant literature that shows that equity relationships (whether wholly-owned subsidiaries or joint ventures) are preferred to contracts for the exchange of intermediate inputs (raw materials, parts and components, knowledge, reputation, financial capital) whenever markets for these inputs are characterized by high transactions costs (see for example Stuckey 1983; Davidson and McFetridge 1985; Hennart 1988b).

Full versus shared equity

The second characteristic of joint ventures is that they are *shared* equity relationships, in contrast to wholly-owned ventures, which are exclusive equity relationships (there is only one parent to the venture). Given the need to use equity relationships rather than contracts, why would two or more parents choose to simultaneously take equity in a given venture? The answer is simple: the markets for the inputs supplied by both parents must be simultaneously subject to high transaction costs (Hennart 1988a).

To go back to our example of product P requiring the combination of inputs I1 and I2 from firms A and B, assume that input I1 is tacit marketing knowledge while I2 is knowledge that is patented and easy to license. The combination of I1 and I2 to produce P can be effected the following way: Firm B, which has 'marketable' knowledge will license its knowledge to firm A, whose knowledge is costly to transact (and vice versa if the input with high transaction costs is I2). Only if both I1 and I2 are costly to transact (if they are both non-marketable) will a joint venture be the efficient mode.

A number of recent empirical studies support these points. Most of the work has been done at the international level, and looks at the choice of foreign direct investors between wholly-owned subsidiaries and joint ventures. Empirical findings show that parents take full ownership of their subsidiaries when they possess or can acquire on the market the complementary inputs they need; they joint venture when the needed inputs are subject to high transaction costs and are costly to acquire on the market (Gatignon and Anderson 1988; Gomes-Casseres 1989). For example, Hennart (1991a) found that Japanese investors were more likely to enter the US through joint ventures if they had little experience of the US market (hence a need for tacit country-specific knowledge) and if they were diversifying into a different industry (hence a need for tacit industry-specific knowledge).

Joint venture versus replication and acquisition

We have established so far that a joint venture can serve to remedy the failure of markets for two or more inputs. A third condition for the existence of joint ventures is that the alternatives of replication or acquisitions must be more expensive than the sharing of existing assets through a joint venture. Consider, for example, a pharmaceutical firm that wants to manufacture a biologically-engineered drug. The necessary knowledge may already be held by a biotechnology firm. If such knowledge is tacit or poorly protected and its sale subject to high transaction costs, the licensing option may not be viable. The pharmaceutical firm has then three choices: (1) it can obtain the needed technology by joint-venturing with a biotechnology firm; (2) it can ask its in-house R&D department to replicate the technology held by the biotechnology firm (replication); (2) it can obtain access to the technology by acquiring the biotechnology firm (acquisition).

Joint ventures versus replication

Consider first replication. Replication will be more costly than a joint venture in two main cases: first, if there are scale and scope economies in the production of one of the inputs, obtaining the services of this input through a joint venture will be much less costly than replicating it, since the marginal cost of using an existing input will be a fraction of the total cost of replicating it. This is the case for intangibles (knowledge, reputation) which are public goods. In that case the fixed cost of replicating the knowledge is high, while the marginal cost is low (it is the cost of transferring the knowledge to third parties). Such is also the case for distribution networks, which are often characterized by scope economies. For example the additional cost of adding one more drug to the list of drugs distributed by a pharmaceutical firm's sales force is typically low within an extended range. Similarly, it is much cheaper for a pharmaceutical company to tap the knowledge of a biotechnology firm through a joint venture than it is to replicate it in-house.[3] Knowledge, reputation, and distribution make up a large proportion of all assets contributed to joint ventures.

Joint ventures versus acquisitions

The other condition for joint ventures to be the most efficient arrangement is that it must be more efficient than an acquisition. The reason for this condition is clear: if the successful sale of a biotechnologically-engineered drug requires the combination of biotechnology R&D and an extensive distribution system, one way to achieve this combination is to have the biotechnology firm buy out the pharmaceutical firm, have the pharmaceutical firm buy the biotechnology firm, or have both merge. For a joint venture to be preferable to this solution, there must be significant costs involved in acquisitions. Since our analysis focuses on the choice between joint ventures and acquisitions, understanding the nature of these costs is an important element of our model.

One can think of five main cases where acquisitions/mergers will be more costly to carry out than joint ventures:

Indivisibilities Hennart (1988a) and Kay *et al.* (1987) have argued that one potential impediment to acquisitions is when the desired assets are hard to disentangle from non-desired ones. Assume that the distribution assets needed by a biotechnology firm to successfully introduce a new drug are a small part of the total assets held by the pharmaceutical firm, but are hard to separate from the other assets held by that firm. If the biotechnology firm were to buy the pharmaceutical firm to obtain its sales force, it would also be buying many assets which are not needed and which, because they are difficult to disentangle from the sales force, are difficult to divest afterwards. It may be difficult to separate the sales force from the research and manufacturing activities of the pharmaceutical firm because of the need for vertical integration between those two activities. Hence it may be impossible to acquire the sales force without acquiring the pharmaceutical business as well. Furthermore, pharmaceutical companies also often manufacture other products, such as veterinary medicines, medical instruments, hospital supplies, cosmetics, and seeds. A small biotechnology company would be encumbered by these assets, and would incur high costs in managing them (Shan 1988). By contrast, through a joint venture, the biotechnology firm is able to obtain use of the sales force without actually managing it. Hence the fact that a partner's desired assets are linked to its non-desired assets, while it makes acquisitions costly, does not cause problems for joint ventures, since the flow of services from the assets counts as a contribution to the joint venture, yet is still available for the parent's other businesses. Joint ventures may therefore be preferred when the desired assets are not easily separable from the many other assets owned by the parent. This is likely to be the case when the parents are large and not organized in quasi-independent divisions which can be acquired separately from the rest of the firm, i.e., when they are not divisionalized. Acquisitions, on the other hand, will be chosen when the parents are small, or if they are large, when they are divisionalized (Kay *et al*. 1987).

Management costs As noted by Kogut and Singh (1988a), full acquisitions involve higher labour management costs than greenfield joint ventures. An acquisition of a previously independent firm transforms erstwhile entrepreneurs into employees, and thus reduces their motivation. When a foreign firm acquires a local firm, the foreign firm acquires an existing set of employees, with their own routines and culture. Integrating such employees is difficult, particularly so if there are cultural differences between the two firms (Jemison and Sitkin 1986). These cultural differences can be due to differences between the national cultures of the home base of both firms, but also to differences between the industries in which these two firms operate. In contrast, the joint venture solution has the benefit of safeguarding the incentives that employees of both firms have to maximize the profits of the joint venture. The management of the joint venture's labour force can therefore be left to the local partner (Kogut and Singh 1988a). Hence, even if the desired assets are not commingled with undesired assets, joint ventures may be preferred over acquisitions by firms which are inexperienced in managing a foreign labour force, and by firms venturing outside their core industry.

Difficulties in assessing the value of the target firm   For Balakrishnan and Koza (1991, 1993), joint ventures arise when acquisitions are difficult because of the acquirer's ignorance of the true value of the assets he needs and wants to acquire. Lack of knowledge of the true value of the assets is likely to lead the acquirer to bid too high (hence making losses) or too low (hence missing the deal). A joint venture, on the other hand, is an efficient vehicle for reducing these information costs because it allows the partners to rescind the relationship at relatively low cost. It also makes it possible to gather additional information on the value of the partner's assets. One implication of the analysis is that joint ventures should be preferred to acquisitions when the firms combining assets have little knowledge of each other's business, i.e., when they are in different industries (Balakrishnan and Koza 1991).

Governmental and institutional barriers   Governmental and institutional barriers in target countries may also impede acquisitions. This is the case in many LDCs, which forbid acquisitions and instead mandate joint ventures (Gomes-Casseres 1990), but most developed countries also put restrictions on acquisitions of domestic firms by foreigners in 'strategic' industries (weapons, telecommunications, banking, transportation, the press, aerospace, computers) (Office of the US Trade Representative 1985). Acquisitions of firms by foreigners may also be barred on antitrust grounds. Acquisitions are also difficult when there are institutional barriers. In some countries hostile takeovers are discouraged by legal restrictions on voting rights, cross-holdings (Japan), and bank and family control (Germany and Italy, respectively) (Lightfoot 1992). Because of these barriers, Kay *et al.* (1996) found that the ratio of acquisitions to joint ventures tends to be larger for transactions between firms domiciled within a member country of the European Union, and lowest for transactions involving European Union firms and firms domiciled outside the Union.

Kogut and Singh (1988a) and Singh and Kogut (1989) provide empirical evidence on the factors that determine the choice between acquisitions and joint ventures. They looked at entries by foreign multinational firms into the United States and argued that a main disadvantage of entering through acquisition rather than joint ventures was the high management cost involved in integrating the target firm's labour force. They hypothesized that the disadvantage would be greater the greater the cultural distance between the investor's home base and the US. As expected, they found that joint ventures were preferred to acquisitions when the entrant's home country was culturally distant from the US. Joint ventures were also preferred to acquisitions when the US operation was large and when the US industry entered was R&D intensive. The parent's experience of the US market was not significant.

The design and the data sources in Singh and Kogut (1989) are similar to Kogut and Singh (1988a), but the emphasis is on the characteristics of entering firms and on those of the US sectors entered. Five structural characteristics of the sectors penetrated by foreign investors were entered as independent variables: R&D intensity, advertising intensity, concentration ratio, import penetration, and growth of shipments. Singh and Kogut hypothesized that the problems of valuing acquisitions were higher in R&D intensive industries and hence that entries in these industries were more likely to be joint ventures. They found that joint ventures were preferred to acquisitions when the US industry entered was R&D intensive, when the foreign investor had little experience of the US market, and when the targeted venture was large.[4]

Neither of these two studies examined what can be called the 'digestibility' of the targeted US assets, i.e. the extent to which the desired assets of the target firm are linked to its other non-desired assets. Kogut and Singh (1988a) argue that acquisitions will be discouraged the larger the assets of the affiliate, but do not provide a rationale for this prediction. In Singh and Kogut (1989), the hypothesis is that large investments are more risky than small ones. Hence foreign investors enter through joint ventures to share that risk with their partners. The size of the venture is defined as the assets of the acquired unit (in the case of acquisition) or that of the US partner (in the case of joint ventures). This specification introduces a bias if, as we expect, acquisitions are systematically associated with small affiliate size (but not necessarily small partner size, since the acquired unit may be a division of a large firm). By measuring affiliate size by the assets of the acquired unit in the case of acquisitions, and by those of the partner in the case of joint ventures, the authors bias the test towards significance of their size variable. A correct specification should be neutral *vis-à-vis* the outcome, i.e., it should consider partner size in the case of both acquisition and joint ventures. Assets are also a poor proxy for the magnitude of post-acquisition management problems. Because of this and other problems with the empirical analysis, further research into the determinants of the choice between acquisitions and joint ventures is warranted.[5]

Taken together, these results suggest that, in an environment with low barriers to acquisitions like the United States, joint ventures are preferred to acquisitions when the value of the target firm is difficult to assess, and when it is difficult to assimilate the target through an acquisition because of its size or because of the inexperience of the acquirer.

Research design and testable propositions

Research design

Based on the theoretical considerations developed above, this section outlines specific testable hypotheses in the context of Japanese investment in the United States. Two types of entries are compared: full acquisitions of US firms by Japanese investors (hereafter acquisitions) and greenfield joint ventures between Japanese and American firms (henceforth joint ventures).

Focusing, as we do, on firms from a single home country entering the

United States has a number of advantages. First, it avoids the difficult problem of having to control for the often subtle governmental and institutional barriers to acquisitions described above. The United States is one of the few countries which has minimal restrictions on foreign ownership, and none for manufacturing enterprises (Price Waterhouse 1991). Even foreign acquisitions of high technology firms have been unregulated.[6]

In contrast to the situation in Germany, France, or Japan, there are also no structural barriers in the United States to the acquisition of domestic firms by foreigners. All in all, most experts agree that the United States is, with the United Kingdom, the only major country with an active and open market for corporate control. In fact, acquisitions are the most common mode of foreign entry (Graham and Krugman 1991). This makes a meaningful comparison between acquisitions and joint ventures possible.

A second advantage of our research design is that studying parents based in a single country controls for the impact of national cultural differences in the mode of entry (Kogut and Singh 1988a). Such differences are very difficult to model.

Lastly, the choice of Japanese entries in the United States is particularly appropriate for two additional reasons. First, Japanese investment in the US has elicited considerable interest and debate. Second, in contrast with other countries, Japanese firms have a remarkably low propensity to enter through acquisitions. For example, acquisitions made up only 31 per cent of the 114 Japanese entries in the United States in the Kogut and Singh sample, compared to 54 per cent for the all-nationality sample (Kogut and Singh 1988a: table 2). One often mentioned reason is the cultural distance between Japan and the United States, which makes the problem of post-merger integration more salient.

We define the American partner as the firm with which the Japanese investor is dealing. When the entry is a joint venture, the partner is the American parent of the venture. When the entry is an acquisition, the American partner may or may not be the same as the acquired firm, as in some cases Japanese firms have acquired divisions of divisionalized US parents. In that case, the partner is the divisionalized parent.[7]

Hypotheses

Given our focus on Japanese entries in the United States, we present the following hypotheses:

H1: Acquisitions will be preferred to joint ventures when the size of the US partner is small, or if it is large, when the US partner is divisionalized.

If the US partner is small, it is likely that the assets desired by the Japanese investor make up 100 per cent of the assets held by the US firm. If the target firm is large but divisionalized, it is possible for the Japanese investor to acquire only the division that owns the desired resources. Acquisitions become problematic when the partner is large, but not divisionalized. Then it is difficult to separate the desired from the non-desired assets, and an acquisition would involve having to operate at a scale and/or in industries which do not fit well with the acquiring firm's business. In contrast, services of the desired assets can be obtained through a joint venture without having to change the ownership of these assets, and hence without having to disentangle them from non-desired assets.

We have seen above that one of the main disadvantages of acquisitions relative to joint ventures is the high cost of integrating the target's firm's labour force. Such costs are likely to be particularly high for Japanese firms because of the large cultural distance between Japan and the United States. Many recent Japanese acquisitions of US firms have fared poorly because of serious problems encountered in integrating the subsidiary. Sanyo was unable to transfer its work and production organization to the television plant it bought from Warwick in Forrest City, Arkansas, because of resistance by unions and by the US management team it left in place, and ended up shifting production of TVs to its other plants in the US and Mexico (Kenney and Florida 1993). The acquisition of Firestone by Bridgestone has also been painful (*The Economist* 1991). By contrast, joint ventures with US firms are a less risky way to test the feasibility of transferring the Japanese system to the United States, as the case of Toyota shows.

Japanese firms are likely to expect their post-acquisition integration costs to vary along two predictable dimensions. The first is their experience in the US market: the longer they have been in the US, the more likely they will choose, everything else constant, an acquisition over a joint venture.

H2: Acquisitions will be preferred to joint ventures when the Japanese investor has a long experience of the US environment.

The second factor is whether or not the US target is in the same industry as the Japanese parent. Company cultures and administrative routines differ systematically across industries. Hence we would expect Japanese investors to have a higher probability to choose acquisitions if the subsidiary manufactures the same product as the parent, and to opt for a joint venture if their products are different.

H3: Acquisitions will be preferred to joint ventures when the Japanese investor is in the same industry as the planned subsidiary.

As noted earlier, Balakrishnan and Koza have argued that joint ventures are a way to reduce the uncertainty concerning the value of the complementary assets brought together, and one implication they have drawn is that joint ventures should occur more frequently between parents who are in industries that are relatively unrelated to one another. Firms that are in unrelated industries are not likely to have sufficient knowledge or may require costly 'help' to evaluate complementary assets.

(Balakrishnan and Koza 1991: 24)

Hence,

H4: Joint ventures will be preferred to acquisitions when the partners are in a different industry.

By contrast, Hennart's (1988a) theory has no strong implications as to whether joint ventures are more or less likely to be preferred to acquisitions when the parents are in the same industry. Link joint ventures are often established to combine the knowledge assets of firms in two different industries, as in the case of biotechnology joint ventures. Partners in scale joint ventures are often in the same industry. The same goes for acquisitions. Hence whether or not the partners are in the same industry should have no impact on the way they choose to combine their assets.

Lastly, we must control for antitrust policies and the rate of growth of the target market. Kay *et al.* (1987), quoting Nelson (1982), argue that while US antitrust authorities frown upon acquisitions and joint ventures between US firms in concentrated industries, they are more tolerant of joint ventures if the partner is foreign. According to Berg and Friedman (1978), US antitrust authorities see horizontal joint ventures in a more positive light than full horizontal acquisitions. If, as seems to be the case, the combination of two firms with market power, one domestic and one foreign, attracts more opposition if it is achieved via an acquisition rather than via a joint venture, then,

H5a: Joint ventures will be preferred to acquisitions for Japanese entries into concentrated US industries.

On the other hand, one advantage of acquisitions is that they do not create additional capacity, and hence are less threatening to incumbents.

H5b: Acquisitions will be preferred to joint ventures when the entry is in a concentrated US industry.

Because of these two offsetting factors, the impact of concentration on entry is unclear.

Because our study compares full acquisitions to greenfield joint ventures, we must control for factors that push firms towards acquisitions over greenfield entry (whether through wholly owned or joint ventured units). Acquisitions have two main advantages over greenfields: they permit faster entry, since it takes longer to build a subsidiary from scratch than to buy a going concern. In contrast to greenfield plants, acquisitions also do not add capacity. Hence acquisitions are encouraged when the US industry entered grows either very fast or very slowly. Acquisitions are desired when the target industry grows very quickly, because then the opportunity cost of greenfield entry is high; acquisitions also make sense when the target industry is growing very slowly or is declining, because a greenfield entry would then add capacity which would depress profits (Caves and Mehra 1986; Hennart and Park 1993).

H6: *Acquisitions will be preferred to joint ventures when the US industry entered is growing very rapidly or very slowly.*

Methodology and dependent variable

Before we discuss our dependent variable, it may be worthwhile to briefly survey what we know about Japanese manufacturing investment in the US. Employment in the manufacturing US affiliates of Japanese companies grew at a compound annual rate of 22.4 per cent between 1980 and 1989. By 1988 Japan was the fourth largest investor in US manufacturing, behind the United Kingdom, the Netherlands, and Germany (US Department of Commerce 1990).[8] Japanese investment has been concentrated in specific sectors, namely industrial and commercial machinery (especially computers), electronic and other electrical equipment (particularly colour TVs and audio equipment), in steel and rolling mills, and in transportation equipment and parts.

In contrast to much received wisdom, recent empirical research on Japanese investment in the US suggests that Japanese foreign direct investment does not differ fundamentally from that of other countries, and can be explained by the modern theory of foreign direct investment.[9] As in the case of US investment abroad, Japanese investment is driven by a combination of location, governance, and strategic factors, namely the overcoming of trade barriers, the exploitation of intangible assets, and rivalry in the home market. The major difference between Japanese and non-Japanese investors into the US is the Japanese reliance on greenfield plants rather than acquisitions. This difference can be explained by the fact that Japanese technological advantages are often embedded into the parent's routines, making post-merger integration problems more acute.

Sample

Our sample of Japanese manufacturing entries in the United States was obtained from two separate censuses of Japanese subsidiaries in the United States undertaken periodically by Toyo Keizai and by the Japan Economic Institute. Data on the status of a Japanese subsidiary at entry (whether it was fully acquired or established as a greenfield joint venture with an American partner) were available for the years 1978 to 1989. An acquisition takes place when a Japanese parent fully acquires an existing US manufacturing company or parts thereof. A joint venture occurs when a Japanese investor establishes a new manufacturing facility and shares the ownership with an American partner (hence partial acquisitions are excluded). The unit of observation is the venture. Entries by Japanese trading companies were excluded because of the fundamental differences in investment strategies between Japanese traders and manufacturers (Tsurumi 1976).

There were 428 affiliates established as a greenfield joint venture between a Japanese and an American firm or fully acquired by a Japanese investor. Two hundred and forty four of these entries were acquisitions (57 per cent), and 184 were joint ventures (43 per cent). Data for the independent variables were compiled from the *Directory of Corporate Affiliations*, the *Japan Company Handbook*, *Predicast's F&S Index Plus Text*, *Predicast's F&S Index Plus Text – International*, and the *Census of Manufacturers*.

Lack of information for the independent variables reduced our sample size to 175 observations. The two sources used for the independent variable did not always provide us with the identity of the ultimate American partner firm. Lack of detailed information on the products, employment, and organizational struc ture of US partners also limited the number of entries considered for further examination. In addition, product mix information was unavailable for small unlisted Japanese companies. The under-representation of these small Japanese investors did not result in a significant bias, since the proportion of joint ventures in our sample (42.9 per cent) is comparable to that of the population as a whole (43 per cent). The distribution of acquisitions and greenfield joint ventures for each entry year in our sample is shown in Figure 6.2.

Table 6.1 shows that at the time of entry the Japanese subsidiaries in our sample operated in sixteen different two-digit SIC industries.[10] About 20 per cent of all entries were in the chemical industry and another 20 per cent in the electrical and electronics industries. The metal and machinery industries are also heavily represented. Most subsidiaries (138 out of 175 observations) were active in a single four-digit SIC industry. The remaining thirty-seven entries were in multiple four-digit SIC industries.

The US partners range in size from 7 to 853,000 employees (between 7 and 367,000 for acquisitions, and between 85 and 853,000 for joint ventures). Eighty-one of the US partner firms (slightly less than half) were found to have a multidivisional structure.

Research design

Mode of entry is captured by a dummy variable which takes a value of zero if the Japanese parent made an acquisition and one if it established a greenfield joint venture with an American firm. Because of the nature of the dependent variable, a binomial logistic model is used in which the probability of joint

127

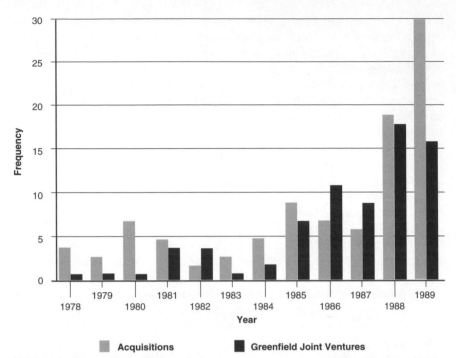

Figure 6.2 Distribution of joint ventures and acquisitions over time (sample only)

Table 6.1 Frequency count of Japanese entries into US industries by two-digit SIC
(single industry entries only)

SIC code: industry name*	Full acquisitions	Joint ventures	Total
20: Food and kindred products	6	1	7
23: Apparel and other textile products	0	2	2
24: Lumber and wood products	1	0	1
25: Furniture and fixtures	1	2	3
26: Paper and allied products	1	2	3
27: Printing and publishing	1	0	1
28: Chemicals and allied products	23	9	32
30: Rubber and miscellaneous plastics products	4	6	10
32: Stone, clay, and glass products	3	4	7
33: Primary metal industries	3	10	13
34: Fabricated metal products	0	12	12
35: Machinery, except electrical	15	6	21
36: Electric and electronic equipment	19	10	29
37: Transportation equipment	1	6	7
38: Instruments and related products	4	1	5
39: Miscellaneous manufacturing industries	1	0	1
Total	83	71	154

Note:

* Classification according to the 1972 Standard Industrial Classification Manual and its 1977 Supplement venture is explained by the variables described below. The regression coefficients estimate the impact of the independent variables on the probability that the entry will be through a joint venture. A positive sign for the coefficient means that the variable increases the probability of a joint venture. The model can be expressed as

$$P(y_i = 1) = 1/(1 + \exp(-a - X_i B)),$$

where y_i is the dependent variable, X_i is the vector of independent variables for the ith observation, a is the intercept parameter, and B is the vector of regression parameters (Amemiya 1981).

Measurement of the independent variables

Table 6.2 provides the mean, standard deviation, and maximum and minimum values of the variables.[11] The dummy INDIG captures the extent to which the assets coveted by the Japanese investor are indigestible if obtained through an acquisition. INDIG is composed of SIZE, a dummy equal to one if the US partner is large, and USSTRUC, a dummy equal to one if the US partner is divisionalized. A large US partner is a US firm with more than 5,000 employees.[12] The cutoff value was empirically estimated by looking at the size distribution of US partners in our sample. Changing the cutoff value to other plausible values (1,000 and 2,500 employees) does not change the results. Number of employees was obtained from the issue of the *Directory of Corporate Affiliations* published in the year before the corresponding Japanese entry.

We ascertained whether the US partner was divisionalized or not (USSTRUC) by looking at the firm's organizational structure, as described in the *Directory of Corporate Affiliations.* USSTRUC takes a value of 1 if the US partner was divisionalized, and 0 if it was not. We would expect joint ventures to be favoured when the US partner is large and not divisionalized. Hence INDIG takes a value of 1 when the US partner is not divisionalized (USSTRUC is 0) and large (SIZE is 1), and 0 otherwise (the American partner is small, or is large and divisionalized). INDIG should enter with a positive sign.

The Japanese investor's experience of the US market at the time entry was made (JEXP) is measured by the number of years between entry and the establishment of the parent's first US manufacturing subsidiary. We therefore assume that the parent's level of experience of the US market is proportional to the number of years it has operated in the US. The sign of the coefficient of this variable should be negative.

The difference in company culture between the Japanese parent and its subsidiary is proxied by COMMON. COMMON is measured by a dummy variable equal to one if any one of the products produced by the affiliate

Table 6.2 Means and correlations (coefficient/(t-statistic)/cases)

	Mean	SD	Frequency*/n	JVAQ	CONCEN	USEMPL	USSTRUC	INDIG	JEXP	PARCOMMON	COMMON	GROWDEV
JVAQ				1.000 n = 175								
CONCEN	611.996	512.703	75/175	0.025 (0.329)	1.000							
USEMPL	42,617	124,064		0.288 (3.932) 173	0.188 (2.499) 173	1.000						
USSTRUC			81/174	0.293 (4.012) 174	0.179 (2.382) 174	0.287 (3.899) 172	1.000					
INDIG			23/175	0.347 (4.861) 175	−0.02 (−0.259) 175	−0.013 (−0.170) 173	−0.364 (−5.129) 174	1.000				
JEXP	5.211	5.803		−0.131 (−1.744) 175	−0.038 (−0.498) 175	0.058 (0.762) 173	0.047 (0.613) 174	−0.052 (−0.688) 175	1.000			
PAR-COMMON			132/175	0.146 (1.936) 175	0.008 (0.100) 175	−0.106 (−1.394) 173	0.027 (0.356) 174	0.065 (0.855) 175	−0.144 (−1.918) 175	1.000		
COMMON			149/175	0.037 (0.488) 175	0.079 (1.046) 175	0.061 (0.802) 173	0.036 (0.468) 174	0.115 (1.522) 175	−0.026 (−0.347) 175	0.284 (3.897) 175	1.000	
GROWDEV	0.782	1.082		−0.153 (−2.032) 175	0.097 (1.283) 175	0.057 (0.744) 173	−0.017 (−0.220) 174	−0.076 (−1.000) 175	−0.021 (−0.279) 175	−0.06 (−0.795) 175	−0.052 (−0.690) 175	1.000

Note:
* Frequency count of dummy = 1.

matched those produced by the Japanese parent, and to zero otherwise. COMMON should have a negative sign.

The extent to which the US and the Japanese firms have divergent information concerning the value of the assets of the US target firm is proxied by PARCOMMON, a dummy variable indicating whether the Japanese *and* the American partners were in the same industry. PARCOMMON was calculated by comparing the products manufactured by the Japanese investor and those manufactured by its US partner. In the case of joint ventures, the partner is the US joint venture partner. In the case of acquisitions, the partner is the parent firm of the acquired unit if the Japanese firm acquired a division or a part of a US firm, or the acquired firm itself.[13] PARCOMMON was coded one if at least one of the products produced by the American partner was also produced by the Japanese parent. The sign of PARCOMMON should be negative.

The concentration ratio of the US industry entered (CONCEN) is measured by the Herfindahl–Hirschman index for the fifty largest companies for each four-digit SIC US industry, as published in the 1982 *Census of Manufactures*. The arithmetic average of the concentration ratio was used for subsidiaries active in multiple SICs. No prediction is made for the sign of this variable.

Following Caves and Mehra (1986) we calculated GROWDEV to describe the conditions that encourage acquisitions. GROWDEV is the absolute value of GROWTH's deviation from its sample mean divided by its standard deviation, with GROWTH equal to the three-year average annual growth rate of shipments of the four-digit US industry two years before entry (US Department of Commerce *US Industrial Outlook*). Average industry growth rate was used for the few observations with multiple SICs. GROWDEV is high when the growth rate of the target US industry is either very fast or very slow. A high value of GROWDEV should encourage acquisitions. Hence the coefficient of GROWDEV should be negative.

The matrix of correlations of the independent variables (Table 6.2) suggests little collinearity. Almost all correlations are low, the two highest correlation coefficients being the ones between INDIG and USSTRUC (− 0.36) and between PARCOMMON and COMMON (0.28).

Results

The results of the binomial logistic regression model are presented in Table 6.3. A positive coefficient for an independent variable means that it tends to increase the probability that a Japanese firm entered through a joint venture.

The model has a high overall explanatory power, with a χ^2 of 31.55 ($p = 0.0001$). One can also measure how well a maximum likelihood model fits the data by using it to classify observations (Amemiya 1981). The classification rate thus obtained can be compared to the rate that would have been obtained by chance (the baseline). The baseline rate is equal to $a^2 + (1 - a)^2$, where a is the proportion of acquisitions (Morrison 1974). In our case, that rate is 51

Table 6.3 Parameter estimates for binomial logit model: greenfield joint ventures versus acquisitions (Joint ventures = 1)

Variable name	Description	Coefficients (t-statistic)
Intercept		-0.4533 (0.80)
CONCEN	Concentration ratio of US industry entered	0.0002 (0.60)
INDIG	Indigestibility of target firm	2.464***
	Dummy for US partners which are large and not divisionalized	(3.74)
JEXP	Number of years of presence of the Japanese partner in the US market	$-0.043*$ (1.43)
PARCOMMON	US and Japanese partners have one common product	0.642* (1.52)
COMMON	Japanese parent and subsidiary have one common product	-0.278 (0.58)
GROWDEV	Deviation from the average of the growth of shipments of the US industry entered	$-0.371**$ (1.67)

model χ^2: 31.55, p value: 0.0001
n = 175

Notes:
*** $p. 0.01$
** $p < 0.05$
* $p < 0.1$ (one tailed)

per cent. Our model correctly classifies 62.3 per cent of the observations, a rate higher than the 51 per cent baseline (Table 6.2).

With the exception of PARCOMMON, all significant variables have the predicted signs. As predicted by *H1*, the coefficient of INDIG, our measure of the extent to which an acquisition would involve the purchase of unwanted assets, is positive and significant at the 0.1 level. Joint ventures are therefore desired when the US firm that holds the assets needed by the Japanese entrant is large and is not divisionalized.

PARCOMMON is weakly significant (at 0.10), but enters with a positive sign, suggesting that Japanese investors tend to prefer joint ventures to acquisitions when the Japanese and American partners are in the same industry. This contradicts Balakrishnan and Koza's (1991) prediction (*H4*) that joint ventures should be preferred when parents are in different industries. Our findings indicate that acquisitions are more likely if the partners are in different industries, and restating them this way points out to a likely explanation: there is a strong connection between diversification and acquisitions, since acquisitions allow entrants to purchase going firms. This is often an expensive option, but it is attractive if entrants do not possess the assets

Table 6.4 Classification table

		Predicted		
		JV	Acquisition	Total
True	JV	20	55	75
	Acquisition	11	89	100
	Total	31	144	175
	Sensitivity:	26.7%		
	Specificity:	89.0%		
	Correct:	62.3%		

needed to operate in the industry, i.e., if they are diversifying (Caves and Mehra 1986).

The coefficient of JEXP is negative and significant at the 0.10 level. As per H2, the longer Japanese firms have been in the United States, the more likely they will choose an acquisition over a joint venture.

GROWDEV, the coefficient of the absolute value of the deviation from the mean in the growth of shipments in the target US industry, is negative and significant (at 0.05). As hypothesized in H6, acquisitions are favoured when the target industry experiences either very high or very low growth rates. Hennart and Park (1993) found this to be also true in their study of the choice between greenfield entries (both wholly-owned and joint ventures) and acquisitions by Japanese investors in the United States, while Caves and Mehra's (1986) found this variable significant for a sample of foreign firms entering the United States.

The coefficient of the concentration ratio of the target US industry is insignificant. The results are consistent with Hennart and Park (1993) who found that the choice of Japanese investors between greenfield entry and acquisitions was not affected by this variable.

The coefficient of COMMON is not significant, suggesting that similarity of products between the parent and the venture does not increase the probability that the Japanese entrant will opt for an acquisition, as we had hypothesized in H3. Both Hennart and Park (1993) and Yamawaki (1992) found that Japanese investors choose acquisitions over greenfield entries when the investment is into a new industry. Our results suggest that acquisitions and joint ventures are both ways to acquire complementary assets, in contrast to greenfield investments, which are used to exploit the parent's advantages.[14] The relative efficiency of these two modes is determined by the significant variables in our model.

Conclusions

Joint ventures are complex organizational structures devised to bring together the resources necessary to perform economic tasks. This is also the purpose of other institutional arrangements, such as contracts and acquisitions. Hence an understanding of joint ventures requires a careful comparison of their costs and benefits *vis-à-vis* these two alternatives. Over the last ten years a number of theoretical and empirical studies have shed light on the circumstances under which joint ventures will be preferred to contracts. They have shown that joint ventures are chosen when firms find it difficult to rent their assets on the market.

On the other hand, we know much less of the factors that determine the choice between joint ventures and acquisitions. While there is an extensive literature on acquisitions, little attention has been paid to the costs and benefits of acquisitions relative to joint ventures. This paper investigates this choice in the context of Japanese investments in the United States.

This topic is particularly interesting because it allows us to compare and contrast two theories of joint ventures. Balakrishnan and Koza (1991, 1993) argue that joint ventures arise to reduce the transaction costs involved in purchasing firms. Joint ventures make it possible to obtain additional information on the value of the target firm, thus allowing the acquirer to decide whether to complete the acquisition or instead to pull back. One implication of their theory is that joint ventures should be preferred to acquisitions when the mutual ignorance of the partners is high because they come from different industries.

An alternative theory is that of Hennart (1988a), who contends that joint ventures are favoured when the desired assets are linked to non-desired assets, thus making an acquisition unwieldy (see also Shan 1988; and Kay *et al.* 1987). The relevant consideration is therefore whether the desired assets are cleanly separable from the non-desired ones, or in other words, whether they are digestible, thus making an acquisition efficient, or whether they are commingled with other assets. In the latter case, a joint venture is preferable.

We tested these two propositions on a sample of recent Japanese manufacturing entries in the United States. Controlling for other relevant factors, our results failed to support Balakrishanan and Koza's view that joint ventures are a mechanism to reduce the information costs of acquisitions. They confirm Hennart and Kay's predictions that joint ventures will be chosen when the desired assets are packaged in a way that would raise the costs of managing the merged unit. In other words, our results suggest that a joint venture is primarily a device to obtain access to resources which are embedded in other organizations, and not so much a way to reduce transaction costs in the markets for firms.

The results also show that a fundamental difference between joint ventures and acquisitions lies in the costs of integrating the labour forces of the two organizations (Haspelagh and Jemison 1991). Much of the literature on the acquisition process has had a domestic focus, but it is clear that the post-acquisition integration process is even more salient in the case of foreign acquisitions. Greenfield joint ventures with local firms significantly alleviate the problem facing investors from culturally distant countries of having to manage an alien labour force because they make it possible for the foreign investor to either select and mould the labour force or to delegate labour management to the local partner (Kogut and Singh 1988a). One implication of this view is that joint ventures would be more desirable, ceteris paribus, for investors based in countries whose cultures are radically different from the US, a hypothesis empirically supported by Kogut and Singh (1988a). Another is that, keeping the origin of investors constant, the benefit of joint ventures would decrease with the investor's familiarity with the US environment, and this is confirmed by our results.

One additional interesting finding is the positive and significant sign of PARCOMMON. This suggests that Japanese investors tend to joint venture with US partners which manufacture at least one common four-digit SIC product. This is consistent with the view that joint ventures with established local firms are a privileged way to enter foreign markets when scale economies are large and domestic firms have a dominant position.[15]

One limitation of the current work is that it is large scale: hence we do not capture well some of the more subtle points raised in the literature (Harrigan 1986). For example, the difficulties of integrating an acquired US concern should vary systematically according to the type of synergies that motivated the acquisition. Hence the post-acquisition challenge is much greater when the resources of the US unit needed by the Japanese investor are embedded in the labour force than when they consist of physical assets. In the first case, the acquirer and the acquired unit must be strategically integrated, yet it is crucial to maintain the acquired unit's autonomy and culture (Haspeslagh and Jemison 1991). Similarly, our modelling of the bundling of assets within US partners is necessarily crude, since it relies on formal organization structures, which may differ from actual patterns of interdependence. Detailed clinical studies could provide much better measures of these concepts, and would further our understanding of the issues raised in this paper.

Lastly, our analysis is static. An interesting topic to explore would be the comparative success rate of these two alternatives, and their determinants.[16]

Notes

We thank Young Ryeol Park, Dixie Zietlow, and Shih-Fen Chen for research assistance, Massimo Colombo, Alessandro Grandi, Ashish Nanda, and Alain Verbeke for useful comments, and the University of Illinois Research Board and the European Science Foundation for financial support.

1 Kogut and Singh (1988a) and Singh and Kogut (1989) use a multinomial logistic regression to compare simultaneously wholly-owned greenfield entry, greenfield joint ventures, and acquisitions.
2 An example of a joint venture is Fuji-Xerox, a 50–50 per cent joint venture between Fuji Photo Film of Japan and the Xerox corporation of the United States. In the initial agreement Xerox provided technology to the venture, Fuji manufactured the

copiers, and each partner was entitled to 50 per cent of the profits. An example of a contractual alliance is the subcontracting agreement under which the Austrian firm Steyr-Daimler-Puch provides marine engines to the US firm Outboard Marine. Steyr is paid on a per engine basis (*Annual Report*, Steyr-Daimler-Puch AG 1991).

3 See Pisano (1990) for evidence on the high cost experienced by established pharmaceutical firms in trying to develop internal biotechnology capabilities.

4 The authors do not provide information on the correlation ratios between the industry characteristics, which we would expect to be high (for example high R&D US industries are also usually fast growing).

5 These two studies also failed to control for another important determinant of the choice between acquisitions and joint ventures: whether acquisitions were more likely when the US investment represented a diversification for the parent. This variable was found to be significant in Hennart and Park (1993). Singh and Kogut also argue that the faster the rate of growth of the US industry entered, the more likely entry through acquisition, neglecting the fact that acquisitions may be preferred in low growth industries because they allow entry without adding to capacity (Caves and Mehra 1986). Lastly, the data set of these two studies includes entries in the manufacturing, extractive, and service industries. Since assets per employee are lower in services and higher in extractive industries, the size variable may reflect systematic interindustry patterns.

6 Until the passage of the Exon-Florio amendment to the Omnibus Trade and Competitiveness Act of 1988 the US government had no power to block the acquisition of a US firm when this was deemed to be a threat to national security. The Exon-Florio amendment stipulates that cases of potential concern are notified to the Committee on Foreign Investment in the US (CFIUS) which initiates an inquiry. If the Committee recommends blocking the acquisition, the President can do so. However, since 1988 only thirteen proposed investments (from 750 notifications) have received more than a cursory review, and only one has been blocked. The consensus of observers is that, in the period under study (1978 to 1989), the United Sates had no really binding restrictions on foreign acquisitions of US firms in technologically advanced industries (Price Waterhouse 1991).

7 This is in contrast to Singh and Kogut (1989) who, in the case of acquisition, measure the size of the US partner by the size of the acquired unit, not by the size of the parent.

8 These data refer to Foreign Direct Investment Position, a balance of payments concept that measures direct capital inflows into the United States.

9 See Caves (1993) for a recent survey of empirical studies of Japanese foreign direct investment, and Hennart (1991b) for a survey of the modern theory of foreign direct investment.

10 For data consistency purposes, we used the 1972 Standard Industrial Classification and its 1977 Supplement.

11 Note that USEMPL and USSTRUC show a different N (number of observations). However this does not present a problem because neither variable enters into the regression model directly, and the combined variable INDIG can, under certain circumstances, be computed with only one component present.

12 We measure size by employees rather than by sales or assets because post-merger acquisitions difficulties arise from the need to integrate and motivate the labour force of the acquired firm (Sales and Mirvis 1984). The larger that labour force, the greater the difficulties. Hence the cost of acquiring a firm should be proportional, everything else constant, to the number of its employees.

13 In the latter case, PARCOMMON and COMMON are identical.

14 This is consistent with Kogut and Chang (1991), who found that differences across industries in the number of greenfield investments were influenced by the Japanese industry's level of R&D expenditures, while this variable had no influence on entries through joint ventures and acquisitions.

15 This is suggested by the high ratio of joint ventures to acquisitions in the metal and transportation equipment industries (see Table 6.1).

16 For analyses of the success rates of joint ventures see Blodgett (1991), Gomes-Casseres (1987), Harrigan (1988) and Kogut (1989).

References

Amemiya, T. (1981) 'Qualitative response models: a survey', *Journal of Economic Literature* 19: 1,483–1,536.

Balakrishnan, S. and Koza, M. (1991) 'Organization costs and a theory of joint ventures', unpublished manuscript, University of Minnesota.

—— (1993) 'Information asymmetry, adverse selection and joint ventures: theory and evidence', *Journal of Economic Behavior and Organization* 20: 99–117.

Berg, S. and Friedman, P. (1978) 'Joint ventures in American industry: an overview', *Mergers and Acquisitions* Summer: 28–41.

Blodgett, L. (1991) 'Partner contribution as predictors of equity share in international joint ventures', *Journal of International Business Studies* 63–78.

Blomstrom, M. and Zejan, M. (1991) 'Why do multinational firms seek out joint ventures?', *Journal of International Development* 3, 1: 53–63.

Buckley, P. and Casson, M. (1976) *The Future of the Multinational Enterprise*, New York: Macmillan.

Byrne, J. (1986) 'At Sanyo's Arkansas plant the magic isn't working', *Business Week* 14 July: 51.

Caves, R. (1993) 'Japanese investment in the United States: lessons for the economic analysis of foreign investment', *The World Economy* 16, 3: 279–300.

Caves, R. and Mehra, S. (1986) 'Entry of foreign multinationals into US manufacturing industries', in M. Porter (ed.) *Competition in Global Industries*, Boston, MA: Harvard Business School Press, pp. 449–81.

Contractor, F. (1990) 'Contractual and cooperative forms of international business: towards a unified theory of modal choice', *Management International Review* 30: 31–54.

Contractor, F. and Lorange, P. (1988), 'Why should firms cooperate? The strategy and economic basis for cooperative ventures', in F. Contractor and P. Lorange (eds) *Cooperative Strategies in International Business*. Lexington, MA: D.C. Heath.

Davidson, W.H. (1982) *Global Strategic Management*, New York: Wiley.

Davidson, W.H. and McFetridge, D. (1985) 'International technology transfer mode', *Journal of International Business Studies*, Summer, pp. 5–21.

Directory of Corporate Affiliations (various years) Wilmette, IL: National Register Pub. Co.

Drake, T. and Caves, R. (1992) 'Changing determinants of Japanese foreign investment in the United States', *Journal of the Japanese and International Economies* 6: 228–46.

The Economist (1991) 'The tyre industry's costly obsession with size', 8 June: 65.

Gatignon, H. and Anderson, E. (1988) 'The multinational corporation degree of control over subsidiaries: an empirical test of a transaction cost explanation', *Journal of Law, Economics, and Organization* 4: 305–36.

Globerman, S. and Schwindt, R. (1986) 'The organization of vertically related transactions in the Canadian forest products industries', *Journal of Economic Behavior and Organization* 7: 199–212.

Gomes-Casseres, B. (1987) 'Joint venture instability: is it a problem?', *Columbia Journal of World Business* Summer: 97–102.

—— (1989) 'Ownership structures of foreign subsidiaries: theory and evidence', *Journal of Economic Behavior and Organization* 11: 1–25.

—— (1990) 'Firm ownership preferences and host government restrictions: an integrated approach', *Journal of International Business Studies* 21: 1–22.

Graham, E.M. and Krugman P. R. (1991) *Foreign Direct Investment in the United States*, Washington, DC: Institute for International Economics.

Harrigan, K. (1986) *Managing for Joint Venture Success*, Lexington, MA: D.C. Heath.

—— (1988) 'Strategic alliances and partner asymmetries', in F. Contractor and P. Lorange (eds) *Cooperative Strategies in International Business*, Lexington, MA: D.C. Heath.

Haspelagh, P. and Jemison, D. (1991) *Managing Acquisitions*, New York: Free Press.

Hennart, J.-F. (1982) *A Theory of Multinational Enterprise*, Ann Arbor, MI: University of Michigan Press.

—— (1988a) 'A transaction costs theory of equity joint ventures', *Strategic Management Journal* 9: 361–74.

—— (1988b) 'Vertical integration in the aluminum and tin industries', *Journal of Economic Behavior and Organization* 9, 3: 281–300.

—— (1991a) 'The transaction costs theory of joint ventures: an empirical study of Japanese subsidiaries in the United States', *Management Science* 37, 4: 483–97.

—— (1991b) 'The transaction cost theory of the multinational enterprise', in C. Pitelis and R. Sugden (eds) *The Nature of the Transnational Firm*, London: Routledge.

Hennart, J.-F. and Park, Y.R. (1993) 'Greenfield vs. Acquisition: the strategy of Japanese investors in the United States', *Management Science* 39: 1,054–70.

Japan Company Handbook (various years) Tokyo: Toyo Keizai Shimposha.

Jemison, D.B. and Sitkin, S.B. (1986) 'Corporate acquisition: a process perspective', *Academy of Management Review* 11: 145–63.

Joskow, P. (1985) 'Vertical integration and long-term contracts: the case of coal burning electric generating plants', *Journal of Law, Economics and Organization* 1.

Kay, N.M., Robé, J-P., and Zagnolli, P. (1987) 'An approach to the analysis of joint ventures', working paper, European University Institute.

Kay, N., Ramsay, H. and Hennart, J.-F. (1996) 'Industrial collaboration and the European internal market', *Journal of Common Market Studies* 34: 3 (September): 465–75.

Kenney, M. and Florida, R. (1993) *Beyond Mass Production: The Japanese System and its Transfer to the US*, New York: Oxford University Press.

Kogut, B. (1989) 'The stability of joint ventures: reciprocity and competitive rivalry', *Journal of Industrial Economics* 38: 183–98.

Kogut, B. and Chang S.J. (1991) 'Technological capabilities and Japanese foreign direct investment in the United States', *Review of Economics and Statistics* 73: 401–13.

Kogut, B. and Singh H. (1988a) 'The effect of national culture on the choice of entry mode', *Journal of International Business Studies* 19: 411–32.

—— (1988b) 'Entering the United States by joint venture: competitive rivalry and industry structure', in F. Contractor and P. Lorange (eds) *Cooperative Strategies in International Business*, Lexington, MA: D.C. Heath.

Lightfoot, R. (1992) *Note on Corporate Governance Systems: The United States, Japan and Germany*, Boston, MA: Harvard Business School, note 9–292–012.

Masten, S., Meehan, J. and Snyder, E. (1991) 'The costs of organization'. *Journal of Law, Economics, and Organization* 7: 1–25.

Morrison, D. (1974) 'Discriminant analysis', in R. Ferber (ed.) *Handbook of Marketing Research*, New York: Wiley, pp. 2,442–57.

Nelson, R. (1982) 'Government stimulus of technological progress: lessons from American history', in R. Nelson (ed.) *Government and Technical Progress: A Cross-Industry Analysis*, New York: Pergamon.

Office of the US Trade Representative (1985) *Barriers to Investment*, Washington, DC: Office of the US Trade Representative (mimeo).

Pisano, G. (1990) 'The R&D boundaries of the firm: an empirical analysis', *Administrative Science Quarterly* 35, 1: 153–176.

Predicasts F&S Index Plus Text on CD-ROM (1992) Boston, MA: Silverplatter Information.

Predicasts F&S Index Plus Text International on CD-ROM (1992) Boston, MA: Silverplatter Information.

Price Waterhouse (1991) *Doing Business in the USA*, New York: Price Waterhouse.

Sales, A. and Mirvis, P.A. (1984) 'When cultures collide; issues in acquisitions', in J. Kimberly and R.E. Quinn (eds) *New Futures: The Challenge of Managing Corporate Transitions*, Homewood, IL: Dow Jones-Irwin, pp. 107–33.

Shan, W. (1988) *Technological Change and Strategic Cooperation: Evidence from the Commercialization of Biotechnology*, PhD dissertation, University of California at Berkeley.

Singh, H. and Kogut, B. (1989) 'Industry and competitive effects on the choice of entry mode', *Academy of Management Proceedings* 116–20.

Stuckey, J. (1983) *Vertical Integration and Joint Ventures in the Aluminum Industry*, Cambridge, MA: Harvard University Press.

Tsurumi, Y. (1976) *The Japanese are Coming*, Cambridge, MA: Ballinger.

US Department of Commerce, Bureau of the Census (1982) *Census of Manufacturers: Subject Series*.

US Department of Commerce, International Trade Administration (various years) *US Industrial Outlook*.

Williamson, O. (1979) 'Transaction cost economics: the governance of contractual relations', *Journal of Law and Economics* 22, 2 (October): 233–61.

Yamawaki, H. (1992) 'International competitiveness and the choice of entry mode: Japanese multinationals in US and European manufacturing industries', unpublished manuscript, Universite Catholique de Louvain.

Yoshida, M. (1987) *Japanese Direct Manufacturing Investment in the United States*, New York: Praeger.

Zejan, M. (1990) 'New ventures or acquisitions: the choice of Swedish multinational enterprises', *Journal of Industrial Economics* 38: 349–55.

7

A SIMULTANEOUS EQUATIONS MODEL OF TECHNOLOGICAL AGREEMENTS AND INFRA-MURAL R&D[1]

Massimo G. Colombo and Paola Garrone

Introduction

Is there a mutual relation between technical co-operative agreements stipulated by firms in high-tech industries and their own R&D effort? Do technological leaders exhibit a greater propensity to engage in collaborative technological ventures than other firms or are laggard firms that have the most powerful incentives to resorting to alliances, with the aim of supporting catch-up technological strategies or more simply of gaining access to process and product technologies which cannot be developed in-house? What impact have such agreements on the R&D expenses of the partners? What other firm-, industry- and country-specific factors influence the relationships between technical agreements and inframural R&D?

Co-operative inter-firm relationships have become the subject of a growing number of studies in the economic and managerial literature. Nevertheless, it seems to us that the literature has so far failed to address the aforementioned issues, in spite of the fact that they are of fundamental importance to extend our understanding of the co-operation phenomenon and to enable us to assess its implications for firm strategy, economic efficiency, and social welfare. The present chapter offers a contribution, mainly of empirical nature, along such line.

The empirical evidence on the relationship between technical collaborations and infra-mural R&D is quite unsatisfactory and largely incoherent with the arguments proposed by theoretical studies; most of the available studies focus alternatively on the former innovative mode or on the latter one, thus failing to recognize existing feedbacks.[2] Even when this happens, such recognition does not result in the use of appropriate econometric tools. Relying on the notion of Granger-causality (Granger 1969), Colombo and Garrone (1996) show that dynamic feedbacks between technical co-operative agreements in which firms are involved and their independent research effort do exist; contrarily to common modelling assumptions, R&D intensity and technical co-operation are far from being strictly exogenous.[3] In accordance with such results, in this chapter we propose a structural simultaneous equations model; the model enables us to point out both the influence exerted by infra-mural R&D upon the yearly number of technical agreements concluded by firms and the impact of this latter variable upon R&D intensity in a subsequent period.

The chapter analyzes technological collaborative agreements concluded by major US, European and Japanese firms in the semiconductor, data processing and telecommunications (SDPT) industries during the period 1980–6, using panel-type data provided by the ARPA database developed at Politecnico di Milano.[4] Considering the central role played by such industries in the co-operation phenomenon and the large number of collaborative ventures that were concluded during the period under examination, as is witnessed by previous studies,[5] we believe that our panel sample offers an ideal testbed of theoretical hypotheses regarding the *mutual* relations between the R&D intensity of firms and the number of co-operative ventures they entered into.

The organization of the chapter is as follows. We synthesize the theoretical literature and formulate the main hypotheses which will be tested, then we present the data sample. We go on to specify the structural simultaneous equations model, and then we describe the findings of the econometric estimates, which highlight the positive impact of infra-mural R&D upon a firm's propensity to resort to technology-based collaborative arrangements. We also investigate how the relations between R&D intensity and the yearly number of agreements concluded by firms depend on other firm-, industry- and country-specific characteristics. The main conclusions of the article are reviewed.

The theoretical hypotheses

The effects of inter-firm co-operation upon a firm's R&D expenses

The effects of co-operation on the amount and efficiency of firms' R&D expenses have recently been addressed by a series of theoretical contributions sharing a game-theoretic approach (see for instance D'Aspremont and Jacquemin 1988, 1990; Kamien *et al.* 1992; Katz 1986; Katz and Ordover 1990; Sinha and Cusumano 1991; Suzumura 1992; Simpson and Vonortas 1994. For a recent survey see De Bondt 1996). By means of two- (or more) stages models of oligopolistic competition, they examine the influence that the decision of rival firms to collaborate in the R&D stage exerts upon the amount of resources devoted to R&D, the production output, the product price, and, more generally, the level of social welfare.

141

Such literature acknowledges that technical co-operative agreements may well result in a decrease of R&D expenses. First, if a firm's R&D leads to process innovations which reduce the innovator's average variable cost, a negative pecuniary externality is created for all rival firms, as their profits will suffer. It follows that firms may find it jointly beneficial to resort to collusive agreements aimed at limiting their own R&D budget.[6] In addition, collaborative arrangements allowing partners to share the results of R&D activity may enable them to eliminate duplicative R&D projects. Consequently, R&D productivity is likely to increase; all other things being equal, this should lead to a reduction of the R&D expenses of the partners.[7] Lastly, joint R&D allows firms to benefit from inexhausted economies of scale and scope, due to the indivisibility of inputs needed to perform R&D activity (for instance, laboratory equipment and administrative personnel).

Nonetheless, it is fundamental to recognize that the game-theoretic literature suggests that if there are positive externalities, co-operation among rival firms has a *positive* effect on R&D expenses. In particular, when there are substantial spillovers, because technology in its own is not appropriable or the imitation costs that rival firms must incur to timely reproduce innovations are negligible in comparison with the costs incurred by innovators, collaboration in R&D is likely to induce firms to increase their R&D budget, as it enables them to internalize the externality connected with the spillovers. The expected positive impact will be greater if the agreement extends forward to the production and marketing of products, and, more generally, if competition is weak. In fact, whether the free rider problem associated with spillovers is important or not, fierce market rivalry deters firms' investments in own and joint R&D, as in very competitive settings consumers are expected to capture most of the surplus created by innovations (see for instance D'Apremont and Jacquemin 1988; Katz 1986; Suzumura 1992).[8] Lastly, we should also consider that the development costs of new technologies and the uncertainty surrounding innovative activities have constantly been increasing since the beginning of the century: research joint venture and consortia contribute to overcoming such cost-of-development barriers, which in some instances have become impenetrable even for the largest firms.

The arguments above can be summarized as follows.

Hypothesis 1: the expected impact of technical collaborative agreements upon infra-mural R&D expenses of partner firms is uncertain. However, the larger are the spillovers and the weaker is market rivalry, the more positive is the alleged effect.[9]

Technological agreements and the need for absorptive capacity

Notwithstanding their interest, the studies in the game-theoretic neo-classic tradition suffer from some shortcomings. First, they tend to neglect the additional costs engendered by technological collaborations: they include additional administrative overhead, organizational inefficiencies arising from the need to co-ordinate work that takes place in various laboratories often located in different regions or countries and is performed by personnel that belongs to different organizations, and transaction costs connected with the need to prevent leakage of relevant technologies to the partners and other firms and to deter opportunistic behaviour. More will be said on this issue later.

Second, and more importantly, they fail to recognize that a firm's own independent R&D effort does influence its propensity to conclude technical collaborative agreements with other firms. The reason probably is to be traced to the assumption by mainstream economics that technology essentially consists in 'information'. In other words, technology is considered as a public good in the sense that once it has been discovered, it is easy to apply and inexpensive to transfer compared with the costs incurred by innovators. In addition, even though it is widely accepted in the neo-classic literature that transactions concerning the results of R&D are affected by market failures due to information asymmetries and moral hazard, as is highlighted by Arrow's paradox (Arrow 1962), the design and enforcement of suitable institutional and contractual mechanisms are believed to enable firms to overcome such transaction difficulties.

On the contrary, it is fundamental to emphasize that while scientific knowledge and the generic aspects of new technologies can indeed be expected to quickly become common knowledge among the *interested* professional community, the same reasoning does not apply to industrial technology (see Nelson 1990). As is pointed out by numerous studies on the economics of technical change (see for instance Rosenberg 1976; Nelson and Winter 1982; Pavitt 1984. For a survey see Dosi 1988), industrial technology in most cases is of little use outside the context where it has been developed, with its transfer involving considerable costs. The reason is that codified knowledge and technology incorporated in components and capital equipment represent only a part of the results of innovative activity. Another part, as significant as the other, consists in disembodied tacit knowledge, skills and capabilities of a very applied nature. To a large extent, their development is a matter of context-specific experience and cumulative adjustments through trials and errors. Accordingly, in order for them to be transferred and tailored to a different application environment, substantial transaction-specific investments and autonomous technological expertise from the parties involved are required (see Teece 1980).

In addition, as is pointed out by Cohen and Levinthal (1989), firms need to develop an 'absorptive capacity' through independent R&D to be able to take advantage of the results of the innovative activity of external sources, whether they are codified or of tacit nature.

The above considerations have important implications for the issue addressed in the present study. In particular, they suggest that infra-mural

R&D is *complementary* to technological collaborations. For one thing, as is illustrated by Mowery and Rosenberg (1989), adequate absorptive capacity is required to reap the benefits of collaborative R&D and transform it in a source of competitive advantage. Furthermore, as is well-known, substantial uncertainty surrounds the outcome of innovative activity: hence, an autonomous R&D capability is essential to making effective decisions as regards co-operative R&D, identifying the most promising research areas, selecting partners, evaluating likely research results and perceiving possible implications.[10] Lastly, an autonomous R&D capability puts firms in a better position to cope with the contractual incompleteness, information asymmetries, and transaction costs typical of R&D agreements. In fact, both the ability to effectively monitor the behaviour of partners and evaluate the resources they contribute to the venture, and the decrease in switching costs that originate from a firm's own expertise in R&D, are likely to help deterring opportunism, thus incentivating collaborations. To sum up, we derive the following hypothesis.

Hypothesis 2: Firms' propensity towards technological co-operative agreements increases with their autonomous R&D effort.

The data

The data on technological agreements are provided by the ARPA database. ARPA monitors agreements focused on technologies, products and production processes pertaining to the SDPT industries, that were concluded all over the world during the period 1980–6. Agreements are classified on the basis of the contractual arrangement used (joint venture, license, *consortium*, etc.), the functional content (technology, production, marketing and distribution), and the (tangible and intangible) resources that partners contributed to the agreement (and which they gained access to).

Previous studies (see for instance Cainarca *et al.* 1992; Colombo 1995) have considered the cross-sectional dimension of the ARPA database; in this paper we also take advantage of the temporal dimension by using a panel data sample. More specifically, in accordance with the results of Colombo and Garrone (1996) which show that both firms' R&D intensity and the yearly number of technological co-operative agreements concluded by them are not strictly exogenous, we investigate the mutual dynamic relations between such variables, an exercise which of course is precluded to cross-sectional models. In addition, the large number of degrees of freedom typical of panel data increases the reliability of the estimates of the coefficients of the explanatory variables.[11]

The study focuses on the technical co-operative agreements concluded by a sample of firms composed of 95 out of the top 150 firms in the SDPT industries. Two categories of technical collaborations are actually considered: (a) agreements involving joint research or joint development of new technologies, products and processes (for instance, research joint ventures and consortia, non-equity joint development agreements, etc.); (b) agreements allowing a sample firm to gain access to scientific and technological knowledge, competencies, and skills developed by the partners (examples include technology transfer agreements, licenses, etc.). In accordance with such definition, agreements allowing sample firms to unilaterally transfer knowledge and technical capabilities to other firms in exchange for royalties or other type of payments are not considered.

The procedure used to select the sample firms can be described as follows. First, we identified the world's 150 largest firms in the SDPT industries on the basis of SDPT sales in 1986. For this purpose, we relied on the lists compiled by specialized magazines (*Datamation, Telecom Magazine, Electronic Business*) and sector studies (*Benn Electronic File Directory, Gartner Group Top 100 Almanac*). These same sources provided time-series data on a number of firm-specific variables: sales, diversification, profits, capital expenditures, R&D expenditures (see below). Such data were complemented with data obtained from firms' annual reports and other publications (e.g., the *Japan Company Handbook*). The coherence of the various sources was also checked.

We excluded firms for which complete time-series relating to the 1981–6 period (1980–6 for R&D expenses) were not available. We also dropped firms which entered the SDPT industries or were incorporated after 1980. Lastly, we excluded two Japanese trading companies (Sumitomo and C. Itoh) which in 1986 realized less than 5 per cent of their total turnover in the SDPT industries and were not involved in production, their activities being confined to distribution and sale.

The final sample consists of ninety-five firms observed during seven years, as concerns R&D expenses and the number of technical collaborative arrangements they entered into (665 observations), and during six years as concerns the remaining firm-specific variables (570 observations). The sample can be regarded as quite representative of SDPT industries, as is apparent from the data presented in Table 7.1. They show the composition of total 1986 sales of the sample firms by industry and geographical area and the estimated shares of the universe accounted for by the sample.

The specification of the structural model

We consider two variables, TCA_{it} and IRD_{it}. The former is assumed to capture firm i's propensity towards technological co-operation in time t, proxied by the yearly number of technical collaboration agreements concluded. The latter measures the ratio of the R&D expenses incurred by the i-firm in the year t to firm sales.

As was said earlier, Colombo and Garrone (1996) suggests that IRD and TCA cannot be regarded as strongly exogenous, since each of the two variables Granger-causes the other one. Whether one may interpret the results of the

Table 7.1 Distribution of 1986 sales of the sample firms by geographical area and sector, and share of the universe[a]

	Industry							
Geographical area	*Semiconductor*		*Data processing*		*Telecommunications*		*Total*	
Europe	3,819	77%	20,438	76%	19,379	87%	43,636	81%
Japan	11,867	93%	20,576	85%	7,979	74%	40,422	85%
USA	14,486	95%	59,047	97%	37,986	64%	111,519	82%
Total	30,172	91%	100,061	89%	65,346	70%	195,579	82%

Note:
[a] Software, data processing services and telecommunications services are excluded. Data on the universe are provided by Humbert (1988).

Granger causality analysis as a prediction of the direct action of a variable on another one is a controversial matter. First, the risk of detecting a 'trivial' endogeneity, with a third variable determining both propensity to co-operation and innovative effort, is never completely ruled out. Second, a bivariate autoregressive model is admittedly not appropriate to estimate the mutual impact between two variables; for this purpose, a structural model would be required.

The aim of this paragraph is to specify a structural econometric model which (a) enables us to investigate the sign and importance of the mutual influence between a firm's R&D expenses and its propensity towards technical co-operative agreements and (b) is consistent with the results of Colombo and Garrone (1996). Accordingly, we will estimate a simultaneous two equations model, where IRD and TCA have been introduced as explanatory variables in the TCA and IRD equations respectively. The present paragraph is devoted to specifying the model, while the outcome of the econometric estimates will be presented in the next paragraph.

The dependent and independent variables

As has already been said, the dependent variables of the model are the yearly number of technical agreements concluded by firm i, TCA_{it}, and the ratio of R&D expenses to firm sales in year t, IRD_{it}.

As concerns the TCA equation, the following explanatory variables have been introduced into the model, in addition to IRD. SIZE measures firm sales (in US$ at 1981 prices) in the SDPT industry.[12] The diversification of a firm's activities is described by DIVE, DIVEREL and DIVESDPT. DIVE coincides with the Utton diversification index of a firm's sales based on the two digit

SIT classification. DIVEREL gives the share of firm turnover in industries related to the SDPT industries.[13] DIVESDPT captures the scope of a firm's activities within the SDPT industrial system by means of the Utton diversification index based on a classification which distinguishes three sectors (semiconductor, data processing and telecommunications). CEXP stands for the ratio of capital expenditures to sales. All these variables, except DIVEREL (and including IRD), are introduced into the model in logarithmic form (see below). In line with the results of previous studies (see for instance Berg *et al.* 1982; Link and Bauer 1987; Arora and Gambardella 1990, 1994; Colombo 1995), they are expected to have a significantly positive effect upon propensity to co-operate. Lastly, PROFIT measures returns on sales. In this case predictions are mixed: on the one hand high profitability on current sales may reduce incentives to looking for new sources of revenues, discouraging technical collaborations, on the other it may also remove financial constraints to investing in several new ventures, with the opposite effect.

In addition, a number of dummy variables have been considered. NICHE aims to capture the expected negative influence that the adoption of a niche strategy relating to products and/or markets exerts on the propensity towards co-operation. The remaining dummies control for industry- and country-specific effects. SEMIC, DP, TELEC and DEF equal 1 when firms are in the semiconductor, data processing, telecommunications and defence industries: they are not mutually exclusive. CC identifies common carriers (such as ATT, BT and STET). US and JAP are equal to 1 for firms located in North America and Japan.

Finally, the cross-products of IRD and the aforementioned variables have also been introduced into the TCA equation, with the aim of capturing possible interaction effects. In particular, we have tried to highlight whether the impact of a firm's research intensity on the propensity to be involved into technical collaborative ventures depends on firm-specific characteristics such as firm size, diversification and profitability, and on the characteristics of firm's industrial environment.[14]

Turning now to the IRD equation, the set of explanatory variables includes the yearly number of technical collaborative agreements concluded by firms, lagged once, the set of industry and geographical area dummy variables described above, the NICHE dummy, and the cross-products of the dummy variables and TCA. These latter terms are instrumental in trying to capture the influence possibly exerted by differences in competitive conditions and extent of spillovers on the relation of TCA to IRD.

The specification of the TCA equation

As TCA_{it} is by definition greater than or equal to zero, we have resorted to a Tobit model to estimate the following equation (for sake of simplicity the subscript t has been omitted from time variant variables):

$$TCA_i = a_0 + a_1 \ln SIZE_i + a_2 \ln DIVESDPT_i + a_3 \ln DIVE_i + a_4 \ln CEXP_i$$
$$+ a_5 \ln IRD_i + a_6 DIVEREL_i + a_7 PROFIT_i + a_8 (\ln SIZE_i)^2$$
$$+ a_9 (\ln DIVESDPT_i)^2 + a_{10} (\ln DIVE_i)^2 + a_{11} (\ln CEXP_i)^2$$
$$+ a_{12} (\ln IRD_i)^2 + a_{13} DIVEREL_i^2 + a_{14} PROFIT_i^2$$
$$+ a_{15} SEMIC_i + a_{16} DP_i + a_{17} TELEC_i + a_{18} NICHE_i + a_{19} DEF_i + a_{20} CC_i$$
$$+ a_{21} US_i + a_{22} JAPAN_i + (a_{23} \ln SIZE_i + a_{24} \ln DIVESDPT_i$$
$$+ a_{25} \ln DIVE_i + a_{26} \ln CEXP_i + a_{27} \ln IRD_i + a_{28} DIVEREL_i + a_{29} PROFIT_i$$
$$+ a_{30} SEMIC_i + a_{31} DP_i + a_{32} TELEC_i + a_{33} NICHE_i + a_{34} DEF_i$$
$$+ a_{35} CC_i + a_{36} US_i + a_{37} JAPAN_i) \cdot \ln R\&D_i + a_{38} t84_i + a_{39} t85_i$$
$$+ a_{40} t86_i + \varepsilon_{it.} \tag{1}$$

The specification of the IRD equation

As is well known, the literature on the 'Schumpeterian hypotheses' has so far failed to provide conclusive evidence as to the determinants of firms' R&D intensity (see for instance Cohen and Levin 1989). Nonetheless, there is some agreement among social scientists interested in the economics of technical change that appropriability conditions, technological opportunities and the degree of rivalry do affect firms' incentives to invest in R&D. In addition, time-series empirical evidence seems to suggest that the share of turnover firms attribute to their R&D budget tends to remain quite stable. As the main purpose of the IRD equation is to disentangle the impact of technical collaborative agreements on R&D intensity, we have resorted to a simple autoregressive bivariate model of the following form:

$$\ln IRD_{it} = b_0 + b_1 \ln IRD_{it-1} + b_2 \ln IRD_{it-2} + b_3 \ln IRD_{it-3} + b_4 TCA_{it-1}$$
$$+ b_5 SEMIC_{it} + b_6 DP_{it} + b_7 TELEC_{it} + b_8 NICHE_i + b_9 DEF_{it}$$
$$+ b_{10} CC_i + b_{11} US_i + b_{12} JAPAN_i + (b_{13} SEMIC_i + b_{14} DP_i +$$
$$b_{15} TELEC_i + b_{16} NICHE_i + b_{17} DEF_i + b_{18} CC_i + b_{19} US_i +$$
$$b_{20} JAPAN_i) \cdot AT_{it-1} + v_{it.} \tag{2}$$

Industry and geographical area dummies are expected to reflect (to some extent) different appropriability conditions, technological opportunities and degrees of rivalry across the sample firms. For this reason we have also included the cross-products of such variables and the yearly number of agreements lagged once.

The results of the econometric estimates

In order to estimate the simultaneous equations model composed of equations (1) and (2), for i = 1,..., 95, and t = 83, 84, 85, 86, we have followed the approach proposed by Smith and Blundell (1986). Numerous nested restrictions have been tested through LR χ^2 tests. Table 7.2 illustrates the estimated value of the coefficients, standard errors and the associated significance levels relating to the best restriction path. Under any restrictions of the model, IRD proved to be weakly exogenous and, hence, inference on the (1) coefficients can rely on conditional maximum likelihood estimates, as was pointed out by Smith and Blundell (1986). Nonetheless the simultaneous equations framework has never been given up, since strong exogeneity of both IRD and TCA was rejected by Colombo and Garrone (1996).

As regards the IRD equation, we are aware that the outcome of the econometric analysis is a bit unsatisfactory. On the positive side, two out of the three lagged variables included in the autoregressive vector are highly significant; in addition, the number of agreements concluded by firms in year t fails to show any explanatory power of the logarithm of the ratio of R&D expenses to firm sales in the subsequent year, a result which is coherent with the predictions of Hypothesis 1. On the negative side, no cross-products introduced into the equation turn out to be statistically significant at standard levels. The reason probably is that NICHE and the industry and geographical area dummies do not effectively reflect differences in appropriability regimes and conditions of competitive rivalry faced by sample firms. Thus, the impact of spillovers and market rivalry upon the relation of the yearly number of agreements concluded by firms to their own research effort remains an empirical question which waits for further, more robust findings. [15]

Let us now turn to the TCA equation. Let us initially examine the coefficients of the control variables. The significantly positive and increasing coefficients of the time dummies t84, t85 and t86 come as no surprise, as they conform to the available evidence on the growing number of agreements concluded by firms in information technology industries during the period examined. The estimated values of the coefficients of the continuous control variables basically are in line with our predictions. In particular, the yearly number of technical collaborations turns out to increase with firm size, with the coefficients of both the first order and second order terms being positive and highly significant. As to the remaining variables, diversification within the SDPT industries and in related industries positively affects firms' propensity towards technical co-operation.[16] The ratio of capital expenditures to sales also has a positive, weakly significant coefficient. Instead, profitability exhibits no explanatory power. As to industry dummies, firms in the data processing industry appears to be more prone to technical co-operation; quite unsurprisingly, the opposite holds true for firms in the defence business.

Table 7.2 Results of the estimates of the structural simultaneous equations model

TCA equation		IRD equation	
Constant	0.4656	Constant	− 0.0727
	(0.3278)		(0.0327)**
ln SIZE	1.0519	ln IRD $_{t-1}$	0.7418
	(0.0788)***		(0.0404)***
ln DIVESDPT	1.0623	ln IRD $_{t-2}$	0.0356
	(0.4172)**		(0.0478)
ln CEXP	0.4001	ln IRD $_{t-3}$	0.1407
	(0.2062)*		(0.0315)***
ln IRD	0.8818	DP	0.0599
	(0.4022)**		(0.0309)**
DIVEREL	0.3559	TELEC	0.0397
	(0.0814)***		(0.0281)
ln SIZE ^{2}	0.1143	CC	0.2524
	(0.0382)***		(0.0454)***
ln DIVESDPT ^{2}	− 1.0233		
	(0.8702)		
DP	0.6673		
	(0.2389)***		
DEF	− 1.1964		
	(0.4690)**		
US	− 0.7090		
	(0.2011)***		
ln DIVESDPT · ln IRD	− 1.9799		
	(0.8274)**		
ln DIVE · ln IRD	− 0.9424		
	(0.6022)		
SEMI · ln IRD	1.3975		
	(0.4224)***		
NICHE · ln IRD	− 1.0952		
	(0.5080)**		
US · ln IRD	− 0.7438		
	(0.5545)		
t84	0.4790		
	(0.2149)**		
t85	0.5713		
	(0.2274)**		
t86	0.6050		
	(0.2039)***		
Log-likelihood	369.93		

Notes:
*** significance level greater than 99%.
** significance level greater than 95%.
* significance level greater than 90%.
Standard errors between brackets.

Lastly, US firms show a significantly lower propensity to be involved in technical agreements than both Japanese and European firms.

For our purposes, the most interesting finding of the econometric analysis is that the estimates of the TCA equation provide clear evidence supporting the argument, synthesized in Hypothesis 2, that the development of an autonomous research expertise plays a crucial role in allowing firms to take full advantage of technical collaborations with other firms. This is made clear by Table 7.3. Table 7.3a gives the value of the marginal effect of the R&D variable with the remaining continuous variables being evaluated at their 1986 mean value, and NICHE, DEF, D84 and D85 being set to zero (of course D86 equals one). The values of the standard errors and confidence levels of the t-statistics for Wald tests of the zero hypothesis that the marginal effect be zero, are also provided. We distinguish eight cases, according to whether firms' parent company is located in the US or in Europe/Japan, and firms are in the semiconductor and/or data processing industries.[17] A similar exercise is carried on in Table 7.3b where we focus on non-US firms; the first column refers to firms pursuing a niche strategy, the second one concerns firms in the defence industry. Lastly, Table 7.3c illustrates the impact of variations in the value taken by DIVE and DIVESDPT, which reflect a firm's diversification within and outside SDPT industries, on the marginal effect of R&D intensity.

Altogether, the results document the positive impact of firms' inframural R&D expenses upon the number of collaborations in which they were

Table 7.3a Marginal effects of infra-mural R&D in the semiconductor and data processing industries: US vs European/Japanese firms

SEMIC	DP	US	Europe/Japan
1	1	1.3453	2.1875
		(0.3516)	(0.3801)
		***	***
1	0	1.1138	2.0129
		(0.3012)	(0.3441)
		***	***
0	1	0.1208	0.8463
		(0.3470)	(0.3867)
			**
0	0	0.1000	0.7787
		(0.2888)	(0.3588)
			**

Notes:
*** significance level greater than 99%
** significance level greater than 95%
* significance level greater than 90%.
Standard errors between brackets. Remaining continuous variables are evaluated at their 1986 mean value. Other dummy variables are set at 0.

Table 7.3b Marginal effects of infra-mural R&D for non-US firms in the
semiconductor and data processing industries – niche strategy; defence
industry

SEMIC	DP	NICHE = 1	DEF = 1
1	1	1.1365	1.7621
		(0.5589)	(0.3965)
		**	***
1	0	1.0457	1.3132
		(0.5005)	(0.4209)
		**	***
0	1	− 0.2048	0.6817
		(0.5929)	(0.3209)
			**
0	0	− 0.1884	0.5080
		(0.5470)	(0.2691)

Notes:
*** significance level greater than 99%
** significance level greater than 95%
* significance level greater than 90%.
Standard errors between brackets. Remaining continuous variables are evaluated at their 1986
mean value. Other dummy variables are set at 0.

Table 7.3c Marginal effects of infra-mural R&D for non-US firms in the
semiconductor and data processing industries – diversification within
and outside SDPT industries

SEMIC	DP	DIVESDPT = 1[a]	DIVESDPT = 2.16[b]	DIVE = 1[a]	DIVE = 2.72[b]
1	1	N.S.	1.2777	2.5945	1.6810
			(0.3580)	(0.5190)	(0.4213)
			***	***	***
1	0	2.2934	N.S.	2.3874	1.5468
		(0.4551)		(0.4710)	(0.3853)
		***		***	***
0	1	1.3270	N.S.	1.2533	0.3398
		(0.4394)		(0.5355)	(0.4088)
		***		**	
0	0	1.1623	N.S.	1.1532	0.3126
		(0.3913)		(0.4952)	(0.3776)

Notes:
*** significance level greater than 99%
** significance level greater than 95%
* significance level greater than 90%.
Standard errors between brackets. Remaining continuous variables are evaluated at their 1986
mean value. Other dummy variables are set at 0.
[a] Once the set of ninety-five firms has been ordered by ascending DIVESDPT (DIVE), the
value of DIVESDPT (DIVE) that characterizes the tenth firm has been chosen for simulation.
[b] Once the set of ninety-five firms has been ordered by ascending DIVESDPT (DIVE), the
value of DIVESDPT (DIVE) that characterizes the eighty-fifth firm has been chosen for
simulation.

involved. The marginal effect of IRD is positive and statistically significant at standard levels, with only a few exceptions.

In general, marginal effects are substantially greater for firms which are in semiconductor and smaller for those pursuing a niche product/market strategy. The largest values pertain to non-US firms operating in the semiconductor and data processing industries. It is worth noticing that the cross-product of SIZE and IRD turns out to have no statistically significant impact upon the yearly number of technical agreements, even though it takes a positive sign. As to diversification, the signs of the coefficients of the cross-product terms involving DIVE (or DIVEREL) and DIVESDPT are negative, with the latter being significant at 95 per cent confidence level. In addition, as is shown in Table 7.3c, while it is quite difficult to isolate the impact of DIVESDPT upon the marginal effect of IRD, that of DIVE is definitively negative. In particular, for widely diversified firms that are not in semiconductor, the positive impact of R&D intensity upon the yearly number of collaborations concluded largely vanishes.

Concluding remarks

In this paper we have analyzed the mutual relationships between the autonomous R&D effort of firms and their inclination to concluding technological collaborative agreements with other firms. We have relied on data concerning the yearly number of technical collaborative projects undertaken by a sample composed of ninety-five large European, Japanese and American firms in the semiconductor, data processing and telecommunications industries over the period 1980–6.

In accordance with the suggestions of Colombo and Garrone (1996), a simultaneous two-equations model of the determinants of both firms' R&D intensity and their propensity towards technical co-operative agreements, has been estimated. The econometric findings highlight that, in accordance with the arguments raised by evolutionary theories of the economics of technical change, own R&D experience plays a crucial role in allowing firms to reap the benefits of technical co-operation. Some initial evidence is also provided that the impact of R&D intensity on the propensity to collaborate depends on firm-, industry- and country-specific characteristics, even though this argument is waiting for more robust and reliable findings. Lastly, as regards the relation of the intensity of R&D expenses to the number of agreements concluded, we obtained mixed results, with the impact of the latter variable upon the former one not being statistically different from zero at standard levels. In addition, we were unable to find out any dependence of such relation on spillovers and competitive conditions, as is suggested by the neo-classical theoretical literature, possibly as a result of use of quite unsatisfactory proxies. Hence, further empirical studies are needed to shed light into this important issue.

We think that such empirical results are interesting on their own. However, they also have important implications for technology policy. In particular, they raise serious doubts on the argument that a policy based on incentives to technological co-operation is effective in allowing laggard firms to catch up. The results of our analysis support the view that technological collaborative agreements are to be regarded as ancillary to the development of an autonomous R&D expertise. In other words, in order to take advantage of collaborative inter-firm relations, firms need to be equipped with an adequate absorptive capacity that originates from independent cumulative investments in the R&D activity. Collaborations among laggard firms are thus unlikely to have any durable beneficial effects on their technological prowess.

Notes

1　The financial support of 60 per cent MURST 1995 funds is gratefully acknowledged. The authors are grateful to Ugo Colombino, Dominique Foray, Alfonso Gambardella, Claudio Leporelli, participants in the 1994 AiIG workshop and the 1994 EARIE meeting for helpful comments to previous drafts of the paper. The usual disclaimer applies. The first three parts have been written by Massimo G. Colombo, while the redaction of the remaining paragraphs is attributable to Paola Garrone.

2　See, among the others Berg *et al*. 1982; Link and Bauer 1987; Pisano 1990; Kleinknecht and Reijnen 1992; Arora and Gambardella 1994.

3　Colombo and Garrone (1996) specify a bivariate autoregressive process for a panel of firms' technological agreements and R&D intensity, building on an econometric model proposed by Holtz-Eakin *et al*. (1988).

4　ARPA includes 2,014 agreements involving 1,574 partners that belong to 1,177 industrial groups (or public institutions). Non-equity agreements represent 70.8 per cent of the total, joint development agreements/consortia and licences being the most prominent categories with shares equal to 24.6 per cent and 20.8 per cent respectively. Within the equity category, joint ventures clearly prevail with a 21.8 per cent share. As concerns firm functions, technological agreements account for a 32.1 per cent share. The majority of such agreements (about 75 per cent) involve joint R&D, with the remaining ones being aimed at technology transfer. Further details on the ARPA database can be found in Cainarca *et al*. (1989).

5　Relying on the CATI-MERIT database, Hagedoorn (1991) estimates that information technology industries account for about 40 per cent of all agreements concluded in the world during the 1980–9 period. In addition, the yearly number of agreements in such industries has rapidly been growing from 1980 up to 1986, remaining quite stable afterwards.

6　A similar result has been highlighted under more general conditions by the literature on patent races of the 'winner-take-all' kind. See for instance Reinganum (1989).

7　For a similar claim, see Spence (1984).

8　For instance, it is easy to show that if (a) firms engage in Bertrand competition in the product market, (b) R&D leads to a reduction of average variable costs and (c) the final good cannot be differentiated, oligopolistic rivalry in the production stage would engender a reduction in the price of the final product equal to the reduction in average production costs obtained through joint R&D.

9　As a corollary, we may expect collaborative projects regarding basic science or

154

aimed at development of generic technologies to stimulate an increase of the partners' R&D effort, as the results of such projects can often be assimilated to 'public goods'. On the contrary, the effect on R&D expenses of collaborative projects that focus on applied research and development of specific products or production processes is likely to be negative.

10 As Rosenberg stresses, 'it frequently requires a substantial research capability to understand, interpret and appraise knowledge that has been *placed* upon the shelf' (1990: 171).

11 It is worth stressing that due to the recent development of large scale use of agreements by firms and the lack of historical data, an approach resting on the analysis of time series would not be viable.

12 Annual figures for sales of European and Japanese enterprises were first converted into US$ on the basis of average annual exchange rates. Afterwards, all data were deflated using prices implicit in the portion of US GNP corresponding to durable goods.

13 Related industries include other electrical and electronic products, transportation equipment, machinery, and measurement, scientific, optical and medical equipment.

14 For instance, Rosenberg (1990) notes that large firms are more oriented towards basic research than small firms. First, only firms that are quite confident of surviving in the long-term would be likely to consider the possibility of investing in basic research projects, the pay-off of such activity being very distant into the future and surrounded by very substantial uncertainty. In addition, firms must also be confident that they will be able to exploit commercially the findings of basic research; other things being equal, this is more likely for large firms, with a diverse range of products, strong marketing capabilities and distribution networks, and a well recognized brand name. In turn, differences in the nature of a firm's research effort may lead to differences in the influence exerted by internal R&D expenses upon the number of agreements concluded.

15 It is worth noticing that some industry dummies prove to have a substantial bearing on R&D expenses: in particular, the coefficient of CC is positive and highly significant, probably as a result of the rapid deregulation of common carrier telecommunication services in the 1980s.

16 The same holds true for DIVE. Actually, such a variable proves to be multi-collinear with DIVEREL; consequently, introducing it into the model makes the estimates worse.

17 SEMIC directly affects the value of the coefficient of lnIRD, as the zero hypothesis that the value of the coefficient of the cross-product term does not significantly differ from zero can be rejected. DP influences the marginal effect of the R&D variable as the probability of being censored (i.e., no agreement concluded in year t) is significantly lower for firms in the data processing industry. US cumulate both effects, with the probability of being censored being significantly higher for US firms.

References

Arora, A. and Gambardella, A. (1990) 'Complementarity and external linkages: the strategies of the large firms in biotechnology', *The Journal of Industrial Economics* XXXVIII: 361–79

—— (1994) 'Evaluating technological information and utilizing it. Scientific knowledge, technological capability, and external linkages in biotechnology', *Journal of Economic Behavior and Organization* 24: 91–114

Arrow, K.J. (1962) 'Economic welfare and the allocation of resources for invention', in *The Rate and Direction of Inventive Activity*, NBER Conference No. 13, Princeton, NJ: Princeton University Press.

Berg, S.V., Duncan, J. and Friedman, P. (1982) *Joint Venture Strategies and Corporate Innovation*, Cambridge, MA: Oelgeschlager, Gunn and Hain Publishers Inc.

Cainarca, G.C., Colombo, M.G., Mariotti, S., Ciborra, C., De Michelis, G. and Losano, M.G. (1989) *Tecnologie dell'informazione e accordi fra imprese*, Milano: Edizioni di Comunità.

Cainarca, G.C., Colombo, M.G., Mariotti, S. (1992) 'Agreements between firms and the technological life cycle model: evidence from information technologies', *Research Policy* 21: 45–62.

Cohen, W.M. and Levin, R.C. (1989) 'Empirical studies of innovation and market structure', in R. Schmalensee and R.D. Willig (eds) *Handbook of Industrial Organization*, Amsterdam: North-Holland.

Cohen, W.M. and Levinthal, D. (1989) 'Innovation and learning: the two faces of R&D', *The Economic Journal* 99: 569–96.

Colombo, M.G. (1995) 'Firm size and cooperation: the determinants of cooperative agreements in information technology industries', *International Journal of the Economics of Business* 2: 3–29.

Colombo, M.G. and Garrone, P. (1996) 'Technological cooperative agreements and firms' R&D intensity. A note on causality relations', *Research Policy* 25: 923–32.

D'Aspremont, C. and Jacquemin, A. (1988) 'Cooperative and noncooperative R&D in duopoly with spillovers', *The American Economic Review* 78: 1,133–7.

—— (1990) 'Cooperative and noncooperative R&D in duopoly with spillovers: erratum', *The American Economic Review* 80: 641–2.

De Bondt, R. (1996) 'Spillovers and innovative activity', *International Journal of Industrial Organization* 15: 1–28.

Dosi, G. (1988) 'Sources, procedures, and microeconomic effects of innovation', *Journal of Economic Literature* XXVI: 1,120–71.

Granger, C.W.J. (1969) 'Investigating causal relations by econometric models and cross-spectral methods', *Econometrica* 37: 424–38.

Hagedoorn, J. (1991) 'Changing patterns of interfirm strategic technology alliances in information technologies and telecommunications', WIK, mimeo, 72.

Holtz-Eakin, D., Newley, W. and Rosen, H.S. (1988) 'Estimating vector autoregressions with panel data', *Econometrica* 56: 1,371–95.

Humbert, M. (1988) *Les stratégies d'industrialisation dans l'électronique*, Rennes: GERDIC.

Kamien, M.I., Muller, E. and Zang, I. (1992) 'Research joint ventures and R&D cartels', *The American Economic Review* 82: 1,293–1,306.

Katz, M.L. (1986) 'An analysis of cooperative research and development', *Rand Journal of Economics* 17: 527–43.

Katz, M.L. and Ordover, J.A. (1990) 'R&D cooperation and competition', *Brookings Papers on Economic Activity: Microeconomics*: 137–203.

Kleinknecht, A. and Reijnen, J.O.N. (1992) 'Why do firms cooperate in R&D? An empirical study', *Research Policy* 21: 347–60.

Link, A.N. and Bauer, L.L. (1987) 'An economic analysis of cooperative research', *Technovation* 6: 247–60.

Mowery, D.C. and Rosenberg, N. (1989) *Technology and the Pursuit of Economic Growth*, Cambridge: Cambridge University Press.

Nelson, R.R. (1990) 'Capitalism as an engine of progress', *Research Policy* 19: 193–214.

Nelson, R.R. and Winter, S.G. (1982) *An Evolutionary Theory of Economic Change*, Cambridge, MA: Harvard University Press.

Pavitt, K. (1984) 'Sectoral patterns of technical change: towards a taxonomy and a theory', *Research Policy* 13: 343–73.

Pisano, G.P. (1990) 'The R&D boundaries of the firm: an empirical analysis', *Administrative Science Quarterly* 35: 153–176.

Reinganum, J.F. (1989) 'The timing of innovation: research, development, and diffusion', in R. Schmalensee and R.D. Willig (eds) *Handbook of Industrial Organization*, Amsterdam: North-Holland.

Rosenberg, N. (1976) *Perspectives on Technology* Cambridge: Cambridge University Press.

—— (1990) 'Why do firms do basic research (with their own money)?', *Research Policy* 19: 165–174.

Simpson, D.R. and Vonortas, N.S. (1994) 'Cournot equilibrium with imperfectly appropriable R&D', *The Journal of Industrial Economics* XLII: 79–92.

Sinha, D.K. and Cusumano, M.A. (1991) 'Complementary resources and cooperative research: a model of research joint-ventures among competitors', *Management Science* 37: 1,091–1,106.

Smith, R.J. and Blundell, R.W. (1986) 'An exogeneity test for a simultaneous equation Tobit model with an application to labor supply', *Econometrica* 54: 679–85.

Spence, M.A. (1984) 'Cost reduction, competition, and industrial performance', *Econometrica* 52: 101–21.

Suzumura, K. (1992) 'Cooperative and noncooperative R&D in an oligopoly with spillovers', *The American Economic Review* 82: 1,307–20.

Teece, D.J. (1980) 'Economies of scope and the scope of the enterprise', *Journal of Economic Behavior and Organization* 1: 223–247.

8

TECHNOLOGICAL CHANGE AND VERTICAL INTEGRATION

Analysis of international vertical integration in multinational companies

John Cantwell and Ivana Paniccia

Introduction

This chapter aims to make a small contribution to a dynamic theory of vertical integration and the boundaries of firms. It enlarges upon the framework of Langlois (1988; Langlois and Robertson 1995), who has argued that rapid economic change leads to vertical integration, rather than to disintegration as in the case of the original Stigler model of industry evolution. This counter-hypothesis can be constructed with reference to a dynamic theory of the firm which differs from the transaction costs approach as well as other static theories. In particular, our contribution relies on a competence-based theory of the firm, which stems from a definition of technology in which the tacit element is emphasized (Cantwell 1989, 1992a, 1994). From this theoretical background, we claim that the nature of the technological paradigm defines the nature of the learning process in each industry, which in turn sets some of the conditions for vertical integration decisions. We then examine data which provide an initial test of this hypothesis, by looking at the evolution of vertical integration at an international level in multinational companies.

The role of technology in static and dynamic theories of vertical integration

In the analysis of the factors explaining why one industry is more vertically integrated across national boundaries than another, or why the same industry exhibits a different degree of vertical integration in different countries, the role of technology has been quite neglected. This omission can be partly explained by the static nature of many of the theories applied (e.g., in most versions of the transaction cost approach), but the dynamic analysis of the vertical integration has not properly taken account of the technological dimension either.

The Stigler (1951) model, which is reputed to be the main contribution to a dynamic theory of vertical integration, depicts a general life cycle for all industries without considering their different technological patterns of development. As is widely known, the main conclusion can be expressed in Stigler's words: 'vertical disintegration is the typical development in growing industries, vertical integration in declining industries'. Empirical evidence on vertical integration has not confirmed this thesis for all industries in different contexts. According to some researchers (Adelman 1958) vertical integration is instead the typical result in a growing industry. Without wishing to enter into the debate over the validity of the Stigler's model, we wish just to propose that an explicit recognition of technological accumulation as a determinant of the structure of the industry and of its cycle of development, could help to reconcile some apparently conflicting results and interpretations. Langlois (1988) has refined the Stigler model, adding the rate of growth of demand as an important variable in explaining different levels of vertical integration across industries. However, the problem is that the rate of growth of demand is an inadequate proxy for the specific course of technological development in an industry.

The nature of technology

This chapter aims to bring technological considerations into vertical integration theory – considered with reference to integrated international production and the international division of labour within multinational companies in Europe. Industries follow different development patterns according to the nature of the dominant technology in the sector in question, and the path of innovation that they tend to follow over time. The pattern of technological advance varies significantly from field to field.

The definition of technology used here is the broad one adopted in the theory of technological competence (Cantwell 1989, 1992a, 1994). Technology is defined as partially tacit, specific to the context in which it has been created or adapted, and tied to the skills and routines of those who have developed and operate it. Technology in any firm is a product of a steady search for improvements and an internal learning process.

The basic proposition is that technology always consists of two elements: the potentially public and the tacit element. The first element includes information, patented blueprints and other codifiable knowledge. The tacit element includes the non-codifiable elements of the skills, routines and operational practices that accrue from collective learning processes. The relative significance of the tacit and the public element of technology varies across

159

industries, influencing their structure and the time path of their growth rate. The source of the competitive advantage of the firm resides essentially in its tacit capability or competence.

This suggests that firms tend to develop and operate technologies internally that are central to their basic competence, to which they attach a very high value, but which typically are of less value to other firms, because these other firms have their own differentiated areas of expertise. It follows that in the cases where combined production processes are sustained by tacit knowledge vertical integration should occur (Cantwell 1992a; Teece *et al.* 1990; Kogut and Zander 1992).

Another implication of the distinction between the two elements of technology is that only the public element of technology is tradable. Internalization theory (Buckley and Casson 1976) – as a theory of exchange – can be applied to flows of potentially public knowledge. The case of the tacit element is different. Technological competence cannot be traded; it is possible only to imitate it through gradual learning processes in other firms, with or without assistance. For this reason, comparisons with a notional market are not relevant to an understanding of why the tacit elements of a technology are exploited internally and give rise to the growth or extension of the firm's own production facilities (Cantwell 1994).

In the same way the emphasis on the firm-specific characteristics of technology in the competence theory suggests that there can be no feasible market for the core technologies of a competent firm since it places a much higher value on them than any potential licensee which would have to bear the costs of adaptation. There need be no 'opportunistic' behaviour or 'lack of trust' between the firm and a potential licensee; the technology is simply worth less to the licensee.

Learning is a cumulative process that occurs in a firm-specific and path-dependent way, so that competences deriving from a learning process are localized and specific. Spillovers can be obtained at a cost, where the extent of the cost depends upon the firm's own past experience. The more closely the technological competence of the recipient and originator are related, and the stronger and more sophisticated the competence of the recipient, the lower the cost.

Technological co-operation can be also explained in terms of the need to co-ordinate similar learning processes in partner companies.

Rate of growth of demand and rate of technological innovation

In his attempt to take account of technological aspects in the theory of vertical integration, Langlois (1988) refers to Teece's (1984) distinction between *autonomous* innovation and *systemic* innovation. He argues that growth – or rapid growth, at any rate – must involve a large degree of systemic innovation, and the evolution of industry structure in response to an increase in the extent of the market will depend crucially on the time path of growth. If growth is gradual and innovation is incremental, vertical disintegration as foreseen by Stigler may occur. If by contrast, growth comes in spurts or is the result of radical innovation, the picture may be rather different. The phases of rapid change are periods of disequilibrium in which the transaction-cost disadvantages of markets outweigh the disabilities of internal management, and so at such times strategies of integration are relatively more favoured.

In our view, the rate of growth of an industry, when it is linked to a technological impetus, seems to be better explained by the nature of the paradigm governing technological opportunities, rather than by the existence of *systemic* innovation in fast growing sectors, unless the term *systemic* is taken to mean the emergence of a new range of technological opportunities relevant to the sector, thus coinciding with the concept of a new technological paradigm.

Together with the category of *systemic* innovation we wish to have some term which could take account of the wide variety of types of technological change among different industries. Across many industries inventions may represent a continuous process of the enhancement or the critical revision of a prior 'dominant design', or they may be part of a sequential chain of incremental improvements, or both. Systemic change in this sense applies to many slow growing as well as fast growing industries, and so it does not enable us to discriminate between them.

In addition, according to Nelson, in different industries like those producing automobiles, aircraft, electric light systems, semiconductors and computers, technical advance is cumulative, in the sense that today's advances build on and interact with many other features of existing technology. To reiterate, what distinguishes rapidly changing from dormant industries is the nature of the paradigm that governs technological opportunities, and which is associated with much greater opportunities for innovation in some sectors than in others.

Langlois seems to fall into a common trap that has characterized much of the literature on the sources of technological innovation until recently. He supposes the growth of demand is an external pull factor, which is generally required to stimulate innovative activity (a view criticized by Mowery and Rosenberg 1979). It may instead be the radical new knowledge and opportunities opened up by an innovation (as in the case of microelectronics) coinciding with the emergence of a new paradigm, that paves the way for a cluster of related innovations and sparks off a virtuous circle between demand and innovative activity.

In addition, Langlois makes the relevant point that rapid economic change or technological change may introduce additional costs of a kind which he calls dynamic transactional costs. In a first statement these are defined as the costs of alerting contractors to and persuading them of the benefits of the new process of production or of the use of a new input (according to the typology of the invention/innovation, Langlois 1988). When the innovation has a systemic nature the inventor needs complementary inputs, which he can produce by himself or buy from an external supplier. In the first case he has to sustain the costs related to communicating the procedures and routines to employees, while in this second case, for the supplier be able to exactly fit his needs, the inventor has to sustain the costs of persuading, negotiating, co-ordinating and teaching outside suppliers (Langlois and Robertson 1995: 37). Because employees can follow more easily the detailed specifications of an end-product than could an independent contractor, the 'dynamic transaction costs' – that is, the costs of teaching or transferring capabilities – are lower internally than between firms, and vertical integration is the preferred choice in the face of economic change or innovation.

From our point of view, this valuable point requires some additional and complementary qualifications. In particular, we will claim that technological change creates new sources of costs which would be better defined in more general terms as learning costs.

If the innovator has only to persuade the subcontractor to do something which has already been specified in a detailed manner, the only remaining problem reduces to one of asset specificity. The new input may require the complete dedication of the productive process to the production of such an input. In this case vertical integration is the natural solution because no independent supplier will be available. Transaction cost theory or internalization theory offers the most appropriate scheme to explain the choice between vertical integration or disintegration, where such a choice exists. But it may be the case that no supplier can be found not because they are unwilling but because as a result of the specificity of the learning process, the innovator alone has the capability needed to develop the input internally. If the input has not yet been specified, it may be difficult to engage in a subcontracting or collaborative relationship, because the potential partner's competence is too far removed from that of the buyer.

In this case the costs of 'transferring capabilities', that is dynamic transactional costs, in the recent restatement, will be too high in comparison with the internal cost of development.

Dynamic transaction costs also occur in the initial stage of development in an industry when different designs are in competition ('the pre-paradigmatic phase'). Subcontractors are reluctant to invest in dedicated assets because of the risk that the chosen design of the contractor will not be the dominant one in the future. In the paradigmatic stage this reluctance is attenuated, so that vertical disintegration can occur, depending upon the characteristics of the external environment.

From the above, it seems that in Langlois' view, the learning process occurs on the supplier's side. In fact, it seems that the firm which takes the initiative to integrate is the buyer, and, more important, this firm has the relevant capabilities. This implies a uni-directional process of capabilities tranferance. Yet it may just as easily be the case that the supplier has the specific and autonomous competencies which are required by the inventor for the development and customization of a component. That is, the supplier itself may be the inventor, but may lack the complementary resources to realize the new idea.

Not all inventions occur in the same way. They can be the result of a collective process of trial and error, rather than the outcome of individual innovative development undertaken in one firm. The convergence of different trajectories (as suggested by Kodama 1992) offers new opportunities of co-operation between firms belonging to different fields of activity. In this way the manner in which technological advance occurs may affect industrial structure, redefining the boundaries of industries as well the boundaries of firms.

When an innovation requires the *joint* development of capabilities or competencies we prefer to talk of learning costs involved in the process rather than of costs of transferring capabilities or teaching. In this case vertical integration is not a necessary outcome, and joint ventures and other collaborative agreements may be more appropriate. Active co-operation in learning is more likely to be feasible, and becomes more effective, the more closely complementary are firms' initial profiles of technological specialization or competence. Joint ventures provide a means by which the learning processes of different companies can be combined in some areas of mutual interest, while cross-licensing agreements focus on the contractual exchange of knowledge. Joint ventures (or integration) may be superior to cross-licensing agreements as a means of mutual assistance towards technological improvements where tacit capability is more complex and more important relative to the sharing of communicable knowledge. This line of argument suggests it is necessary to look deeply at the diffusion of related, complementary competence in an area when assessing the feasibility of inter-firm partnerships.[1]

The distinction between a simple exchange of knowledge and co-operative learning may give rise to a distinction between firm-specific paths of development which are complementary, and those that are closely complementary (Loasby 1991; Cantwell and Barrera 1996). The fruitful exchange of knowl edge requires the complementarity of activities, but co-operative learning creates a closer complementarity between those activities. Closely complementary activities may remain quite operationally distinct, and hence difficult to manage within a single organizational structure (Loasby 1991, with reference to Richardson 1972), and if so joint ventures will be preferred over vertical integration. In more general terms, if the patterns of learning being followed by firms are closely complementary to one another, joint ventures or vertical integration may be the chosen organizational form. If the competencies are unrelated or only weakly related, arms length exchanges and a separation of learning processes will be the result.

From what we have said it is apparent that the concept of learning costs is close to that of dynamic transactional costs, but slightly different since it allows one to take into account a mutual interaction between the capabilities of buyer and seller, and the further development of these capabilities themselves. Learning costs arise in each situation where the firm is engaged in a process of upgrading its own knowledge, competencies, and abilities. More specifically, it is the development of tacit capability that requires investments in processes of learning, which can be carried out at an individual (firm) or joint level. The costs of learning are the costs of developing collective expertise in teams (or of team-building) within the firm, or combined and interactive learning process in joint ventures or other forms of agreements between different firms. They may encompass the costs of communicating, of developing common codes of understanding, teaching each other, and meeting.

They emerge in situations of high uncertainty and a high degree of competitiveness, where the need to explore new technological opportunities is particularly urgent. These periods may follow the 'pre-paradigmatic stage' referred to by Langlois, and they are characteristic of many industries affected by technological change, affecting incumbents, entrants and suppliers.

The correct interpretation of learning costs is as the costs of investments whose benefits are expected to be realized only in the long-term. It is also possible to contrast them with static transaction costs, by saying that learning costs are the costs of processes that have a positive impact upon the value of underlying production activity, while transaction costs are conceived simply as expenses to be subtracted from the value of the transaction, which has already been established. Conversely, when learning costs are incurred, the value of the transaction increases proportionately to the expense of undertaking learning activities.

When innovation is complex and systemic, it is less likely that the knowledge of one component of it would lead to the comprehension of the whole system. Thus, there is less likelihood that the risks of disclosing reserved information or the risk of opportunistic behaviour will occur. The variety of processes leading to technical innovation, the multiplicity of actors, the regime of appropriability and the stage of development of the industry give rise to a range of industry-specific development paths which cannot be summarized by rate of growth of demand as a comprehensive descriptive variable for technological development. Even in situations where problems of appropriability are at work, the risk of disclosure can be overcome by the matching risk of supplier's dependence. In addition, as has already been underlined, complementary assets are more relevant to the aim of exploiting the fruits of innovation. Questions of market power between contractors must also be taken into account.

In more concise terms, if we suppose that the process of discovery is undertaken internally, and then technological co-operation with other firms is conceived as a means of enlarging the range of application of the discovery, it is possible to incur the dynamic transaction costs of convincing external contractors to specialize in a new field or of transferring capabilities. But since further innovations are the objective of collaboration we do not have a settled new product as in the case described previously by Langlois. The inventor is not simply trying to convince the contractor or some other external source to develop a new component suitable for a given new process or product, sustain the costs to accommodate himself in a relationship where the external supplier has the capabilities he needs. The mastery of the new discovery requires a joint process of learning and further technological development. The extent to which the process of learning can be speeded up through internal routines or through the co-ordination of two autonomous firms with different cultures (and different codes of communicating, routines, etc.) determines the choice between integration or co-operation.

In introducing the concept of learning costs we take into account situations in which the relevant capabilities are not entirely in the hands of the firm which has the choice to integrate or to co-operate, such as the inventor, the client or the leader. In determining the degree of vertical integration, the technological paradigm governing innovation opportunities, the nature of the learning process as well as the nature of diffused capabilities, and the form of institutions are important variables. Taking them into consideration would also lead to a better appreciation of the role of the more traditional factors considered by the dynamic theory of vertical integration (the extent of the market, age of the industry and rate of growth of demand).

Indeed, the growth of firms horizontally or vertically is the result of an interaction between different economic factors. The theory of technological competence can offer a contribution towards a dynamic theory of vertical integration on the basis of a different definition of technology and by paying greater attention to the varying rates of growth achieved by different industries as a consequence of the prevailing technological paradigm.

Economic and technological factors explaining vertical integration at an international level

We have argued firstly that the degree of vertical integration depends upon learning costs as well as transaction costs – i.e., upon the extent to which firms operating in different stages of a production process have complementary competencies or separate and less related competencies. The more that their fields of competence overlap the less vertical integration will occur (and the more firms will co-operate in complementary learning processes), while the less their fields of competence overlap the greater will be vertical integration as each firm attempts to establish its own specific chain of learning relationships in production.

Second, for some given spectrum of competencies across the firms that operate in the different stages of production in an industry, the degree of vertical integration depends on the rate of technological change (and hence the speed of learning) within the industry in question. When the rate of technological change is low, vertical integration may be low even when the competencies of firms at different stages of production are unrelated, since learning costs (because of few technological opportunities) remain low and the conventional transaction cost considerations dominate the extent of vertical integration. Conversely, when the rate of technical change is high the management of learning comes centre stage, and vertical integration may be high even when firms have overlapping fields of competence.

We examine this latter hypothesis in the case of the degree of cross-border vertical integration within the operations of US MNCs in Europe. We expect MNCs to be more vertically integrated in industries in which technological change is greater. This factor should be added to the other influences upon vertical integration that have been considered traditionally in the literature on intra-firm trade.

In an international context trade can be organized through arm's length exports or within a multinational company through direct investments. For a foreign affiliate the choice between internal production or subcontracting is further complicated because it has also the option to procure inputs locally. Imports may be sourced either from other parts of the MNC, that is, from the parent company or a sister affiliate, or from independent foreign sellers. In an international context the issue of vertical integration has a slightly different meaning, because it refers to a vertical division of labour, that is a process of specialization, that occurs in global space. The specialization of production in each plant can occur whether horizontally (certain products or parts of the product range being confined to production in a single location) or vertically (the separation of intermediate products and final assembly).

A link between the theory of vertical integration and the international division of labour can be found by observing that intra-firm trade is an alternative to arm's length trade and so is an index of international vertical integration. The more that industry-specific factors encourage vertical integration, the higher the percentage of international trade is likely to be within firms (Casson 1987). In what has already been said, we have paid attention to the impact of industry-specific paths of technological change on the degree of vertical integration. In the case of MNCs, the attention paid to technology must be even greater because it has been recognized that MNCs are particularly strong agents of technological advance (Dunning 1988; Cantwell 1994).

The industry characteristics which tend to promote intra-firm trade have been described in the relevant literature on this topic (Casson 1987; Doz 1986; Williamson 1985). We do not want to discuss this literature, but rather to complement it by incorporating technological factors, which instead we are going to describe in more detail.

The factors related to the nature of the technological paradigm in an industry can be summarized by the following.

Economies of experience Industries characterized by economies of experience are those where the benefits of learning by doing and learning by using are related to the increase of production over time. In such industries the cost of producing a given product in a single firm or location is lower than the cost of spreading its production among different plants or locations. The economies of experience may be either location-specific or firm-specific. Where they are location-specific they are more likely to lead to MNC rationalization, as there is an incentive to specialize by both products and processes according to which centres provide the most conducive environments for each type of activity. Production of each kind can then be allowed to grow most rapidly where the potential for improvements in productivity or product quality in the process or product concerned is at its greatest. To the extent that learning is cumulative and is only transferred to new locations at some costs, a process of vertical specialization may result. Economies of experience are likely to be significant in sectors which are capital-intensive, or in which the rate of product innovation is high.

Research intensive production   Traditionally, it has been affirmed that R&D activity is subjected to the same scale effects as manufacturing plants. Therefore a concentration of R&D in a single location where manufacturing activity is also concentrated – for learning by doing opportunities to improve R&D – can result in major efficiencies. Recent evidence conversely suggests that large laboratories incur bureaucratic costs that lower the creative level of researchers. But reasons why research activity should not be geographically concentrated are even wider when considering the benefits of diversity of related learning activities and the ability to respond in a more flexible way to changes in the firm's environment.

Rate of growth of technological opportunities   The rate of growth of technological opportunities is a factor discussed earlier. Technological paradigms governing the distribution of technological opportunities have effects on the organizational structure of firms at a national and international level.

From what we have said we expect a high value of intra-firm trade in industries characterized by growing technological opportunities, but with different directions of the trade of intermediate products according to the nature of the capabilities diffused among affiliated and parent companies.

Technological change and vertical integration in US MNCs in Europe: the evidence

In order to attempt a rough test of our hypothesis we look at the intra-firm trade of US MNCs, paying special attention to their manufacturing trade in Europe.

Different patterns of intra-firm trade may apply to firms originating from different countries. There is simply more evidence on the extent to which US MNCs rely on intra-firm trade than there is for the firms of other countries.[2] Therefore, the data used here must be understood as perhaps representing a pattern of intra-firm trade that is specific to US companies.

Europe, as a location of US affiliates, offers an interesting illustration because it has been shown that in previous years up to 1987 both horizontal and vertical international integration of US foreign affiliates located in the EC have been rising (Cantwell 1992b). In addition, this corporate rationalization has proceeded faster within the EC than elsewhere, and affiliates here have become more closely integrated with other EC firms and markets than with firms and markets outside the EC. If these trends have been confirmed in detail through to 1982, we now look to the evolution in the last decade, observing how the integration strategies of firms have evolved according to the evolution of the life cycle of industries, taken as a change in the availability of technological opportunities.

The international linkages of foreign-owned affiliates can be measured by the value of their export sales. These are to be distinguished from local sales within the country in which they are located, which represent the local market-oriented (or import-substituting) element of their production. The data on US foreign affiliate exports also enable us to make a loose distinction between the international horizontal and international vertical integration of US-owned firms. The data are classified by industry and are reported separately for US parent companies and for their overseas affiliates, so that it is possible to observe by industry the flow of exports from affiliates to parents and vice versa.[3]

The extent of international horizontal specialization is roughly given by the value of the export sales to unaffiliated firms or individuals, while international vertical integration can be measured by the value of export sales to other affiliates which are part of the same MNC or the parent company itself. For these reasons, the Benchmark Survey on US intra-firm trade is the best available data on intra-firm trade of MNCs. Data are available about every seven years from 1966 to 1992, as the last available year.

Some additional definitions are necessary in order to understand the following tables. A foreign affiliate is defined in the US data as a business enterprise in which one foreign person owns, directly, or indirectly, 10 per cent or more of the voting securities or the equivalent.[4] Affiliates report on a consolidated basis; the consolidation for a given affiliate includes all other affiliates in the same host country owned more than 50 per cent by that affiliate. When a consolidated affiliate has operations in more than one industry, it is classified in the industry that accounts for the largest proportion of its sales.

In the following tables we give an overall picture of the evolution of horizontal and vertical integration of MNCs. First, we contrast affiliated versus unaffiliated exports and local sales. Second, we look at intra-firm trade within MNCs belonging to different industries of the manufacturing sector, for which we provide an index. Lastly, we distinguish between exports of intermediate and exports of final goods as different components of intra-firm trade.

Table 8.1 shows the evolution of international horizontal and vertical integration in all industries for the period of observation. Horizontal integration recorded a more sustained increase between the mid-1970s and the early

1980s than did international vertical integration, but the latter strongly recovered in the 1980s. Unaffiliated exports rose from 9.1 of affiliated sales in 1966 to 16.5 per cent in 1982, before falling back close to their initial value by 1989 (11.9 per cent), while intra-firm exports increased from 17.0 per cent to 20.3 per cent in 1989, but still remain below their peak value of 26.4 per cent in 1977.

Table 8.1 The geographical distribution of sales and the structure of exports of US majority owned foreign affiliates 1966–89 (%)

	1966	1970	1977	1982	1989
Local sales	73.9	70.5	61.8	65.5	67.7
Total exports	26.1	29.5	38.2	34.5	32.2
to third countries	20.1	23.0	19.8	24.0	21.0
to USA	6.0	6.6	18.5	10.5	11.2
Unaffiliated exports	9.1	11.3	11.8	16.5	11.9
to third countries	8.0	10.2	9.9	14.7	9.8
to USA	1.2	1.1	1.9	1.8	2.1
Affiliated exports	17.0	18.2	26.4	18.0	20.3
to third countries	12.1	12.8	9.8	9.3	11.2
to USA	4.8	5.4	16.6	8.7	9.1

Source: US Department of Commerce data in Cantwell 1992b; US *Direct Investment Abroad* 1989; Benchmark Survey 1992.

Table 8.2 The geographical distribution of sales and the structure of exports of US majority owned foreign affiliates in manufacturing 1966–89 (%)

	1966	1970	1977	1982	1989
Local sales	77.2	74.4	69.2	66.1	62.2
Total exports	22.8	25.6	30.8	33.9	37.8
to third countries	16.2	18.0	21.7	24.2	24.0
to USA	6.7	7.6	9.1	9.7	13.8
Unaffiliated exports	8.9	9.2	10.9	11.4	10.2
to third countries	7.8	8.2	9.2	10.1	8.5
to USA	1.1	1.0	1.7	1.3	1.7
Affiliated exports	14.0	16.4	19.9	22.5	27.7
to third countries	8.4	9.8	12.5	14.1	15.5
to USA	5.6	6.6	7.4	8.3	12.2

Source: US Department of Commerce data in Cantwell 1992b; US *Direct Investment Abroad* 1989; Benchmark Survey 1992.

In manufacturing – considered separately – the picture is quite different, as reported in Table 8.2. The trend toward international vertical integration is stronger and less subject to fluctuations. The value of affiliate exports in 1989 is nearly double the corresponding value in 1966. The greatest increase over the period considered has taken place between 1982 and 1989. Unaffiliated exports rose only moderately, from 8.9 per cent of the value of affiliate sales in 1966, to 10.2 per cent in 1989.

In general, US-owned affiliates located in the EC have a similar distribution of international vertical and horizontal integration as applies to all affiliates. However, Table 8.3 shows that the evolution of intra-firm trade has been different between 1977 and 1989. Local sales of US affiliates located in the EC (ten countries) have decreased, although slightly, to the advantage of affiliate export growth. The increase has in any case been lower than for the EC6 (six original countries) share of affiliated exports from an EC location. It is worth noting, though, that there was a much greater increase in international integration from 1977 to 1989 amongst affiliates located in the original EC 6, for which exports rose from about 27% to about 35%, than among those located in countries joining subsequently.

Table 8.3 The geographical distribution of sales and the structure of exports of US majority owned foreign affiliates located in the EC (10) 1977–89 (%)

	1977	1982	1989
Local sales	68.9	67.0	65.8
Total exports	31.1	33.0	32.8
to third countries	27.7	29.3	28.0
to USA	3.4	3.7	4.8
Unaffiliated exports	12.4	15.4	11.8
to third countries	11.9	14.5	11.0
to USA	0.5	0.9	0.8
Affiliated exports	18.7	17.6	21.0
to third countries	15.8	14.8	17.0
to USA	2.9	2.8	4.0

Source: US Department of Commerce data in Cantwell 1992b; US *Direct Investment Abroad* 1989; Benchmark Survey 1992.

In manufacturing, the proportion of total affiliate exports is higher than for all industries, both in Europe and elsewhere throughout the period considered (see Table 8.4).

Returning to our central theme, it is important to observe the degree of vertical integration across the different industries of the manufacturing sector.

Tables 8.5a and 8.5b present the distribution of intra-firm trade by industries in two periods of time 1982 and 1989. In all manufacturing industries the proportion of affiliated exports is greater than that of unaffiliated exports.

Table 8.4 The geographical distribution of sales and the structure of exports of US majority owned foreign affiliates in manufacturing located in the EC (10) 1977–89 (%)

	1977	1982	1989
Local sales	61.4	58.1	58.2
Total exports	38.6	41.9	41.9
to third countries	36.3	39.4	36.4
to USA	2.3	2.5	5.5
Unaffiliated exports to third countries	15.0	15.8	10.1
Affiliated exports to third countries	21.3	23.6	26.3

Source: US Department of Commerce data in Cantwell 1992b; US *Direct Investment Abroad* 1989; Benchmark Survey 1992.

Exports to US parents in 1989 are at a similarly significant level in the transportation (23.1 per cent), machinery (18.2 per cent), electrical and electronic equipment (17.2 per cent) industries. In 1982, the industries most dependent on exports to US parents were also the transportation (19.6 per cent) and electrical industries (16.8 per cent).

In 1989, transportation (essentially motor vehicles and equipment), machinery (including office and computing machines), and electrical and electronic equipment have the highest shares of affiliated exports, that is 41.6 per cent, 37.0 per cent and 32.9 per cent respectively. In other words, this suggests that industries in which the extent of vertical integration within the MNC may be high tend to also be areas in which technological opportunities are high. The same industries report an above-average value in 1982 as well, but with lower shares in line with the lower average share of affiliated exports: transportation (36.8 per cent), electrical (28.3 per cent) and machinery (28.3 per cent). However, it must be said that the large share of affiliated exports in the electrical industry in 1989 is much more at the expense of local sales rather than unaffiliated exports, as unaffiliated exports account for 12.5 per cent (compared to 10.2 per cent on average). By comparison, the metals, chemicals and 'other' industries are more dependent on unaffiliated exports, but the food industry is strongly dependent on local sales (80.5 per cent).

Table 8.6 shows that from 1982 to 1989, exports to affiliates increased more than 23 per cent, while the total export increase is about 12 per cent. The major part of this increase is due to the flow of sales to US parents (+ 46 per cent). Exports to US parents grew from a share of 8.3 per cent to 12.2 per cent in the period considered. As a consequence, local sales diminished.

The most dynamic industry in affiliated sales is metals (+ 52.6 per cent), followed by food (+50.1 per cent), and machinery (+ 30.9 per cent); all other industries, with the exception of 'other' industries, reported a positive variation very close to the average value. Sales to US parents have risen by most in machinery (165.23 per cent), metals (79.2 per cent), and food (64.4 per cent). Symmetrically, food exhibits the highest increase in exports to affiliates in

Table 8.5a The geographical distribution of the sales of all US majority owned foreign affiliates in manufacturing by industry – 1989

	All industries	Food	Chemicals	Metals	Machinery	Electric	Transportation	Other
Local sales	62.2	80.4	66.6	64.6	55.1	55.0	53.2	69.3
Total exports to third	37.8	19.6	33.4	35.4	44.9	45.0	46.8	30.7
countries	24.0	17.3	29.2	25.9	25.8	25.5	22.0	21.6
to USA	13.8	2.3	4.2	9.5	19.1	19.5	24.8	9.1
Unffiliated exports to third	10.2	9.5	12.4	20.2	8.0	12.0	5.3	13.8
countries	8.5	9.3	11.6	16.4	7.0	9.8	3.5	10.5
to USA	1.7	0.3	0.8	3.9	0.9	2.3	1.7	3.3
Affiliated exports to third	27.7	10.0	21.0	15.2	37.0	32.9	41.6	16.9
countries	15.5	8.0	17.6	9.6	18.8	15.7	18.5	11.1
to USA	12.2	2.0	3.4	5.6	18.2	17.2	23.1	5.8

Source: US *Direct Investment Abroad*, 1989 Benchmark Survey, Washington DC, 1992.

Table 8.5b The geographical distribution of the sales of all US majority owned foreign affiliates in manufacturing by industry – 1982

	All Industries	Food	Chemicals	Metals	Machinery	Electric	Transport	Other
Local sales	66.1	84.4	68.3	74.3	59.4	59.3	56.7	69.3
Total exports to third	33.9	15.6	31.7	25.7	40.6	40.7	43.3	30.8
countries	24.2	13.9	28.0	20.8	33.0	22.4	22.0	24.2
to USA	9.7	1.7	3.7	4.9	7.6	18.3	21.3	6.6
Unaffiliated exports to third	11.4	9.0	13.7	15.8	12.3	12.4	6.5	13.9
countries	10.1	8.4	12.9	14.0	11.6	10.9	4.7	11.5
to USA	1.3	0.5	0.8	1.8	0.7	1.5	1.8	2.3
Affiliated exports to third	22.5	6.7	18.0	9.9	28.3	28.3	36.8	16.8
countries	14.1	5.5	15.1	6.8	21.4	11.5	17.2	12.6
to USA	8.3	1.2	2.9	3.1	6.8	16.8	19.6	4.2

Source: US *Direct Investment Abroad*, 1982 Benchmark Survey, Washington DC, 1985.

Table 8.6 Variations between 1982 and 1989 (%)

	All Industries	Food	Chemicals	Metals	Machinery	Electric	Transportation	Other
Local sales	−6.0	−4.6	−2.5	−13.0	−7.4	−7.2	−6.3	0.0
Total exports	11.7	25.1	5.4	37.6	10.8	10.5	8.2	−0.1
to third countries	−0.8	24.3	4.4	24.7	−21.6	14.0	0.3	−10.6
to USA	42.6	30.9	13.3	92.3	151.6	6.1	16.4	38.5
Unaffiliated exports	−10.6	6.4	−9.2	28.1	−35.4	−2.9	−18.6	−0.3
to third countries	−15.6	9.7	−9.8	17.0	−39.4	−10.2	−25.0	−8.6
to USA	23.2	−47.5	1.1	115.0	26.5	49.5	−1.5	40.4
Affiliated exports	23.1	50.1	16.4	52.6	30.9	16.3	13.0	0.4
to third countries	9.6	46.9	16.3	40.4	−12.1	37.0	7.2	−12.0
to USA	46.1	64.4	16.8	79.2	165.?	?.?	18.0	37.5

third countries, as a consequence of a gradual trend towards geographical integration. Such dynamism in the food industry can be viewed as a consequence of the shift in consumers' tastes towards a greater cross-country homogeneity, in the last period.

We can distinguish industries more prone to vertical integration as those that exhibit a share of affiliate exports larger than the average value for manufacturing as a whole. The US benchmark survey enables us to analyse the composition of affiliate trade by a more detailed disaggregation of industries.

For this purpose, we can calculate an index of intra-firm trade defined as the ratio between the sum of international affiliate exports to other sister affiliates plus the affiliates' exports to their US parents, plus the exports of parent companies to their affiliates, on the numerator, and the sum of the total sales of affiliates plus the total parents' exports at denominator (Table 8.7).

The ratio can be expressed as follows:[5]

Aff Exports to Aff + Aff Exports to Parents + Parent Exports to Aff
—————————————————————————————————
Affil Sales + Parent Exports

In 1989 the industries showing a degree of intra-firm (affiliate) trade above the average are the following (the distance from the mean in manufacturing appears in brackets):

Table 8.7 Index of intra-firm trade. US majority owned affiliates in manufacturing

	1989	*Mean differences*	1982
Manufacturing	34.5	0.0 mean=34.5	
Food and kindred products	12.4	−22.1	
Grain mill and bakery	12.6	−21.9	7.7
Beverages	8.7	−25.8	8.6
Other (meat, dairy, kindred products)	13.6	−20.9	9.0
Chemical and allied products	25.8	−8.6	0.0
Industrial chemicals synthetics	34.1	−0.3	25.8
Drugs	24.2	−10.3	21.2
Soap, cleaners toilet goods	11.9	−22.6	13.6
Agricultural chemicals	23.1	−11.4	13.0
Chemical products	20.5	−14.0	19.6
Primary and fabricated metals	20.2	−14.3	0.0
Primary metal industries	27.1	−7.4	0.0
Ferrous	20.6	−13.9	6.1
Non-ferrous	28.7	−5.7	22.8
Fabricated metal products (cans, forgings, stampings, cutlery, etc.)	17.4	−17.0	14.8
Machinery	42.8	8.3	34.4
Farm and garden machinery	52.4	17.9	20.9
Construction and mining machinery	39.7	5.3	38.4
Office and computing machines	48.0	13.5	19.0
Other machinery	22.2	−12.3	0.0
Electric and electronic equipment	42.6	8.1	10.7
Household appliances	18.0	−16.5	40.4
Radio and communication equipment	38.1	3.6	38.5
Electronic components	57.0	22.5	14.0
Other Electrical machinery	26.3	−8.1	0.0
Transportation equipment	50.2	15.7	43.5
Motor vehicles	51.1	16.6	8.4
Other	19.4	−15.1	0.0
Other manufacturing	22.2	−12.3	0.0
Tobacco	5.2	−29.3	12.2
Textile	25.4	−9.0	16.7
Lumber, wood, furniture	21.8	−12.6	14.5
Paper and allied products	13.3	−21.2	9.9
Printing and publishing	5.6	−28.9	12.2
Rubber products	24.7	−9.8	17.0
Plastics	19.8	−14.6	15.2
Glass	17.6	−16.8	11.1
Stone, clay, cement and concrete	13.0	−21.5	17.6
Instruments	39.4	4.9	26.1
Other	23.3	−11.1	6.0

Source: 1989 US Benchmark Survey; 1982 US Benchmark Survey

Electronic components   57.00% (+ 22.5)
Farm and garden machinery   52.40% (+ 17.9)
Motor vehicles   51.06% (+ 16.6)
Computing   47.96% (+ 13.5)
Construction machinery   39.75% (+ 5.3)
Instruments   39.41% (+ 4.9)

We find some support here for the view that intra-firm trade takes place mostly in industries where technological opportunities are growing faster, where technology has a cumulative nature, economies of experience are relevant, such as electronics, computing and some categories of instruments (e.g., photographic, medical instruments) or in industries particularly influenced by phenomena of globalization of products (farm and garden machinery). The high value of intra-firm trade in motor vehicles can be explained by the US/Canadian automobile agreement, which has created a virtually open market in automobiles in North America since the late 1970s. In fact, about 80 per cent of US exports to affiliates in 1989 went to Canada (and 85 per cent in 1982).

The undifferentiated flow of intermediate products between affiliates implies a multiplicity of interactions between them that could be depicted by the notion of user-producer relationships. The dense exchange of non-codifiable information and the real process of communication requires a common code or generally a common culture which normally can be better developed within a MNC. This fact can explain why in technologically changing or globalizing industries interactions that are not exhaustively described by the exchange of products but extend to more intangible assets, happen inside the network of a MNC rather than with independent companies. Also, as noted earlier in the rough review of the literature on vertical integration, we had occasion to quote authors who praised the benefits of varied strategies of learning within the firm in order to avoid lock in effects in the long run.

The high proportion of affiliate exports to US parents as well as the significant patent activity resulting from US-owned research facilities in the EC countries historically (Cantwell 1995) suggests that 'innovators' are not located exclusively in the home country. The fact that affiliate exports to US parents retain a consistent share of total affiliate exports, especially in industries in which technological innovations are taking place more rapidly and in which US MNCs compete world-wide, suggests instead that the technological capability of home parents is also supported through the activity of affiliates located elsewhere.

These results contrast with the theory of the product life cycle (Vernon 1966), which suggests that innovations are as a rule located in the home country of the parent company, and usually close to the site of the corporate technological headquarters. If we accept further that innovative activity is more dispersed than is supposed by the product life cycle theory, partly because of the advantages of tapping into international centres of technological innovation (Cantwell 1995), the higher proportion of affiliated exports represents an organization of an internal network of centres of technological innovation, and an organizational form devised to share the benefits of a network strategy in innovation. It seems to be the case that 'collective' processes of learning and consequent innovations are taking place between the affiliates of such industries.

MNCs seem to represent an efficient solution to the choice between internal or external learning and manufacturing because they are able to combine the advantages of a common culture internal to all the affiliates, with the benefits of the variety of learning sources located in different national contexts. Each affiliate expresses the corporate culture as well as the local culture. If we suppose actors and sources of innovations are not circumscribed to the firm, but extend to institutions, strategies of varied learning can be efficiently pursued by also tapping into 'national systems of innovations'. This option is closed to a uni-national firm for which the range of freedom is restricted to internal resources.

Anyway, other possible explanatory variables among those listed before cannot be ignored: large economies of scale at an international level (as a consequence of the globalization of the demand) are relevant in some of these industries, high quality concern (especially in motor vehicles and machinery), and the complexity of products (made of different parts and components) are as well features typical of all these industries.

Symmetrically, the lowest values of the index can be found in industries such as tobacco (-29.6 per cent respect to the average), printing (-28.9), beverages (-25.8), soap (-22.6), grain (-21.9), stone, clay, etc. (-21.5) *et al.*, which are more resource-based (closest to the initial stage of production), and where the national differentiation of demand impairs strategies of globalization and the harmonization of products (industries such as food, where demand is differentiated across countries, pursue what can be defined as a multi-domestic strategy).

In 1982 the ranking of industries according to their value of the index of vertical integration does not seem to change our conclusions:

Motor vehicles	43.5
Communication	40.4
Electronics	38.5
Computers	38.4
Farm machinery	32.4
Photographic	32.4
Industrial chemicals	25.8
Construction	20.9

In dynamic terms, although the comparison between 1982 and 1989 is impaired by the non-availability of some data, we observed generally a high increase in intra-firm trade (Table 8.7) specifically for the following industries:

Construction
Electronic components
Farm machinery
Other manufacturing (leather)
Ferrous metals
Other electrical machinery
Other vehicles
Agricultural chemicals.

These industries are again those we described earlier as having the characteristics which favour international vertical integration. In fact, as can be inferred from Table 8.8, the rate of growth of technological opportunities (measured by the growth rate of patenting for the world's largest firms) is proportionately much higher in this same group of industries.

The role of technological advance has been recognized also in other literature on international intra-firm trade (Siddharthan 1990; Kobrin 1991), but besides the fact that our starting point is a broader one concerning the issue of

Table 8.8 Proportional growth of US patenting for the world's largest firms 1969–72 to 1986–90 (%)

Food	11.04
Chemicals	11.83
Pharmaceuticals	12.61
Metals	– 5.11
Mechanical engineering	– 27.04
Non-electrical machinery	52.69
Computing	24.52
Motor vehicles	68.85
Other transport equipment	5.26
Textiles and clothing	78.50
Printing and publishing	25.86
Rubber and plastic products	– 23.89
Non-metallic mineral products (Construction materials)	– 18.57
Instruments	124.98
Other manufacturing	– 39.14
Total, all industries	19.88

Source: US patent database compiled by John Cantwell at the University of Reading with the assistance from the US Patent and Trademark Office.

vertical integration, we are more interested in dynamic factors. We claim that it is especially in a dynamic perspective that such variables can be properly appreciated. We propose to use as a proxy of the rate of growth of technological opportunities the rate of growth of patent activity in different industries.

Having identified the industries in which intra-firm trade is greatest, it is necessary to analyse the nature of products traded, whether they are intermediate or final products, and the geographical destination of exports (for example, whether they run between Europe, the EC and other countries). The stage of the production process in which the industry can be positioned, determines the nature of inputs to the manufacturing process, whether they are raw materials as in food or metal industries, semi-processed components as in electronics, machinery, motor vehicles, or capital equipment in which the extent of independent purchasing depends more on the technological stage of development of the industry than on the organization of the manufacturing process. Obviously, the very fact that technological innovation is taking place means that a new or modified division of labour is under way, implying the creation of a new flow of intermediate products. The division of labour between firms cannot be divorced from the division of labour among countries. Thus, the analysis can be extended to consider the source countries of such intermediate products, as Casson (1986) has done, but we prefer here to stick to the effects of technological innovation on vertical integration.

In Tables 8.9, 8.10 and 8.11 respectively the composition of intra-firm trade between 1989 and 1982 and relative variations are presented. The first column gives the value of exports from US parents to affiliates in 1989 and 1982 (Tables 8.9 and 8.10). Exports are only one component of the intra-firm trade calculated in Table 8.7, and only for this component has it been possible to distinguish the different nature of intermediate products. The disaggregation allows us to separate the export of finished products ready for resale from those that need further manufacturing as applies in the case of a division of labour between affiliates.

The data on motor vehicles presented previously may have overstated the extent of vertical integration, judging by the fact that only 68 per cent of the shipments are subject to further manufacturing. Otherwise, the figures given in the fifth and sixth columns reinforce the conclusions drawn in our comments on Table 8.7, because the exchange of products subject to further manufacturing assumes very high values in industries such as radio and communication equipment, agricultural chemicals, other machinery (metalworking machines), and electronics. So a high proportion can be found also in what we have called resource-based industries such as lumber, textile, leather, ferrous metals and chemicals.

Conclusion

In this chapter we have claimed that vertical integration is affected by the rate of technological advance and by the nature of the technological paradigm

Table 8.9 US exports shipped to affiliates, by industry of affiliate and intended use – 1989

	1 (US$, million)	2 (%)	3 (%)	4 (%)	5 (%)	6 (%)
Manufacturing	57,707	86.8	1.4	18.6	80.1	85.2
Food and kindred products	1,465	70.5	0.8	7.9	91.3	70.3
Grain mill and bakery	768	72.3	D	D	96.0	69.4
Beverages	71	47.6	D	D	90.1	43.0
Other	626	72.2	D	D	85.5	61.7
Chemical and allied products	6,500	88.5	1.0	16.7	82.3	88.6
Industrial chemicals synthetics	3,509	88.2	1.5	24.3	74.2	87.9
Drugs	1,637	92.7	0.4	8.4	91.1	84.5
Soap, cleaners toilet goods	341	77.3	1.2	13.5	85.3	76.0
Agricultural chemicals	233	85.7	0.0	2.1	97.9	83.8
Chemical products	780	88	0.3	5.4	94.4	83.1
Primary and fabricated metals	1,409	80.2	3.7	5.0	91.3	80.9
Primary metal industries	627	83.4	0.5	0.2	99.4	83.7
Ferrous	63	90	0.0	0.0	100.0	90.0
Non-ferrous	564	82.7	0.5	0.2	99.3	83.1
Fabricated metal products	782	77.9	6.3	9.0	84.8	78.5
Machinery	10,837	92.8	1.5	7.3	91.2	92.2
Farm and garden	321	80.2	*	D	D	80.3
Construction	1,169	90.2	0.3	4.1	95.6	89.9
Office and computing machines	7,694	95.8	2.1	6.0	92.0	95.6
Other	1,653	84.4	0.2	0.0	99.8	84.5
Electric and electronic equipment	7,286	89.7	0.8	3.7	95.5	89.6
Household appliances	394	70.5	D	D	85.8	60.5
Radio and communication equipment	1,047	91.8	*	(*)	99.9	94.7
Electronic components	5,085	91.8	0.9	3.6	95.5	91.7
Electrical machinery	760	82.7	D	D	94.2	77.9
Transportation equipment	23,841	85.5	D	29.9	68.5	81.0
Motor vehicles	23,635	86.1	D	D	68.1	59.1
Other	206	49.2	D	D	56.3	27.7
Other manufacturing	6,370	83.4	D	19.4	77.6	77.4
Tobacco	123	67.96	D	D	87.0	59.1
Textile	307	74.70	0.3	1.0	98.7	73.7
Lumber, wood, furniture	184	82.1	*	0.5	99.5	83.6
Paper and allied products	674	63.9	1.6	12.5	85.9	63.4
Printing and publishing	94	87.8	*	6.4	93.6	89.8
Rubber products	581	85.4	D	59.7	36.1	63.4
Plastics	468	87.6	1.3	6.4	92.3	87.8
Glass	276	82.6	9.1	D	83.0	77.4
Stone, clay	192	75	0.5	18.8	80.7	70.8
Instruments	3,232	89.9	2.2	21.2	76.6	87.8
Other	239	91.2	0.4	2.5	97.1	91.3
All industries	86,050	88.3	1.7	42.2	56.0	85.0

Source: US Benchmark Survey 1992

Key:
1 Value of US parent company exports to affiliates
2 US parent company exports to affiliates as a percentage of total US exports to affiliates

179

3   US parent exports of capital equipment to affiliates as a % of total US parent exports
4   US parent exports to affiliates for resale without further manufacture as a % of total US parent exports
5   US parent exports to affilaites for further manufacture as a % of total US parent exports
6   US parent exports to affiliates for further manufacture as a % of total US exports to affiliates

Table 8.10 US exports shipped to affiliates, by industry of affiliate and intended use – 1982

	1 (US$, million)	2 (%)	3 (%)	4 (%)	5 (%)	6 (%)
Manufacturing	20,510	81.6	2.6	55	42.4	70.4
Food and kindred products	454	46.6	2	26	72	41.2
Grain mill and bakery	132	38.6	0.8	D	D	D
Beverages	24	63.2	4.2	D	D	D
Other	297	50.1	2.4	25	72.6	D
Chemical and allied products	2,655	88.3	1	41.6	57.4	83.2
Industrial chemicals synthetics	1,321	88.8	1.2	61.1	37.7	78.1
Drugs	698	96.1	0.3	16.8	82.9	95.9
Soap, cleaners toilet goods	207	67.2	1.9	24.6	73.5	61.1
Agricultural chemicals	151	88.8	2.6	33.8	63.6	85
Chemical products	279	88.6	0.3	27.6	72.1	87
Primary and fabricated metals	632	74.8	2.7	28.2	69.1	72.9
Primary metal industries	276	84.9	1.4	10.5	88.1	85.3
Ferrous	38	90.5	7.9	6.8	85.3	69.2
Non-ferrous	238	84.1	0.4	1.3	98.3	86
Fabricated metal products	357	68.6	3.6	41.7	54.7	61.6
Machinery	2,810	92.6	9.4	39.4	51.2	90.7
Farm and garden	245	92.8	D	D	D	D
Construction	607	87.8	D	36.1	D	D
Office and computing machines	1,263	94.7	D	43.5	D	D
Other	694	92.8	D	D	D	D
Electric and electronic equipment	1,986	85.7	2	31.3	66.7	84.6
Household appliances	261	76.3	1.1	53.6	45.3	69
Radio and communication equipment	239	68.1	3.8	27.2	69	62.7
Electronic components	1,119	93.6	1.7	19.7	78.6	95.4
Electrical machinery	367	85.9	1.9	53.7	44.4	77.2
Transportation equipment	9,483	80.3	0.7	74.8	24.5	56.3
Motor vehicles	9,407	80.7	0.7	75	24.3	57.1
Other	76	48.7	1.3	61.9	36.8	27.9
Other manufacturing	2,490	78.8	4.4	42.3	53.3	70.6
Tobacco	n/a	n/a	D	D	D	D
Textile	194	63.6	2.1	40.2	57.7	53.1
Lumber, wood, furniture	30	47.6	3.3	D	D	D
Paper and allied products	353	60.5	5.4	D	D	D
Printing and publishing	58	89.2	1.7	82.8	15.5	76.9
Rubber products	305	81.5	17.1	51.1	31.8	61.8
Plastics	50	80.6	6	44	50	75.8
Glass	76	80.8	D	21	D	D
Stone, clay	100	71.9	1	52	47	58
Instruments	1,045	94.6	1.6	45.9	52.5	96
Other	n/a	n/a	D	D	D	D
All industries	29,275	81.7	4.1	63.2	32.7	69.5

Source: Authors' calculations based on Casson (1986).

180

Key:
1 Value of US parent company exports to affiliates
2 US parent company exports to affiliates as a percentage of total US exports to affiliates
3 US parent exports of capital equipment to affiliates as a % of total US parent exports
4 US parent exports, to affiliates, for resale without further manufacture as a % of total, US parent exports
5 US parent exports to affilaites for further manufacture as a % of total US parent exports
6 US parent exports to affiliates for further manufacture as a % of total US exports to affiliates

Table 8.11 Proportional change in US parent exports to affiliates, 1982–9

	1 %	2 (%)	3 (%)	4 (%)	5 (%)
Manufacturing	6.4	−47.1	−66.3	88.8	21.0
Food and kindred products	51.3	−59.0	−69.5	26.8	70.7
Grain mill and bakery	87.3	D	D	D	
Beverages	−24.7	D	D	D	
Other	44.1	D	D	17.7	
Chemical and allied products	0.2	0.0	−59.9	43.4	6.5
Industrial chemicals synthetics	0.7	23.5	−60.3	96.9	12.6
Drugs	−3.5	42.5	−49.8	9.9	−11.9
Soap, cleaners toilet goods	15.0	−38.3	−45.2	16.1	24.4
Agricultural chemicals	−3.5	−100.0	−93.7	53.9	−1.4
Chemical products	−0.7	−14.5	−80.5	30.9	−4.5
Primary and fabricated metals	7.2	36.7	−82.1	32.1	11.0
Primary metal industries	−1.8	−65.8	−98.5	12.8	−1.8
Ferrous	−0.6	−100.0	−100.0	17.2	30.1
Non-ferrous	−1.7	33.0	−86.4	1.0	−3.4
Fabricated metal products	13.6	74.1	−78.5	55.0	27.4
Machinery	0.2	−83.8	−81.4	78.0	1.7
Farm and garden	−13.6				
Construction	2.7		−88.6		
Office and computing machines	1.2		−86.3		
Other	−9.1				
Electric and electronic equipment	4.7	−60.9	−88.1	43.2	5.9
Household appliances	−7.6	D	D	89.4	−12.4
Radio and communication equipment	34.8			44.8	51.1
Electronic components	−1.9	−49.1	−81.5	21.5	−3.9
Electrical machinery	−3.7			112.2	0.9
Transportation equipment	6.5		−60.0	179.7	43.9
Motor vehicles	6.7			180.0	3.5
Other	1.0			53.0	−0.8
Other manufacturing	5.8	45.6	9.7		
Tobacco					
Textile	17.4	−84.5	−97.6	71.1	38.8
Lumber, wood, furniture	72.5				
Paper and allied products	5.6	−69.8			
Printing and publishing	−1.6		−92.3	504.0	16.8
Rubber products	4.8		16.9	13.6	2.7
Plastics	8.7	−78.6	−85.4	84.6	15.8
Glass	2.2				
Stone, clay	4.3	−47.9	−63.9	71.8	22.0
Instruments	−5.0		−53.8	45.9	−8.5
All industries	8.1	−57.4	−33.2	71.3	22.4

181

Key:

1 % change in US parent company exports to affiliates as a share of total US exports to affiliates
2 % change in US parent exports of capital equipment to affiliates as a share of total US parent exports
3 % change in US parent exports to affiliates for resale without further manufacture as a share of total US parent exports
4 % change in US parent exports to affiliates for further manufacture as a share of total US parent exports
5 % change in US parent exports to affiliates for further manufacture as a share of total US exports to affiliates

governing the industry. We find a good correlation between the increase of vertical integration and the overall rate of technological development. This result contrasts with the Stigler hypothesis, and it is closer to other approaches (Adelman 1958; Langlois 1987).

However, a more specific methodology would be necessary in order to relate technological factors in a more thorough way to the degree of international vertical integration. In particular, we are aware that to test more fully the counter-hypothesis to Stigler's, the analysis should embrace a longer period of time in order to follow the time-path of development in such industries.

In addition, we think that the factor of 'multinationality *per se*' in the form of the wider geographical dispersal of activity and the eventual corporate gains from integrating such, is another determinant of vertical integration. It seems that MNCs, conceived as networks of centres of technological innovation, may benefit, at the same time, from an internal as well a collective (and decentralized) process of learning. Hence, our results point the way towards an interesting direction for future research.

Notes

1 The past history and experience of firms helps to explain the extent of the similarity of codes among firms. Much attention in empirical studies of the motivations of partnerships and agreements among firms should be devoted to the similarity of their past experience, as a requisite for successful co-operation. Sustaining the creation of complementary technological competencies in partner companies may often be the result of a combined process of learning.
2 The same seems to be true for Japanese MNCs, although the EC Commission reports a growing propensity for Japanese MNCs in Europe to buy parts and components for manufacturing production from unaffiliated firms in Europe (EC 1992).
3 In summary, from that source we have data on affiliate exports to parents, affiliate exports to other affiliates, parent's export to affiliates, local sales of affiliates.
4 After the 1977 survey, earlier data on the 1966 benchmark basis had to be revised to exclude those affiliates where no individual foreigner held at least 10 per cent, but together foreigners of the same nationality (US citizens in the case of outward investment) between them held 50 per cent or over.
5 The index can be split in two components: one being Exports of Affiliates alone, the other including US Parent Company Exports. The shares in Tables 8.9 and

8.10 and in earlier tables referred to Affiliate Exports alone (they correspond to the first component).

References

Adelman, M.C. (1958) 'Concepts and statistical measurement of vertical integration', in G.J. Stigler (ed.) *Business Concentration and Price Policy*, Princeton, NJ: Princeton University Press, pp. 318–20.

Buckley, P.J. and Casson, M. C. (1976) *The Future of the Multinational Enterprise*, London: Macmillan.

Cantwell, J.A. (1989) *Technological Innovation and Multinational Corporations*, Oxford: Basil Blackwell.

—— (1992a) 'The theory of technological competence and its application to international production', in D.G. McFetridge (ed.) *Foreign Investment, Technology and Economic Growth*, Calgary: University of Calgary Press.

—— (1992b) 'The effects of integration on the structure of multinational corporation activity in the EC', in M.W. Klein P.J.J. Welfens (eds) *The New Europe and Global Trade*, Berlin: Springer Verlag.

—— (1994) 'Introduction', in J.A. Cantwell (ed.) *Transnational Corporations and Innovatory Activities*, London: Routledge.

—— (1995) 'The globalisation of technology: what remains of the product cycle model?', *Cambridge Journal of Economics* 19, 1: 155–174.

Cantwell, J.A. and Barrera, P. (1996) 'The localisation of corporate trajectories in the interwar cartels: cooperative learning versus an exchange of knowledge', *University of Reading Discussion Papers in Economics*, No. 340.

Casson, M.C. (1987) *Multinationals and the World Trade*, London: Allen and Unwin.

Doz, Y. (1986) *Strategic Management in Multinational Companies*, Oxford: Pergamon Press.

Dunning, J.H. (1988) *Multinationals, Technology and Competitiveness*, London: Unwin Hyman.

—— (1992) *Multinational Enterprises and the Global Economy*, Washington, DC: Addison-Wesley.

Klein B., Crawford, R. and Alchian, A. (1978) 'Vertical integration, appropriable rents, and the competitive contracting process', *Journal of Law and Economics* 21, 2.

Kobrin, J.S. (1991) 'An empirical analysis of the determinants of global integration', *Strategic Management Journal* 12: 17–31.

Kodama, F. (1992) 'Japan's unique capability to innovate: technology fusion and its international implications', in *Japan's Growing Technological Capability: Implications for the US Economy*, Washington, DC, National Academy Press.

Kogut, B. and Zander, U. (1992) 'Knowledge of the firm, combinative capabilities, and the replication of technology', *Organization Science* 3: 383–97.

Langlois R.N. (1988) 'Economic change and the boundaries of the firm', *Journal of Institutions and Theoretical Economics* 144, 4.

Langlois R.N. and Robertson, P.L. (1995) *Firms, Markets and Economic Change*, London and New York: Routledge.

Loasby, B.J. (1991) *Equilibrium and Evolution: An Exploration of Connecting Principles in Economics*, Manchester: Manchester University Press.

Mowery, D.C. and Rosenberg, N. (1979) 'The influence of market demand upon innovation: a critical review of some recent empirical studies', *Research Policy* 8: 103–153.

Richardson, G.B. (1972) 'The organisation of industry', *Economic Journal* 82: 883–96.

Siddharthan, N.S. and Kumar, N. (1990) 'The determinants of inter-industry variations in the proportions of intra-firm trade: the behaviour of US multinationals', *Weltwirtschaftliches Archive* 126: 581–91.

Stigler, G.J. (1951) 'The division of labour is limited by the extent of the market', *Journal of Political Economy* 59, 3.

Teece, D.J. (1984) 'Economic analysis and strategic management', in L.G. Thomas (ed.) *The Economics of Strategic Planning*, Lexington, MA: D.C. Heath.

Teece, D.J., Pisano, G. and Shuen, A. (1990) 'Firm capabilities, resources and the concept of strategy', Working Paper, No. 90–8, Berkeley, CA: Center for Research in Management.

Vernon, R. (1966) 'International investment and international trade in the product-cycle', *Quarterly Journal of Economics* 80: 190–207.

Williamson, O.E. (1985) *The Economic Institutions of Capitalism*, New York: Free Press.

US Department of Commerce (1992) *Direct Investment Abroad* 1989 Benchmark Survey, Washington, DC.

Part III

SUPPLY RELATIONS

9

COST, QUALITY, AND LEARNING BASED GOVERNANCE OF BUYER–SUPPLIER RELATIONS

Bart Nooteboom

Introduction

In the past, many authors have reported fundamental differences in practices of outsourcing by firms in the West (US, EU) and Japan, mostly on the basis of studies in the auto industry. While in some respects European practice is somewhat closer to Japanese practice, it remains more similar to American practice. The past success of Japanese industry appears to be due to some, perhaps considerable, extent to their subcontracting relations (Helper 1991; Helper and Levine 1992; Dyer and Ouchi 1993; Cusumano and Fujimoto 1991; Dore 1989; Womack *et al.* 1990; Lamming 1993).

To analyse these differences rigorously, we will specify clear-cut stereotypes which are intended to approach traditional Western practice and Japanese practice. From the literature, we approximate Japanese practice by the following stereotype, which we label the 'quality based' form of contracting: emphasis on quality and innovation rather than price; high involvement of suppliers in design and development activities; high levels of relation-specific investments; long-term relations; orientation towards mutual gain (win–win), subject to demands on quality, improvement, cost; guarantees for recovery of specific investments; exchange of staff, technology and information on costs; single supply in the sense that only one 'first tier' supplier is engaged for a given input for the life time of a given model of a given product (which yields multiple suppliers of a given input across different models and products); governance based on mutual commitment and cross-ownership or trust rather than detailed contracts. This is a not a realistic characterization of all Japanese buyer–supplier relations. It applies only to selected first tier suppliers (Kamath and Liker 1994). It is based on reports from the literature, but perhaps it is partly a myth. In our analysis we will investigate how viable this stereotype is.

In many respects, past Western practice is the opposite. Currently, in the West, a novel practice is evolving, which adopts features from Japanese practice. We approach traditional Western practice with the following stereotype, which we label the 'cost based' form of contracting: oriented primarily at lowest cost of supply; adversarial bargaining on price; no concern for mutual profit ('win–lose'); specification, design and even part of the engineering of inputs is performed by the user, as a blueprint for production by the supplier; 'closed' with respect to exchange of information on costs and technology; multiple sourcing (for a given input for a given model of a given product); 'distant' with respect to commitment in terms of investments. For the buyer, control of design, quality and cost takes precedence over utilization of supplier competence.

In the 'quality based' (or 'Japanese') form, outsourcing is driven primarily by considerations of quality, in the sense of a good fit to requirements for differentiated demand, given a maximum price. The user aims to utilize as much as possible the capacities of the supplier. Therefore one leaves part of the design and engineering, as well as production, to the competence and often the initiative of the supplier, and invites them to contribute to the determination of optimal specifications. This requires specific investments (in the sense of TCE), particularly on the part of the supplier, and to cover for this, the user gives certain guarantees (long-term contracts, sufficient minimum volume of purchase), but then requires openness on the part of the user concerning technology used, costs and supply to other customers, in order to control for misuse of such guarantees ('open book contracting'). This openness is also required for effective information exchange for cooperation in development and production. Such openness may have negative effects on the bargaining position of the supplier, and to cover for this, the user grants a profit margin to the supplier, deducts this from the price he can afford to pay, thus arrives at the cost at which the input is to be produced ('price minus costing'), transfers knowledge, technology and staff to the supplier, and jointly they invest in development in order to achieve production of the desired quality at this price-minus-profit cost.

For the development of policy of firms, nations and the EU, it is of some importance to answer the following questions:

- How can these differences be understood: why do they arise; what is their rationale?
- Is 'Japanese practice' indeed better?
- Should US and EU firms emulate the Japanese, and to what extent are they able to do so, and if not, what are the obstacles?
- Is there perhaps a 'third way', better than both 'Western' and 'Japanese' practice?
- What would be required to shift to the latter practice?

With our analysis we aim to provide a basis for answering those questions.

For a theoretical perspective, we will employ transaction cost economics (TCE), but that theory will have to be extended with a dimension of learning, which is absent from the comparative statics of 'normal' TCE.

This extended TCE will be formalized. Returns and risks are specified as functions of variables that define a subcontracting relation. The coefficients of those variables vary between different 'worlds'. This allows us to explore the efficiency and viability of different relations in such different worlds. Use is made of game theory to identify stable pairs of strategies, for the two sides in a subcontracting relation, in the form of Nash equilibria. This allows us to see which generic forms of subcontracting are viable in what worlds, and to compare their efficiency.

TCE

Before we consider extensions and formalization of TCE, a brief summary of its relevant points is perhaps needed. Readers familiar with TCE can skip this section. We concentrate on the main issues, discussed in TCE as developed by Williamson (1975, 1985, 1989), and we will not at each point discuss the criticisms and extensions offered in the literature. However, a crucial extension will be added in the following paragraph.

TCE explains how transaction partners can get 'locked in' to each other as a result of transaction specific investments causing switching costs, and thereby incur risks of opportunistic behaviour ('hold-up'), which cannot be prevented due to bounded rationality. These risks are part of the costs of transactions. Note that transaction specificity, (possibility of) opportunism and bounded rationality each form a necessary condition for these risks. For modelling this, it is straightforward to adopt a multiplicative specification: if any of the variables (specificity, opportunism, boundedness of rationality) is zero, their joint effect is zero.

TCE has implications, in particular, for vertical transactions between suppliers and users of goods and services. In the first version of TCE, as set out in Williamson (1975), the central issue was whether a firm should make some input itself, in which case it chooses 'hierarchy' as the 'form of governance', or buy it from an outside producer, in which case it chooses the market as form of governance. In this decision the costs of transaction are to be traded off against the advantages of outsourcing. According to TCE these advantages lie in scale advantages of a specialized outside producer, who produces for a larger market than the needs of a single user, and market incentives arising from the need for the supplier to maintain efficiency for the sake of survival. As a result, when investments are highly transaction specific, the advice from TCE is: make rather than buy, since in the case of buying transaction costs are high while specialization advantages of an outside producer are small.

In a later development of the theory (Williamson 1985), it is recognized

189

that outsourcing may be desirable even when investments are moderately specific, and the ensuing risks involved in dependence may be controlled in a form of governance 'between market and hierarchy'. When transactions are sizeable and frequent it is worth while to institute detailed controls in 'bilateral governance'. In case of a smaller volume and frequency of purchase such investments in governance are not efficient, and it is better to call in a third party as arbitrator, in 'trilateral governance'.

The controls in bilateral governance include: reciprocal supply in which both sides incur transaction specific investments symmetrically; joint ownership of transaction specific investments; the provision of guarantees to the most dependent party to ensure that the cost of one-sided specific investment is recouped. Typically, but not necessarily, the weight of specific investments lies with the supplier, who invests in specific machinery, knowledge, procedures, locations in order to offer a product that is specific to the user. The implicit assumption here is, that specific (i.e., differentiated) products require specific investments on the part of the supplier. Nooteboom (1993) shows that the two don't necessarily go together. However, they typically do, and it is then that interesting, problematic issues of governance arise.

Guarantees then include: guaranteed volume, frequency or period of purchase; severance payment in case purchase is stopped prematurely (before the investment is amortized); posting of hostages. If a user participates in the payment for a specific asset for the production of an input, or guarantees volume of purchase, he will want to ensure that the asset is not employed for production for a competitor. He will want to monitor this, which requires sufficient openness on the part of the supplier.

Learning

Due to the force of the emerging economies in east Asia, world markets have become more competitive. In order to escape from extremes of price competition, firms are seeking to further differentiate their products. Differentiation is feasible only if several conditions are satisfied: in consumer demand, production, marketing and supply. In consumer demand, ongoing individualization provides opportunities for differentiation. In production, application of information and communication technology (ICT) yields flexible manufacturing systems, that allow for product differentiation by reducing set-up costs. In logistics, an explosion of stocks, one for each differentiated product, can be prevented by means of 'just-in-time delivery', which also is enabled by ICT.

But to successfully offer many different products to different, increasingly fragmented market segments, one needs complex, detailed and up to date information and competence concerning those market fragments, and concerning technological opportunities in the supply of inputs. Supply is complicated, in particular, by the proliferation of new materials (plastics, metals, ceramics, composites, bio-materials). For a single firm, such a detailed and fast changing stock of knowledge concerning market fragments and supply opportunities is not 'sustainable', as Zuscovitch (1994) put it. One needs partner firms that are close to specific markets, and partner firms close to specific sources, who specialize in the required knowledge and make it profitable by sharing it with partners, in networks of partial cooperation. Increasingly, it is impossible to combine product differentiation with organizational autonomy. ICT provides the technical means for rapid, efficient, frequent and increasingly rich communication in networks.

TCE lacks a dynamic perspective of innovation, because it does not consider the question of how firms build competence. Here we adopt the competence based view of firms (Penrose 1959; Nelson and Winter 1982): firms build up distinctive competencies (or routines) in time, in interaction with their environment. Nooteboom (1992) suggested an underlying epistemological perspective, along the following lines. Epistemological subjects perform cognition, which consists of perception, interpretation and evaluation, on the basis of categories which they have developed on the basis of interaction with their physical and social environment. By consequence, cognition is path-dependent and to some extent idiosyncratic. Cognition varies across subjects to the extent that they have developed their categories in different environments. Conversely: cognition will be more uniform in stable, shared environments. In present conditions of rapid technological and market change cognitions vary considerably.

You cannot react to opportunities and threats if your categories are not fit to deal with them. Thus firms may make rather than buy inputs simply because no external firm has the proper ability to acquire the necessary competence, and conversely firms may have to buy rather than make because they themselves lack such ability. In the short term competence may be bought by taking over a firm, but then there is a risk of a break-down of the acquired competence when it is adjusted to fit in the firm that does the takeover. From the constructivist view, the merging of different firms entails a possibly very difficult integration of different categorial systems. There may be an impossibility here which is comparable to the impossibility of crossing different species, arising from different evolutionary paths. This is reflected in the experience that many mergers and acquisitions fail.

In fact, a whole new dimension is added to the existence of the firm and the value of external partners. Due to increased volatility of technology and markets firms need to focus more on core competencies (Prahalad and Hamel 1990). In order to be effective, one needs a focus of cognition and action. Trying to see, understand and do everything yields inaction and certain defeat in the market. Quite apart from transaction costs, a firm is needed to function as a focusing device. The problem of such a focus is, however, that one is in danger of missing out on the perception and interpretation of relevant threats and opportunities. Thus one needs outside partners, with a different but complementary categorial apparatus, to pick up and translate relevant developments, as a form of external intelligence. Since partners will also differ among themselves in their cognitive abilities (due to our epistemological assumption of idiosyncracy of knowledge), there is a premium on having multiple partners, even in a given area of technology (although there are likely to be diminishing returns in increasing the number of partners).

Firms are needed to focus and thereby limit perceptions in order to produce action; transactions between firms serve to complement limited perceptions. The crux of the argument lies in what could appropriately be called 'external economy of cognitive scope' (EECS):

> Level of competence is enhanced if at least two different entities connect their activities, on the basis of different, complementary cognitive abilities.

Learning may take four different forms:

1   *Multiple partners, no intentional technology transfer*: even if partners do not engage in active technology transfer to each other, having multiple partners yields a more varied experience and hence a richer source of learning than exclusive, single partnerships.

2   *Single partners, unilateral technology transfer*: the focal partner may receive knowledge from his partner, who actively contributes to the transfer of his knowledge, derived from his experience with the focal partner. This is limited to documented (as opposed to tacit) knowledge.

3   *Multiple partners, unilateral technology transfer*: the partner engages in multiple transaction relations, in addition to the one with the focal partner (in the same field), which makes him a richer source of knowledge. Note that if the receiving partner also has multiple partners, the partner who yields the technology incurs a spillover risk (see below).

4   *Reciprocal technology transfer*: two partners both transfer technology to each other, which opens up the possibility of joint development and transfer of not only documented but also tacit knowledge.[1] An additional attraction of reciprocal transfer, where one benefits more from the partner's knowledge to the extent that one also contributes knowledge, is that there is less risk of free riding (Nooteboom 1995).

We should note that there are several possibilities concerning 'absorptive capacity' (Cohen and Levinthal 1990). Here, we consider two:

A   Every player in the field can absorb the technology from every other player without delay.

B   Absorptive capacity is both cumulative and specific to the source.

The second possibility yields the complication that the utility of transfer for the receiver increases in time, which creates additional switching costs and related opportunities for hold-up. To keep complexity within bounds, here we will assume A, and we will keep B in reserve for future work. In other words: while we assume idiosyncrasy of knowledge, we assume uniformity in the ability to absorb knowledge from others.

As noted in the literature (see e.g., Williamson 1991), information or technology transfer also entails a risk. This risk is that through the contact with a supplier or user competitive advantage in the form of proprietary knowledge or technology may indirectly 'spillover' to competitors. The risk is greater to the extent that knowledge consists of codified information, and smaller to the extent that it is tacit. However, even in the case of tacit knowledge, spillover may occur if cooperation entails that specialist teams are stationed at the partner's location. Transfer of competence requires control of this risk. The size of this risk depends on the pattern of the network of relations in which a firm is embedded. In particular, spillover risk is higher to the extent that your partner has multiple partners who might be your competitors.

As indicated, the perspective sketched here belongs to the competence based view of the firm, which is quite different from the perspective taken in TCE. One may think that this makes TCE useless (or even irrelevant), but we think that the issues of hold-up raised in TCE, and some of the instruments for dealing with them, as indicated above, are still relevant in a competence based view. So we set out to bring them together in one model.

Specification of the model

We now proceed to formalize our extended TCE. We do this on the basis of the following design principles:

1   We specify discrete alternatives for contracting, in terms of binary vari ables (0–1), which indicate whether a given policy or environmental condition obtains or not. Thus we look at extremes that identify the boundaries within which reality appears.
2   We specify net returns as a function of the binary variables that define the form of contracting, weighted by coefficients that vary across 'possible worlds', and binary variables that belong to the definition of those worlds. Net returns are determined by returns and risks, with the latter taken as costs
3   In our formalization we take boundedness of rationality for granted, under all conditions, so that it need not be indicated. In the present setting, we also go along with the assumption that opportunism prevails, but we will also consider a possible world where it does not.
4   We recognize three types of risk in transaction relations:

    – Spillover risk: if the focal partner transfers technology to the other partner, and the latter has multiple partners, beside the focal partner

(in the same area), then the latter incurs a spillover risk.
– Monitoring hold-up: one-sided risk for the supplier of losing bargaining position due to monitoring: if the supplier opens up to monitoring by the user of the supplier's technology, capacity utilization and costs ('open-book contracting'), he makes himself vulnerable to loss of bargaining position regarding price. This is eliminated if the user guarantees a profit margin (in 'price minus costing').
– Specificity hold-up: one-sided risk due to specific investments by the supplier. This is eliminated if the user shares the risk in joint ownership of the specific assets, or provides guarantees of custom to allow the supplier to recoup the investment.

Note: we focus on the characteristic case of user–supplier relations, where the user produces a differentiated product, and in order to provide high quality of adjustment to user needs the supplier needs to conduct more specific investments than the user. Note that the user may also need to make specific adjustments, to receive the product or to contribute to its development. We assume that the size of these specific investments is so much less than those for the supplier as to be negligible. Note also that even if the user requires no specific investments at all, specificity of investment on the part of the supplier also makes the user dependent to some extent: if supply is discontinued, the user will incur loss of quality, because he has to buy a substitute that conforms less closely to specifications, or higher cost, because conformance to specifications requires purchase at a more expensive source, or delay, because a substitute source first needs to invest to conform to specifications, or some combination of these. However, typically this risk is smaller than the risk of loss of investment and switching costs faced by the supplier. If symmetry of specific investments does occur, the problem of the risk of hold-up becomes much less because there is a threat of retaliation. So it is both more realistic and more interesting to assume asymmetry in the form of larger specific investments and resulting switching costs on the part of the supplier.

The binary variables that define forms of governance, and are thus at the discretion of buyers/suppliers are as follows:

PMCOS: whether (1) or not (0) the user engages in price-minus costing
OPEN: w.o.n. the supplier engages in open-book contracting (OPEN)
SPEC: w.o.n. the supplier engages in partner-specific investments
COV: w.o.n. the user covers the risk of specific assets on the part of the supplier by either participating in their ownership or giving guarantees in terms of duration or total value of purchase, or severance pay
MULSUP: w.o.n. there are multiple suppliers for the user
MULCUS: w.o.n. there are multiple customers for the supplier
UTRAN: w.o.n. the user transfers knowledge to the supplier
STRAN: vice versa.

Binary variables that represent characteristics of possible worlds are the following:

SPEED: w.o.n. the speed of product change is 'radical', exceeding the speed of spillover.

An important side condition is the following:

one cannot have information transfer without openness. In other words: STRAN = 1 implies OPEN = 1.

$$(1)$$

We normalize the surplus of exchange at 2 for a standard product, i.e., if it is not tailored to the specific demand of the user, and is produced at the volume required for the user. In this case each side will obtain a return of 1 if the surplus is distributed equally. Deviations from this 'focal point' depend on bargaining positions, which are determined by price-minus costing, open-book contracting and access to alternative transaction partners, as will be explained below.

In a world where scale effects obtain and are important, both sides obtain additional benefits when the supplier produces at a larger volume. This requires that assets are non-specific (can be used for production for other customers) (SPEC = 0) and that there are multiple users (MULCUS = 1). In a world where product quality and differentiation is important, both sides obtain additional benefit when there is specificity of assets (which is assumed to be required for differentiated products) (SPEC = 1). In other words: we are creating a choice between specialized production for a differentiated product and large scale production for a standard product.

Having multiple partners (MULCUS; MULSUP) can yield benefits for several reasons: better bargaining position (as already indicated) and greater flexibility, due to opportunities to switch between partners, spread of risks and learning from varied transactions. Note that this form of learning is not based on transfer of competencies from one partner to the other, but internal learning due to dealing with varied partners. Another form of learning obtains when a partner actively contributes to the transfer of competence ('transfer': STRAN or UTRAN = 1). This requires a certain duration of the relationship. When variety of sources of competence is important, the utility of a partner for this type of learning is increased to the extent that he himself has multiple partners ('varied learning': STRAN.MULCUS = 1; UTRAN.MULSUP = 1). A yet more intensive form of learning arises when the two partners jointly produce competence ('joint development': STRAN.UTRAN = 1). This allows for the mutual transfer of tacit knowledge and the joint development of new knowledge. Next to these positive benefits, transfer of competence carries risk of spillover: the risk that through the partner information or competence spills over to a competitor. This can happen only if the partner himself has multiple partners (STRAN.MULSUP = 1; UTRAN.MULCUS = 1).

With respect to bargaining position we choose an asymmetrical specification: only the supplier risks loss of bargaining position and hence share of the surplus due to being open ('open-book contracting'; OPEN = 1). This risk can be eliminated by the user (U) granting a profit margin to the supplier (S) (PMCOS = 1), or by S keeping access to multiple customers (to create a credible threat of switching to another customer; MULCUS = 1). The size of this risk is indicated by the parameter b. If S has strong and unique competencies to offer, b is small or zero.

Hold-up risk as a result of specific investments entails one or more of the following:

- loss of specific assets, to the extent that one participates in their finance
- payment of guarantees, or loss of hostages committed to protect specific assets of the partner
- loss due to pressure to compromise on cost, price or quality, due to opportunism which preys on dependence created by unprotected specific assets (hold-up).

This risk arises only if there is opportunism. The risk for S is that if they engage in specific investments (SPEC = 1) while their risk is not covered by U either participating in ownership or giving guarantees (COV = 1). It arises for U if they participate/guarantee (COV = 1), while S does not provide openness for U to control for misuse of ownership or guarantees (OPEN = 0) (in our design principles we assumed that U has no switching costs if they do not give guarantees to cover specific assets, which in this model are assumed to only arise on the part of S).

Concerning the risk of spillover, note that spillover can be blocked by exclusive relations (MULCUS = MULSUP = 0): by requiring the partner not to engage in other contacts for the same product. Note that even when there is no direct linkage of one's partner to one's competitors, information might still spillover to competitors through other linkages, such as through a customer in a different but related market, or a customer of the customer, who is strongly linked to a competitor. But at least direct spillover is blocked: it will take longer for information to reach a competitor, and in the longer process of transmission there is more attrition of meaning (i.e., distortion through interpretation in different categorial systems) and a greater chance of obsolescence. In case of 'radical' speed of change of technology and/or products (SPEED = 1), there is no spillover risk: by the time sensitive information has reached a competitor, it is out of date with respect to current products or technology.

The inclusion of all these effects yields the following specification of net returns, under side condition (1):

for the supplier:

$$SRET = 1 - b(1 - PMCOS).OPEN.(1 - MULCUS) \quad \text{bargaining}$$

$+ s_S.(1 - SPEC).MULCUS$	scale
$+ d_S.SPEC$	specific product
$+ m_S.MULCUS$	multiple partners
$+ t_S.UTRAN$	transfer
$+ v_S.UTRAN.MULSUP$	varied learning
$+ j_S.UTRAN.STRAN$	joint development
$- r_S.STRAN.MULSUP(1 - SPEED)$	spillover risk
$- h_S.\{(1 - COV).SPEC\}$	specificity (hold-up) risk

$$(2)$$

where: SRET = the return for the supplier; $b \leqslant 1$, s_S, d_S, m_S, t_S, v_S, j_S, r_S and h_S are coefficients indicating the weights of the several components of returns to the supplier, which vary between 'possible worlds'.

For the user:

$$URET = 1 + b(1 - PMCOS).OPEN.(1 - MULCUS) \quad \text{bargaining}$$

$+ s_U.(1 - SPEC).MULCUS$	scale
$+ d_U.SPEC$	differentiated product
$+ m_U.MULSUP$	multiple partners
$+ t_U.STRAN$	transfer
$+ v_U.STRAN.MULCUS$	varied learning
$+ j_U.UTRAN.STRAN$	joint development
$- r_S.UTRAN.MULCUS(1 - SPEED)$	spillover risk
$- h_S.COV.SPEC.(1 - OPEN)$	specificity (hold-up) risk

$$(3)$$

where: URET = return for the user.

The subscript U refers to the user.

When the coefficients are used without subscripts (S, U), they refer to both partners.

The items of 'transfer, varied learning and joint development' represent a specification of the concept of 'external economy of cognitive scope' (EECS) that we developed before.

The past: a Fordist world

We now proceed to specify possible worlds in terms of the model variables and coefficients. We construct possible worlds that are interesting and relevant in the sense that they either reproduce, approximately, the recent past, the present and a plausible future, or could arise, with interesting consequences. Next, we see what forms of governance in those different worlds are 'viable', and which are Pareto optimal. By form of governance we mean a pair of strategies for the two sides (buyer and supplier), specified in terms of values of the binary variables that are at their discretion. By viability we mean stability: given the governance form, neither side can improve its net returns by switching the value of one or more of the variables at its discretion. Now this yields precisely the definition of a Nash equilibrium. In other words: in the possible worlds that we define we look for Nash equilibria. A governance form that yields a Nash equilibrium in a given world is called a 'Nash governance' in that world. 'Pareto optimal' means, as usual: one cannot raise net return for one partner without reducing it for the other.

In particular, we want to investigate whether and in what worlds our stereotypes of 'cost-based' and 'quality based' governance, which are intended to approach past Western and Japanese practice, are optimal and viable (Nash equilibria), and we will explore whether a 'third way' exists that may be superior to both in any of the worlds.

We start with a 'Fordist world', defined as follows:

The *Fordist world* (W1): SPEED = 0, s>d, t = v = j = 0.

$$(4)$$

This world is intended to give a reconstruction of the past. In this world, technology and markets are fairly stable, so that one does not need learning from partners (no 'external economy of cognitive scope': t = v = j = 0). Products are homogeneous and economy of scale prevails over product differentiation (s>d), so that there is little need for specific assets. There is a focus on price and cost, which yields an advantage of having multiple partners (to maintain flexibility and bargaining position).

In this world, let us consider 'cost based contracting', which was described before, and is intended to represent an approximation of traditional 'Western' contracting. In terms of our model it is specified as follows:

Cost based contracting: PMCOS = OPEN = STRAN = UTRAN = SPEC = COV =0; MULCUS = MULSUP = 1; URET = SRET = 1 + s + m.

$$(5)$$

We propose that in this world this governance is Pareto efficient and viable (Nash equilibrium). The reader can verify this, but we will give some indications.

It is not advantageous to switch to specific assets (SPEC = 1), because although that yields the return of specialized products, it destroys scale, and in this world the latter dominates. Also, note that S would then require protection for his specific assets (COV = 1), but the buyer would yield that only if he can monitor against misuse (OPEN = 1). In spite of such openness, S does not risk his bargaining position, because he maintains that by maintaining multiple customers. But again: scale is more important than product differentiation, so this option is not chosen. Alternatively, one could consider to switch to technology transfer (UTRAN and or STRAN = 1). STRAN = 1 is feasible after OPEN is set to 1 (see (1)). But in this world learning from partners carries no value (no EECS; t = v = 0). Furthermore, that would create risks of spillover.

We conclude that cost based contracting is optimal, Pareto efficient and viable. In so far as it does represent a realistic approximation of past Western practice, and the Fordist world is a realistic approximation of the past, we can conclude that in the past cost-based contracting was appropriate.

The present: efficient quality

We now turn to a world which is intended to represent an important segment of the present world, or the recent past. In terms of our model:

The *world of efficient quality* (W2): SPEED = 0, d>s; d − h<s and d − b<s; t + j>m; t + v + j − r<m; d + r + j − b<s + m.

$$(6)$$

In this world, as discussed before, globalization, increased competition and developments in technology and consumer demand yield pressures towards product differentiation, to the extent that it becomes more important than scale (d>s). Differentiation requires more attention to quality in one of its usual senses of conforming to the demand of specific customers. This requires access to various complementary competencies. While due to differentiation scale is less feasible, costs and scale remain important. But differentiation requires specific assets, and as discussed in TCE, this yields problems of hold-up and bargaining. When risk of hold-up or loss of bargaining occurs, differentiation is less attractive than scale (d − h<s, d − b<s). If loss of bargaining position occurs, even the combined advantages of differentiation and learning are less than the advantages of variety and scale (d + t + j − b<s + m). But we will also consider the case where this latter condition does not apply. Due to the complexity resulting from product differentiation in input and output markets and increased competition, firms must concentrate on core competencies, in order to have a chance of winning races in technology and markets. Firms seek a solution to the paradoxical, combined demands of concentration on core competence, access to complementary competencies,

low costs (still partly based on scale). They find this in alliances with other firms. These offer mutual exchange of technology (t) and cooperation in the joint development of technology and the sharing of tacit knowledge (j). Together, these are more important than variety of partners (t + j>m), but core competence is so important that if transfer of technology leads to spillover, the benefit of all forms of learning become less attractive than variety of partners(t + j + v − r<m). It is a difficult world.

In this world, let us consider 'quality based contracting', which is supposed to approximate present or recent Japanese practice, and in part is being copied by Western companies. In terms of our model, it is specified as follows:

> *Quality based contracting*: PMCOS = OPEN = SPEC = COV = STRAN = UTRAN = 1; MULSUP = MULCUS = 0; URET = SRET = 1 + d + t + j.

$$(7)$$

We propose that this is Pareto efficient and optimal in this world, but has only a fragile viability, due to two complications.

The first problem is that both sides are tempted to switch to multiple partners. This yields the following game (Figure 9.1), which we label 'the subgame of promiscuity'.

With the parameter settings of this world (t + j>m; t + v + j − r<m), we are facing a prisoner's dilemma (PD): there is a temptation to switch to multiple partners, in order to gain an extra advantage (m). This also yields an additional advantage to the partner (v), but also a risk of spillover, yielding a net loss. To prevent this, the partner prefers to eliminate the risk of spillover by stopping technology transfer, but then there is no sense in maintaining transfer oneself. This yields a breakdown of mutual technology transfer (t + j>m), but this is preferred to the risk of spillover (t + v + j − r<m).

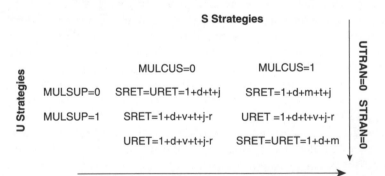

Figure 9.1 Subgame of promiscuity

Note that both sides adhere to product differentiation, with S offering specific assets (SPEC = 1), U eliminating the resulting threat of hold-up to S by providing coverage (COV = 1), and S eliminating the resulting threat of hold-up for U by maintaining openness to monitoring (OPEN = 1). This makes the outcome superior to cost-based governance, which in this world is less attractive then product differentiation. But they have lost the benefits of mutual technology transfer (t, j). The outcome can be characterized as:

differentiation without co-operation in technology: PMCOS = OPEN = SPEC = COV = MULCUS = MULSUP = 1; STRAN = UTRAN = 0; URET = SRET = 1 + d + m.

(8)

It constitutes a Nash equilibrium, and a powerful 'attractor'. Now, as is well known, there is a possibility to get out of a PD in a repeated game, by threatening to retaliate if the partner does not maintain exclusiveness (MULCUS = MULSUP = 0), say in a tit-for-tat procedure. But while over many such games this is a robust strategy, it may fail in individual cases (Axelrod 1984), particularly if there is any expectation that cheating by promiscuity may remain undetected.

A second problem is that there is a temptation for U to refuse price-minus costing (PMCOS = 0), and thereby try to obtain a bargaining advantage (+ b for U, – b for S), in the following game, which we label the game of:

badgering the supplier: PMCOS = 0. S has three options for a response:

1   accept the loss of bargaining position (b), with SRET = 1 + d + t + j – b, URET = 1 + d + t + j + b
2   recover bargaining position by switching to multiple partners, whereby they set in motion the PD of promiscuity, with the result SRET = URET = 1 + d + m
3   recover bargaining position by closing themselves off from monitoring (OPEN = 0). But by (1) this implies STRAN = 0. As shown in Appendix I, this completely unravels the co-operation, with a surrender not only of mutual technology transfer, but also product differentiation. In other words: it results in a regress to cost-based contracting, with the outcome SRET = URET = 1 + s + m.

(9)

By the definition of this world (d > s; d + t + j – b < s + m), 2 dominates both 1 and 3. But since this is worse than the starting point (7), also for U (URET = 1 + d + t + j), this is likely to deter U from playing this game.

But b, which denotes the loss that S may incur as a result of loss of bargaining position, can be influenced by U. U could lower b to just below

$t_s + j_s - m_s$. Then it is better for S to accept the loss. In other words: U can appropriate all the benefits from transfer (t) and joint production (j), and we end up at the equilibrium:

> *One-sided benefit in exclusive cooperation*, with OPEN = SPEC = COV = STRAN = UTRAN = 1; PMCOS = MULSUP = MULCUS = 0; STRET = $1 + d_s + m_s$; URET = $1 + d_u + t_u + t_s + j_u + j_s - m_s$
>
> (10)

Is this, rather than the original reconstruction (7), the reality of Japanese contracting? Summing up: in this world, the viability of quality-based contracting is fragile. The PD of promiscuity may often be held off by tit-for-tat (or some comparable procedure). Users will be deterred from badgering suppliers if the latter catch on that they can deter this with a threat of reverting to the PD of promiscuity. If suppliers do not catch on to this, or users do not take the threat seriously, they will fall back into differentiation without co-operation in the exchange of technology. But U can limit the bargaining loss for S in order to deter him from reverting to promiscuity, and then we wind up in an equilibrium in which U appropriates all the advantages from technology transfer and joint production. This raises doubts concerning the idealized view of mutually beneficial Japanese supplier relations. It confirms suspicions voiced by suppliers that if they open up to the partner for the sake of co-operation in exchange of competence and co-operation in development, on the condition that the buyer allows for a profit margin for the supplier (price minus costing), the buyer will renege on this. The analysis shows that probably the buyer will allow only a profit margin which is sufficient to keep the supplier from escaping to other customers.

The future: a raplex world

Now we consider a world which seems a plausible scenario for the future (or even the present). It is designed to capture conditions that are presently emerging in the industrialized world. In this world we are curious to see what viable optima come out, perhaps as some 'Third Way', next to the 'Western' and 'Japanese' forms of contracting, and to see in what respects it differs from those two.

> *A rapidly changing and complex (raplex) world* (W3a): SPEED = 1, d>s, t,m,v,j>0.
>
> (11)

In this world there is intense competition in global markets, product differentiation prevails (in both input and output markets), which makes differentiation more important than scale (d>s), and radical speed in the change of products and markets (SPEED = 1), which makes all forms of learning crucially important. Speed of change is so high as to exceed the speed of spillover, so that risk of spillover is eliminated. That makes this world much easier than W2.

We recognize two alternative conditions that may eliminate spillover risk:

monitoring against spillover (W3b): there are technologies to monitor what happens to competence transferred so that their spillover can be controlled,[3]

radical differentiation (W3c): competing producers are so radically differentiated they cannot greatly benefit from information that spills over from them.

In these worlds we propose a form of contracting that may be characterized as 'co-operation with multiple partners for full learning':

Cooperation with multiple partners for full learning: COV = OPEN = SPEC – STRAN = UTRAN = MULSUP = MULCUS = 1; PMCOS = 0; SRET = URET = 1 + d + m + t + v + j.

$$(12)$$

We also call this form of contracting the 'Third Way', since it presents an alternative to the stereotypes of Western and Japanese contracting, while carrying elements of both.

We propose that this is optimal and viable. Its optimality follows directly from the definition of this world. Its viability follows from its being a Nash equilibrium. With no risk of spillover, there is no reason why agents should not set the relevant parameters to achieve 'full learning' (m + t + v + j): STRAN = UTRAN = MULSUP = MULCUS = 1. By (1) this requires OPEN = 1, but according to (2) the loss of bargaining position by S that this might entail is averted by MULCUS = 1, and there is no need for a guaranteed margin for S (PMCOS = 0). To achieve advantages of differentiated product requires SPEC = 1, but to eliminate hold-up risk for S (4) this requires COV = 1, but to eliminate hold-up risk for U (5) this requires OPEN = 1.

World of the clan

Finally, we define the following world:

World of the clan (W4): b = 0, h = 0.

$$(13)$$

This world is governed by loyalty and trust(worthiness), based on a reputation mechanism, social control, bonding by friendship or kinship, or shared values and norms, which eliminate or prevent opportunism (Ouchi 1980). As a result, there is no risk of hold-up (h = 0), and partners always equally share returns (b = 0). This is an easy world, and the best of all possible worlds. Here, we consider what we call 'clan contracting':

> *Clan contracting:* COV = OPEN = STRAN = UTRAN = MULSUP = 1
> if s>d + m_S: SPEC = MULCUS = 0, URET = SRET = 1 + s + m_U/2 +
> t + v_S/2 + j
> if s<d + m: SPEC = MULCUS = 1, URET = SRET = 1 + d + m + t +
> v + j.

$$(14)$$

If the advantage of scale exceeds those of differentiation plus varied customers for S (s>d + m_S), then S will have single partners, while U has multiple partners. This yields U a benefit of multiple partners (m_U), and S a benefit of varied learning (v_S), but these will be shared, so that each obtains half of both. If the advantage of scale does not exceed that of differentiation and variety of customers for S, then they will opt for product differentiation and varied contacts also for S. This form of governance is optimal and viable (Nash equilibrium).

Since this is the best of all possible worlds, the question arises whether in evolution it might not emerge as the survivor (Hill 1990). But the question is whether such lack of opportunism is viable or utopian. Especially when many people are trustworthy, it becomes more attractive (and to yield more evolutionary strength) to be opportunistic, and this seems likely to yield some intermediate value of the occurrence of opportunism, rather than to its complete absence. But we will not go into that issue here (see Nooteboom 1996).

Discussion

In our reconstruction of the past, in the 'Fordist world', we found that 'cost-based contracting', which we propose as a reconstruction of recent 'Western' practice, is both optimal and viable. In our reconstruction of the present, in the world of 'efficient quality', we found that 'quality based' contracting, which we proposed as approximating at least part of Japanese practice, is optimal but of dubious viability. It is plagued by a prisoner's dilemma of 'promiscuity', and temptations for the buyer to 'badger the supplier'. In our proposal for the near future (which may already have begun), in the form of a 'raplex world', we found a 'learning based' form which is both optimal and viable.

What are the policy implications? First of all: forms of governance or contracting are not good or bad irrespective of the conditions. In other words: we propose a contingency view of contracting. 'Western' contracting was optimal and viable in the Fordist world, but not now. 'Japanese' contracting is optimal in the present or recent world, but its viability is debatable; it is fragile and likely to break down. In any case, if we are moving into the 'raplex' world, we should no longer try to imitate the 'Japanese way', because it is no longer appropriate. Exclusive relations restrict learning too much. More varied learning is needed to cope with rapid change, and change may be so rapid as to eliminate the need for restrictions on multiple partnership for the sake of controlling for spillover, or techniques for controlling such spillover may be available. We identify a 'Third Way', which combines the close co-operation from the 'Japanese' way (with exchange of knowledge, specific investments and guarantees to cover them), with multiple partnership of the 'Western way'. Perhaps firms are already pulling in that direction. Note that this may reinforce the tendency towards the PD of 'promiscuity' in the 'Japanese way'

Many questions can be raised concerning the specification of the model, and possibilities for further studies. Are our reconstructions of past, present and future realistic? Should we consider other possible worlds? Are our reconstructions of 'Western' and 'Japanese' practice adequate? We already noted that there is some hesitation to accept 'quality based contracting' as a realistic model of Japanese practice. But the analysis showed possible reasons for this: its viability is fragile, and it can break down into sub-optimal outcomes. We predict lapses into 'promiscuity', 'badgering the supplier' and occasionally even complete regress into cost based contracting. Is this what we observe? Perhaps that is why we hesitate to accept it as a universally valid reconstruction of Japanese practice. There are many ways in which the analysis can be varied and extended.

Most fundamentally, we may apply the approach, *mutatis mutandis*, to horizontal rather than vertical alliances.

Within the scope of buyer–supplier relations, we could revise our design principles of the model. We may look at intermediate strategies between the discrete alternatives. We may reconsider the assumption of only one-sided switching costs due to specific investments, and extend them also to the buyer. We may add complexity by assuming that absorptive capacity is both cumulative and specific with respect to the source of knowledge, which raises an additional source of hold-up.

Within the scope of the design principles, we could explore variations. We may define more possible worlds. For example: a world where there is an option to choose for either a standard product, in a cost strategy, or a differentiation strategy, in a world with a dual market. We may add further complexity to governance. For example: a reconstruction of trilateral governance. We may further extend types of knowledge and their transfer. We could be more explicit about the network structure of 'multiple partners'. We might allow for lack of information on strategies and outcomes, and open up issues of 'signalling'. We might make models of the evolution of different forms, in constant or shifting worlds, towards evolutionary equilibria.

In fact, it seems that we have opened up a whole area of research.

Appendix I

The option for S to maintain bargaining position by closing off

In the main text we discussed the possibilities for S to regain bargaining position if badgered by U. One is to (threaten) switch to multiple customers (MULCUS = 1), while maintaining co-operation in product differentiation. The alternative is for S to close themselves off (OPEN = 0). We posited there, and show here that this is worse. In Figure 9.A1 we present the tree of the corresponding sub-game. We start from the reaction of U to the decision of S to close off from monitoring (OPEN = 0). Note that by (1) OPEN = 0 forces STRAN = 0. But then there no longer is a reason for U to maintain technology transfer either, and they set UTRAN = 0. But since the stopping of technology transfer eliminates spillover risk, both sides might as well switch to multiple partners: MULSUP = MULCUS = 1. U now faces the decision whether or not to withdraw cover for the risk of specific assets for S (COV = 0), and thereby avoid hold-up risk but thereby also make the step to a breakdown of differentiation.

In backward induction, every time the right hand branch is chosen, given the parameter settings of this world (W2): d − h<s. So, if S close themselves off

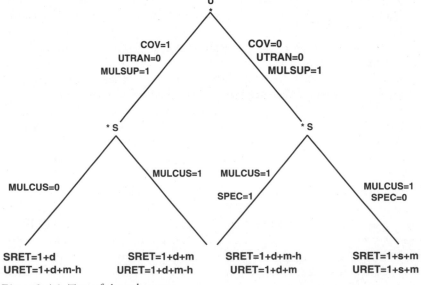

Figure 9.A1 Tree of the sub-game

(OPEN = 0), that leads to an unravelling of co-operation: no co-operation in differentiation and no co-operation in technology transfer. It yields a regress into cost-based contracting.

Notes

1 The idea is that tacit knowledge is implicit and embedded in local routines, and can be transferred only by close, hands-on observation, imitation and interaction on the spot.
2 An example is given in Lamming (1993). In the car industry, a buyer can find out whether a supplier has spilled over proprietary technology to a competitor, by reverse engineering the cars of competitors. Or as Lamming aptly said: in competitors products spillovers get 'publicized'. The threat of this disciplines suppliers to guard against spillover. Of course this does not eliminate unintended leakage.

References

Axelrod, R. (1984) *The Evolution of Cooperation*, New York: Basic Books.
Cohen, W.M. and Levinthal, D.A. (1990) 'Absorptive capacity: a new perspective on learning and Innovation', *Administrative Science Quarterly* 35: 128–152.
Cusumano, M.A. and Takeishi, A. (1991) 'Supplier relations and management: a survey of Japanese, Japanese-transplant and US auto plants', *Strategic Management Journal* 12: 563–88.
Dore, R. (1989) *Taking Japan Seriously*, Stanford, CA: Stanford University Press.
Dyer, J.H. and Ouchi, W.G. (1993) 'Japanese-style partnerships: Giving companies a competitive edge', *Sloan Management Review* 35: 51–63.
Helper, S. (1991) 'Strategy and irreversibility in supplier relations: the case of the US automobile industry', *Business History Review* 65 (Winter): 781–824.
Helper, S. and D.I. Levine (1992) 'Long term supplier relations and product-market structure', *Journal of Law, Economics and Organization* 8, 3: 561–81.
Hill, C.W.I. (1990) 'Cooperation, opportunism and the invisible hand: implications for transaction cost theory', *Academy of Management Review* 15, 3: 500–13.
Kamath, R.R. and Liker, J.K. (1994) 'A second look at Japanese product development', *Harvard Business Review* November–December, 154–170.
Lamming, R. (1993) *Beyond Partnership*, New York: Prentice Hall.
Nelson, R. and Winter, S. (1982) *An Evolutionary Theory of Economic Change*, Cambridge: Cambridge University Press.
Nooteboom, B. (1992) 'Towards a dynamic theory of transactions', *Journal of Evolutionary Economics* 2: 281–99.
—— (1993) 'An analysis of specificity in transaction cost economics', *Organization Studies* 14, 3: 443–51.
—— (1995) 'Towards a learning based model of transactions', in J. Groenewegen (ed.) *TCE and Beyond*, Deventer: Kluwer, pp. 327–49.
—— (1996) *Will Opportunism Go Away?*, research report, SOM research school, P.O. Box 800, 9700 AV Groningen, The Netherlands.
Ouchi, W.G. (1980) 'Markets, bureaucracies and clans', *Administrative Science Quarterly* 25: 129–142.

Penrose, E. (1959) *The Theory of the Growth of the Firm*, New York: Wiley.
Prahalad, C. and Hamel, G. (1990) 'The core competences of the corporation', *Harvard Business Review*, May–June.
Williamson, O.E. (1975) *Markets and Hierarchies: Analysis and antitrust implications*, New York: Free Press.
—— (1985) *The Economic Institutions of Capitalism; Firms, Markets, Relational Contracting*, New York: Free Press.
—— (1989) Transaction cost economics, in: R. Schmalensee and R.D. Willig, *Handbook of industrial organization*, Amsterdam: North Holland, pp. 135–182.
—— (1991) 'Comparative economic organization: the analysis of discrete structural alternatives', *Administrative Science Quarterly* 36: 269–96.
Womack, J., Jones, D. and Roos, D. (1990) *The Machine that Changed the World*, New York: Rawson.
Zuscovitch, E. (1994) *Sustainable differentiation: Economic Dynamism and Social Norms*, conference paper Joseph A. Schumpeter Society, Münster, 19–21 August 1994.

10

JAPANESE 'TRANSPLANT' SUPPLIER RELATIONS: ARE THEY TRANSFERABLE? SHOULD THEY BE?[1]

Susan Helper

Introduction

In recent years Japanese firms have invested a great deal in the United States automobile industry. Starting with Honda in 1982, Japanese auto-assemblers had invested $9 billion in building or substantially re-tooling nine plants in the US by 1994. Many of these firms' suppliers have followed; in 1993 there were 322 Japanese or Japanese-US joint-venture auto supplier plants, which employed over 30,000 American workers and represented an investment of over $8 billion.(Kenney and Florida 1991: 28; 1994: 126).

This influx has been the subject of much debate. Some authors argue that the Japanese production system is both efficient and is being transferred to the United States by the transplants. In this view, the transplants might be thought of as missionaries of continuous improvement. (This perspective has been developed by authors such as Womack *et al.* 1990; Kenney and Florida 1991; Florida and Kenney 1991, 1994; Cusumano and Takeishi 1991.) In contrast, others argue that the Japanese system relies to a significant extent on shifting the costs of production to others, and that the Japanese are transferring mostly these unfair aspects of the system to the US. In this view, the transplants are more like Trojan horses: their US factories are simply a cover for importing Japanese technology, and their invasion has caused the loss of many good jobs for Americans.(Howes 1993a, 1993b; Kearns 1992; Monahan and Pickens 1991; Economic Strategy Institute 1992).

In this chapter I use survey data to test hypotheses contained in these alternative perspectives. The data come from surveys I conducted for MIT's International Motor Vehicle Program. I shall briefly review the literature on transplants, and present a conceptual framework for supplier relations based on Hirschman's (1970) distinction between 'exit' and 'voice' responses to problems. I shall then provide evidence that long-term, 'voice' relationships typically improve performance, and look at the extent to which such policies are characteristic of US-owned firms, Japanese-owned firms in Japan and Japanese transplants. I find that while these policies are more characteristic of Japanese-owned firms, they are far from ubiquitous, and differences between US- and Japanese-owned firms have been shrinking over time.

Next I look at the issue of whether the transplants are transferring valuable new skills to US workers, or whether they are instead causing a loss of good jobs, by substituting low-wage, non-union workers. The conclusion argues that Japanese transplants in the US combine efficient and cost-shifting mechanisms. However, in this respect they are no worse (and in some cases are better) than new US-owned entrants into the industry.

Data

The data discussed below draw on four surveys of automobile suppliers in the United States and Japan, all conducted with the sponsorship of the MIT International Motor Vehicle Program:

(1) In spring 1989, a survey was mailed to every automotive supplier and automaker component division that was either named in the 1988 *Elm Guide to Automotive Sourcing in the United States*, or was a member of the Motor and Equipment Manufacturers' Association (MEMA) who sold components directly to an automaker. Thus, the survey was mailed to virtually every domestically-owned first-tier supplier to manufacturers of cars and light trucks in the United States. The survey asked about relationships with customers, internal firm strategy, and performance.

The target respondent was the divisional director of marketing at independent firms, and the divisional business manager or director of strategic planning at automaker components divisions. I selected these individuals on the grounds that they would have the broadest knowledge about both customer relationships and about their firm's products and processes.

Because many companies supply their customers with several different types of products, and their relationships with their customers differ by product, respondents were asked to answer the survey for *one* customer using *one* product which was typical of their company's output. Companies with multiple divisions selling auto parts received more than one survey. In order to preserve confidentiality and to minimize the time required to fill out the survey, respondents were not asked to provide exact data on their firm's sales, etc., but rather to check boxes indicating ranges (such as 'under $4 million sales', '$4–25 million sales', etc.)

The response was about double the norm for business surveys; 499 completed questionnaires were received, for a response rate of 47 per cent. Furthermore, response rates for many subgroups of interest were close to their proportions in the population, as measured by the original mailing list. The sample was representative both of business organization – automaker components divisions, MEMA members (who tend to be small and medium-sized independent firms), and large independent firms – and of business location by state.

(2) In 1993, I conducted another survey of marketing directors with a similar focus, this time including Canada as well as the United States. The response rate was 55 per cent; 673 surveys were received.

(3) The 1993 survey of plant managers had the same product- and customer-specific structure as the sales manager surveys, but asked questions regarding shop-floor management and human-resource practices. The response rate was 30 per cent; 454 surveys were received.

(4) In 1993 Dr Mari Sako of the London School of Economics surveyed first-tier auto suppliers in Japan using an instrument similar to the US-Canada sales manager questionnaire. The response rate was 30 per cent; 471 surveys were received (for more detail, see Helper and Sako 1995).

These data allow us to test using a larger sample the hypotheses of Cusumano and Takeishi (1991), who surveyed a small group of US, Japanese transplant, and Japanese auto suppliers. In contrast to Florida and Kenney's (1991, and Kenney and Florida 1991) survey, this chapter uses data from both US-owned auto suppliers and Japanese firms in Japan, as well as Japanese transplants.

Literature review

Japanese transplants: missionaries of continuous improvement or Trojan horses?

As discussed above, the arrival of the Japanese transplants has elicited a variety of responses. In the first view, the transplants might be categorized as 'missionaries of continuous improvement'. That is, they diffuse a production system which has proved highly successful in Japan. Prime exponents of this view are Womack et al., who argue that Japanese lean production

> is a superior way for humans to make things. It provides better products in wider variety at lower cost. Equally important, it provides more challenging and fulfilling work for employees at every level, from the factory to headquarters. It follows that the whole world should adopt lean production, and as quickly as possible. [This diffusion will occur naturally] since this mode of production achieves its highest efficiency, quality, and flexibility when all activities from design to assembly occur in the same place . . . . Lean producers in the 1990s will need to create top-to-bottom, paper-concept to finished-car manufacturing systems in the three great markets of the world – North America, Europe, and Asia.
>
> (Womack et al. 1990: 225, 200)

Similarly, Kenney and Florida state 'of course the Japanese production system is efficient' (1994: 8). The Japanese transplants are 'rebuilding the rust belt (by) . . . making long-term commitments where US business leaders had seemed to give up hope' (Kenney and Florida 1991).

In contrast, others argue that the Japanese transplants are more like Trojan horses. The Japanese production system in Japan has a large measure of exploitation, these authors say, and it is largely these unfair aspects which the Japanese are bringing to the US. For example, Howes (1993a: 31) argues that an important part of the Japanese production system are the 'contingent workers and suppliers (which) build cost flexibility into a system otherwise characterized by high fixed costs'. It is this 'market' system that the Japanese are bringing to the US. For every hour spent producing in a US-located transplant, almost twice as many hours are worked in Japan, doing design, engineering, high-technology parts fabrication, and research and development. 'There is no reason why the creative parts of the system should be transferred and a lot of reasons why the exploitative parts of the system would fit well in the United States' (Howes 1993b: 76).

Arguments in this vein are also made by the Economic Strategy Institute (1992) and McAlinden (1992), which characterize Japanese cars assembled in the US as having little more US content than imports. Kearns (1992) says that the Japanese are creating a 'separate auto economy' in the US, one which imports high-value added parts from Japan, and uses low-wage non-union workers to produce standard parts. In this view, the expansion of the transplants comes at the expense of the traditional US auto sector, which has been a large employer of well-paid production workers and highly-educated engineers.

Supplier relations: a conceptual framework

The above authors raise two sets of issues. First, what sorts of production practices are efficient?[2] Second, what is the nature of the practices the Japanese are transferring to the US? In this chapter I will focus on two types of practices: (1) supplier–customer relations, and (2) the wages and training of workers.[3] Below, I will briefly describe a conceptual framework for customer–supplier relations.

Traditional studies of purchasing have focused on analysing the choice between 'make' and 'buy' (see for example, Kaserman (1978), Williamson (1975)). However, in order to analyse different options within the 'make' and 'buy' alternatives, another framework is necessary. Here, we employ the exit-voice framework, adapted from Hirschman (1970) to classify supplier relations according to the methods used to resolve problems which arise between the parties. In an 'exit' relationship, a customer who has a problem with a supplier finds a new supplier. In a 'voice' relationship, the customer works with the original supplier to resolve the problem.

In most cases a voice relationship is more efficient, since a rich flow of information between the parties makes possible effective use of techniques such as value analysis and value engineering.

However, a customer who wants to have a voice relationship with its suppliers must make some amount of commitment to them. Commitment refers to the supplier's degree of certainty that the customer will continue to buy its products for some length of time. This assurance can be provided by any mechanism that makes it harder for the customer to exit from the relationship, such as vertical integration, long-term contracts, or desire to retain suppliers' trust (Sako 1992). Commitment is necessary both to obtain suggestions for improvement (which may be based on proprietary information) and to make investments that respond to these suggestions.

Supplier relations: performance and trends

Linkages between supplier relations and performance

Japanese cars are widely regarded as the best in the world in their price range. They consistently have fewer defects and lower frequency of repair than do US automobiles. Japanese automakers are also the fastest introducers of new models and the most productive assemblers in the world (Abernathy et al. 1983; Clark 1989; Womack et al. 1990).

Many studies find that Japanese supplier relationships play a key role in the automakers' performance. For example, Kim Clark (1989) has estimated that supplier contributions account for one-third of the Japanese automakers' advantage over their US counterparts in total engineering hours required to develop a new car. Defect rates of parts supplied by Japanese companies are on the order of one-tenth the rate of those supplied by US firms (Cusumano and Takeishi 1991).

The Japanese success is not based entirely on cultural factors. Where US firms have adopted voice relationships, they have also experienced improved performance. For example, Helper (1995) finds that US automotive suppliers with explicit long-term contracts are more likely to invest in flexible automation, even after controlling for such organizational characteristics as skill in introducing new processes. Furthermore, firms that meet more frequently with their customers have lower inventory levels (Lieberman et al. 1995).

Many of the Japanese performance advantages disappear when supplier relations variables are controlled for. For example, supplier participation in product development has been found by Clark (1989) to be a significant source of Japanese competitive advantage, allowing Japanese automakers to use 11 per cent fewer engineering hours to design a new car than do their US or European counterparts. Using 1989 survey data, Helper (1996) shows that after controlling for the nature of the design task and the nature of information exchanged, Japanese suppliers participate significantly more in product design. However, when commitment variables are included, the coefficient on the Japan variable falls by one-third and becomes insignificant. Thus, Japanese techniques for involving suppliers are at least partially imitable by US firms.

The 1993 survey data also provide evidence on firm performance. Table 10.1 presents survey data describing firm performance across the dimensions of technology use, inventory management, and quality control. Comparable data from the Japanese firms in Japan is not available for high CNC use, defect rates, or number of parts assembled.

Table 10.1 defines several sub-groups to facilitate comparison among those whose most important customer was a member of the Big Three (n = 533); those whose most important customer was Ford or Chrysler (n = 302); those US-owned suppliers whose most important customer was Japanese (n = 41); Japanese transplants (n = 76); and Japanese suppliers in Japan (n = 473).[4] Among the transplants, thirty-one listed a member of the Big Three (Ford, GM, or Chrysler) as their most important customer; the other forty-five principally supplied a Japanese-owned automaker.

It might be argued that performance differences reflect the impact of factors other than the nationality of the supplier's ownership. For example, customers may have different policies toward suppliers. In particular, since

Table 10.1 Performance measure summary results

Performance Variables	US with Big Three	US with Ford/Chrysler	US with Japanese customer	Japan owned	Japanese in Japan
Robot use	0.5467	0.5621	0.6341	0.8028	0.83
High CNC use, 1993	0.1825	0.2215	0.4118	0.2564	n/a
Median delivery batch size in days, 1989	7	6	4	2	0.5
Median delivery batch size in days, 1993	3.25	3	2	1	0.5
Median production batch size in days, 1989	10	10	10	4.8	1
Median production batch size in days, 1993	6	5	5	3	1
Median defects in parts/million, 1993 (less those not noticing or using regardless)	135	85	69	121	n/a
Median number of parts assembled to make final product	4	6	6	8	n/a

1992 General Motors has adopted a more exit-based approach than the transplant assemblers, Ford, and Chrysler, who have continued to move toward voice (Helper 1994). Other performance differences may simply reflect exogenous characteristics of the supplier base. In particular, the Japanese get the chance to start fresh; they are not weighed down by the adversarial legacy toward both their customers and their workers borne by older US suppliers. In addition, it might be that the products the assemblers chose to have their suppliers produce in the US,[5] are more conducive to voice relations than the ones they continue to import from Japan.

To investigate these possibilities, I ran three sets of regressions on the variables in Table 10.1. In the first set, the only regressor was a dummy 'JOWN', which was 1 if the supplier was Japanese-owned, and 0 otherwise. The second set added variables which controlled for the respondent's most important customer: JCUST was one if this customer was Japanese, and FC was one if this customer was Ford or Chrysler. The third set added variables controlling for the complexity of the product and the age of the supplier (either the age of the plant or the length of the business unit's relationship with its customer).[6]

The first column in Table 10.2 gives the coefficients on JOWN in the simple regression; the second column gives the coefficients after the customer variables have been included. The third column gives the coefficient after the age and complexity controls have been added. The fourth provides the ratio of the first column to the third column, thus providing a measure of how much of the effect of being a Japanese-owned supplier can be explained by factors other than ownership, such as customer, age, and product complexity.

As Table 10.1 shows, Japanese firms in Japan report the highest usage of robots; 83 per cent of them report at least one robot in the plant they use to make the product for which they answered the survey. The US firms which supply Japanese customers also have more firms with robots than the Big Three suppliers (63 per cent versus 55 per cent), although they still lag the transplant firms (80 per cent versus 63 per cent). Even after the complexity of their products and the age of their plants is taken into consideration (Table 10.2), the transplants' advantage in robot use remains significant at better than the 1 per cent level.

US suppliers with Japanese customers report a significantly larger percentage of firms with high CNC use,[7] than any other group (41 per cent). Ford and Chrysler have more high CNC suppliers (22 per cent) than the average for Big Three suppliers (18 per cent). In comparison to Japanese transplants, US suppliers with Japanese customers are much more likely to have high CNC use (0.41 versus 0.26).

Japanese in Japan reported median lot sizes between one-half and one-fifth of the nearest comparison group. While their lot sizes have been stable from 1989 to 1993, the other groups all produce and deliver in equal to or smaller batches now than they did in 1989.

In 1989, Japanese transplants and US suppliers with Japanese customers

Table 10.2 Performance measure regression results

Performance variables	JOWN	JOWN, JCUST, FC	JOWN, JCUST, FC, Complex, Age	Ratio of columns 2 and 4
Robot use	1.202 (0.0001)	1.158 (0.0008)	1.214 (0.0008)	1.01
High CNC use, 1993	−0.06112 (0.3732)	−0.001526 (0.9845)	0.01623 (0.8357	−0.2655
Delivery batch size in days, 1989	−6.632 (<0.0001)	−5.172 (0.0061)	−5.204 (0.0064)	0.7847
Delivery batch size in days, 1993	−4.713 (0.3664)	−3.433 (0.5674)	−3.035 (0.6153)	0.644
Production batch size in days, 1989	11.87 (0.1119)	25.67 (0.0033)	22.14 (0.0090)	1.865
Production batch size in days, 1993	13.6 (0.0481)	25.4 (0.0014)	22.18 (0.0040)	1.631
Defects in parts/million, 1993 (less those not noticing or using regardless)	−1894 (0.8331)	−544 (0.9589)	−1390 (0.9018)	0.73
Median number of parts assembled to make final product	1.171 (0.9177)	2.854 (0.8222)	6.52E-14 (1.000)	5.56E-14

Note
Probability values are in parentheses

reported delivering in lot sizes smaller than those of Big Three suppliers (the batches would last customers 2 days and 2.5 days instead of 7). Over the next four years, each group would roughly cut in half the size of the batches they delivered.

Suppliers also reported reductions in the median size of the batches they produced. However, for all groups of suppliers the reduction in production lot size was smaller than the reduction in delivery lot size. That is, suppliers were not able to reduce the amount of inventory they carried.

While median batch sizes produced by Japanese transplants were slightly smaller than those produced by other groups in both 1989 and 1993, mean batch sizes are higher than for the rest of the sample. This difference increases after controlling for age and complexity. In contrast, the impact of having a Japanese customer is to reduce production lot sizes, an impact that is significant at the 1 per cent level.

Transplants also report the highest rates of defects found by the customer, except for suppliers to GM. In part this may be due to the stricter standards maintained by transplant assemblers, but it is noteworthy that transplant suppliers' defect rates are higher than those of US suppliers to transplant assemblers. Additionally, we have partially controlled for more lax Big Three inspection standards by excluding from the sample those suppliers who report that their customers either 'would not notice' or 'would use anyway' a batch containing minor defects. These differences in defect rates between the Japanese transplants and Ford/Chrysler suppliers are not statistically significant, however.

The number of parts assembled to make the final product is the same for Japanese transplant firms and suppliers to Ford and Chrysler at six. Suppliers to GM assemble less than half as many parts. The greatest use of modularization is found among Japanese suppliers to Japanese customers. However, only the GM effect is significant.

To summarize, Japanese transplants exhibit significant differences from the other groups of US-located suppliers on key performance measures, such as robot use and 1989 delivery batch size. Only in the case of delivery batch size do the controls (complexity of products, age of plant, and most important customer) reduce the JOWN coefficient very much. Overall, the US-owned suppliers to the transplants perform as well as the Japanese supplier transplants, suggesting that it is Japanese-owned *assemblers*, not suppliers, who are the most effective missionaries of continuous improvement.

Japanese and US supplier relations practices: a comparison

The 1989 survey found that Japanese transplant supplier relations practices were very different from the US-owned firms': the distribution of the transplants' responses differs from the US distribution at the 10 per cent level or better on 120 of 234 (51 per cent) measures contained in the sales manager survey. This is five times the number of significant differences one would expect by chance.[8] However, by 1993, only 112 of 444 (25 per cent) were significantly different.

Below, I describe three types of trends in supplier relations: information exchange with customers, commitment from customers, and 'exploitation' by customers.

Information exchange with customers

The data show an impressive increase in the amount of information which suppliers provide to customers, particularly among US-owned firms. In 1989, the differences in patterns of information exchange between the supplier firms with no Japanese contact and those who either were Japanese or who supplied to Japanese firms, were meaningful. Japanese transplants were three times as likely to provide their customer with the cost of process steps as were suppliers to the Big Three (33 per cent versus 11 per cent), and US firms who supplied

Japanese automakers were equally likely to provide this information as Japanese firms in Japan (50 per cent).

Over the past four years, all groups increased this type of formal information sharing, with US firms making the largest gains. Although US firms supplying Japanese customers still share significantly more information than the other firms in the US, the differential among the other groups has diminished.

The gain is particularly large when compared with 1984. The percentage of US-owned suppliers who provide their customers with a breakdown of the cost of each step in their production process increased from 3 per cent in 1984 to 43 per cent in 1993.[9] However, the low absolute level means that in over half of the cases, customers and suppliers are still unable to effectively use techniques such as value analysis, which can lead to significant cost reductions and performance improvements through careful consideration of the cost and functionality of detailed aspects of a part's design.[10]

The extent to which customers share information with suppliers has also increased, although from a very low base. Interestingly, transplant assemblers are equally likely to share confidential financial information with their US-owned suppliers and with Japanese-owned firms.

Face to face meetings are another important type of information exchange. The suppliers to the Big Three and to Ford and Chrysler have increased the frequency of such interaction in the past eight years; in 1989, 74 per cent 'exchange visits on matters regarding this product' at least every two months (and 36 per cent do so at least every two weeks). In 1984, the figures were 50 per cent and 22 per cent, respectively. In 1984 and 1989, Japanese-owned suppliers in the US had significantly more frequent meetings with their customers; this difference disappeared by 1993.

The firms who are Japanese or who supply the Japanese have maintained the same or slightly less face to face contact with customers. While the Japanese in Japan have less face-to face contact with suppliers than do US customers, they use other types of communication (phone, fax, and e-mail) far more frequently.

Commitment

As noted above, in order to manage the voice strategy's increased information flow and to assuage suppliers' fears of leakage of proprietary data to competitors, customers must increase their commitment to their suppliers.

In general, US-owned suppliers received slightly more commitment from their customers between 1984 and 1989. However, GM suppliers saw their customer's commitment decrease markedly between 1989 and 1993.

Suppliers to the Big Three devoted less than one-fourth of their assets for making their product to a specific customer. Japanese in Japan and transplant firms are most likely to have a high percentage of assets which do not have alternate uses (36 per cent). The difference among the US-located firms, however becomes insignificant after controlling for the customer.

Japanese transplants also report the longest time needed for their customers to switch to another supplier, approximately 21 per cent higher than any of the other groups (including Japanese in Japan). This difference remains highly significant between the transplants and the rest of the sample even after including the controls.

US-owned suppliers' perception of the probability that their customer would treat them fairly fell well below 3, the neutral value in a 5-point scale where 1 equals 'can't depend on customer to treat us fairly' and 5 equals 'customer always treats us fairly'.[11] In contrast, Japanese suppliers' average level of trust remained above 3.6. These figures do not exactly reflect the love-fest image of some accounts of Japanese supplier relations, but they do show a greater commitment to voice than found among US automakers.

A differential still exists between suppliers to US automakers and firms who are either Japanese-owned or supplying Japanese. The highest trust score of US automakers (3.17) is significantly lower than the lowest Japanese-influenced group (3.61). US suppliers to Japanese firms are second only to Japanese suppliers in Japan in the degree to which they feel they will be treated fairly by their customers (3.81 versus 3.91).

One reason for the difference in trust levels is in suppliers' perception of their customer's response if one of their competitors came up with a superior component at a similar price. In 1989, only 32 per cent of the US owned suppliers said their customer would help match the competitor's efforts (compared to 14 per cent in 1984). The percentage of customers who would switch to a rival as soon as technically feasible actually *rose*.[12]

Between 1989 and 1993, four of the five groups became more likely to receive help from their customers if a competitor came up with a lower priced product. The only group which faced a reduced likelihood of receiving help from customers when faced with price competition was the Japanese firms in Japan (from 45 per cent to 40 per cent). In 1989, there were marked differences between the lowest likelihood of receiving help (Ford and Chrysler = 0.24) and the most likely (US firms with Japanese customer = 0.55). In 1993 these differences ranged more narrowly, with GM suppliers at the low end with 35 per cent expecting help and the US firms with Japanese customers at the high end with 67 per cent anticipating help.

Another measure of the commitment of the customer to the supplier is their propensity to switch suppliers immediately if a lower-priced alternative becomes available. In 1989, suppliers to Ford and Chrysler felt most at risk in this situation, and a clear distinction between suppliers to the Big Three and Ford/Chrysler (0.27, 0.37) and firms who were Japanese or supplied Japanese customers (0.07, 0.03) was apparent.

GM suppliers are now most likely to report that their customer would switch suppliers immediately if a lower priced alternative came available

(0.63). Ford and Chrysler are less likely to switch than four years ago (0.22 versus 0.35) but Japanese transplants are now more likely to switch than reported in 1989 (0.21 versus 0.06). US firms supplying Japanese automakers also reported an increase, although less pronounced, in the expectation that their customers would switch immediately (0.03 versus 0.05).

Japanese in Japan expect their relationships to last at least twice as long as suppliers in the US. Second to this group, Japanese transplants at 12.8 years, though US firms with Japanese customers believe 'there is a high probability of continuing to do business' for almost 11 years into the future. Big Three suppliers have the most conservative expectations regarding the length of their relationships (7.8 years).

Exploitation

Both US-owned suppliers and Japanese transplants harbour suspicions that JIT is exploitative in the sense that it transfers responsibility for inventories from the customer to the supplier. Japanese transplants believe this less strongly than those who supply the US firms (3.17 versus 3.34), but significantly more than US firms with Japanese customers or Japanese in Japan. Combined with the evidence that suppliers usually deliver in batches which are smaller than the ones they produce in, it seems to be the case that many of JIT's benefits come at the expense of suppliers, even in Japan.

In contrast, respondents firmly believe that their plant does not face a cost-quality trade-off; this belief is strongest among the US suppliers to Japanese automakers. Suppliers to Ford and Chrysler are similar to Japanese-owned firms in their attitudes.

In summary, US firms have almost matched Japanese transplants on the information flow dimension of supplier relationships: they provide information to their customers in roughly the same proportion, and they meet face-to-face almost as frequently. The commitment dimension is another story: the Japanese automakers show higher levels of commitment on every measure discussed. In general, about half of the JOWN coefficient on the commitment variables is due to the GM effect; the age and complexity controls have a relatively small impact on the size of the JOWN coefficient.

Are the transplants creating good jobs – or a 'separate auto economy'?

Womack *et al.* (1990) and Florida and Kenny (1994) see the transplants' missionary efforts as being especially beneficial in the human resource area – even production workers are empowered and trained. In contrast, Kearns and Howe see the transplants' Trojan horse as having particularly bad consequences for labour. In their view, the transplants are creating a 'separate auto economy' (Kearns 1992). This economy is low-wage, non-union, and Japanese-owned; it

Table 10.3 Supplier relations variable summary results

	US with Big Three	US with Ford/Chrysler	US with Japanese Customer	Japan owned	Japanese in Japan
Information exchange					
Provide customer with cost of process steps, 1989	0.1142	0.1026	0.5	0.3333	0.4989
Provide customer with cost of process steps, 1993	0.4295	0.3974	0.7619	0.5139	0.5159
Customer shares non-public financial info, 1989	0.1311	0.1424	0.381	0.3611	0.2706
Customer shares non-public financial info, 1993	0.3876	0.4007	0.4762	0.5	0.2937
Frequency of face-to-face meeting [days], 1989	40.26	35.96	35.32	23.91	45.24
Frequency of face-to-face meeting [days], 1993	28.7	23.5	45.07	26.46	49.42
Commitment					
% of assets specific to customer	28.81	28.8	31.28	36.16	36.88
Months required for customer to switch, 1993	12.56	14.22	13.9	22.15	14.35
Help match if lower price, 1989	0.3169	0.2544	0.5	0.4	0.45
Help match if lower price, 1993	0.5039	0.5788	0.6667	0.6087	0.4
Switch immediately if lower price, 1989	0.276	0.3534	0.02632	0.07246	0.07
Switch immediately if lower price, 1993	0.3564	0.2179	0.05263	0.2039	0.13
Expected length of relationship, 1993	7.804	8.818	10.03	12.8	25.07
Trust, 1989 (1 = low; 5 = high)	3.279	3.031	3.595	3.606	3.887
Trust, 1993 (1 = low; 5 = high)	2.791	3.172	3.805	3.676	3.908
Exploitation					
JIT transfers responsibility, 1993*	3.335	3.272	2.85	3.169	2.703
Lower defect rates mean lower costs*	1.351	1.367	1.294	1.36	n/a

Note:
*   1 = strongly disagree, 5 = strongly agree

Table 10.4 Supplier relations variable regression results

	JOWN	JOWN, JCUST, FC	JOWN, JCUST, FC, Complex, Age	Ratio of columns 2 and 4
Information exchange				
Provide Customer with Cost of Process Steps, 1989	1.084 (<0.0001)	−0.03462 (0.9217)	0.05117 (0.8875)	0.0472
Provide Customer with Cost of Process Steps, 1993	0.2644 (0.2911)	−0.511 (0.1046)	−0.383 (0.2333)	−1.449
Customer Shares Non-Public Financial Info, 1989	1.165 (<0.0001)	0.6847 (0.0347)	0.6384 (0.0538)	0.5481
Customer Shares Non-Public Financial Info, 1993	0.4187 (0.0951)	0.4085 (0.1590)	0.4675 (0.1156)	1.117
Frequency of Face-to-Face Meeting [days], 1989	−16.17 (0.0303)	−16.49 (0.0639)	−17.16 (0.0549)	1.027
Frequency of Face-to-Face Meeting [days], 1993	−4.076 (0.5333)	−11.9 (0.1114)	−11.93 (0.1121)	2.927
Commitment				
% of Assets Specific to Customer	7.215 (0.0398)	4.919 (0.2250)	4.461 (0.2778)	0.6183
Months Required for Customer to Switch, 1993	9.561 (<0.0001)	9.381 (<0.0001)	8.519 (<0.0001)	0.891
Help Match if Lower Price, 1989	0.2905 (0.2648)	−0.22 (0.4796)	−0.2252 (0.4758)	−0.7752
Help Match if Lower Price, 1993	0.3577 (0.1707)	0.16 (0.5948)	0.1508 (0.6216)	0.4216
Switch Immediately if Lower Price, 1989	−1.508 (0.0015)	−0.7249 (0.1543)	−0.8547 (0.1016)	0.5668
Switch Immediately if Lower Price, 1993	−0.6736 (0.0317)	0.07129 (0.8504)	0.005373 (0.9890)	−0.007977
Expected Length of Relationship, 1993	4.862 (0.0002)	3.164 (0.0304)	2.935 (0.0422)	0.6037
Trust, 1989 (1 = low; 5 = high)	0.5588 (0.0211)	0.1489 (0.5987)	0.08596 (0.7639)	0.1538
Trust, 1993 (1 = low; 5 = high)	1.255 (<0.0001)	0.6804 (0.0130)	0.64 (0.0211)	0.51
Exploitation JIT Transfers Responsibility, 1993*	−0.1825 (0.4155)	0.05567 (0.8297)	0.08578 (0.7438)	−0.47
Lower Defect Rates Mean Lower Costs*	−0.1692 (0.6365)	−0.02791 (0.9438)	−0.04099 (0.9193)	0.2423

Notes:
* 1 = strongly disagree, 5 = strongly agree.
1 Coefficients for binary dependent variables from logistic regression.
2 Probability values are in parentheses.

uses non-efficiency based advantages such as access to a low-wage, young workforce and large state subsidies to undermine the existing US auto sector at great social cost.

I investigate the following issues: (1) Who supplies the transplant assemblers? That is, to what extent are Japanese assemblers transforming existing suppliers as opposed to just replacing them with either imports or suppliers brought from Japan? (2) Are transplant supplier jobs good jobs?

Who supplies transplant assemblers?

The 1989 survey asked a few questions about respondents' dealings with transplant assemblers. The results are reported below. (These questions were not repeated in the 1993 survey.) Overall, 46 per cent of US-owned respondents sold at least one product to a Japanese auto-assembly plant in the United States.[13] The degree of technical complexity of the typical product produced by such firms is not significantly different from that of firms without Japanese customers.[14] Because respondents were asked only if they supplied 'any' product to Japanese assemblers in the US, the survey data cannot tell us if the product supplied to the Japanese was more or less complex than the supplier's 'typical' product.

However, of firms who won Japanese business and whose typical product is high-tech, far more answered that they formed 'a joint venture with a Japanese firm in order to supply this customer' than did such firms whose products are low-tech.[15]

The firms who won Japanese business are better-performing on average than their counterparts who did not. They are significantly more likely to both deliver and produce on a just-in-time basis. In contrast to Japanese-owned suppliers, they are also more automated than the US average. Of those respondents who felt the technology was appropriate for their firm, US-owned firms with transplant business were much more likely to be using all of the types of automation asked about in the survey: computer numerically-controlled machine tools, computer-aided design, robotics, and manufacturing cells.

US-owned suppliers felt that their relationship with the Japanese had a great deal of potential to be a mutually benefical one. Only 4 per cent agreed with the statement,[16] 'We have little to learn from our Japanese partner; all they provide is access to Japanese customers'. Conversely, only 12 per cent agreed that 'The Japanese partner has little to learn from us; all we provide is access to US customers'. The survey data did reveal, however, some indications of unease among suppliers selling to transplants. Only 56 per cent disagreed with the statement,[17] 'the Japanese transplant views us as a temporary supplier only; soon a Japanese supplier will open a plant here and they will get the business'. Only 39 per cent felt they had received 'very useful technical assistance from [their] Japanese customer'. And respondents were evenly divided on the question of whether their profits were less than those received from selling to US-owned customers: 41 per cent said they were less; 38 per cent said they were greater, and 31 per cent said they were the same.

These indications of unease came out as well in interviews with both US-owned and Japanese-owned suppliers selling to transplant assemblers. The consensus was that transplant assemblers are not in general willing to accept design modifications made by US-based suppliers, regardless of ownership. 'Toyota is very worried about customer acceptance of US production,' one American manager at a transplant supplier said to me in April 1990. 'Toyota wants to assure its customers that the cars they make in Kentucky are *exactly* the same – just as good as – the ones they ship from Japan.' This fear has caused some Japanese suppliers to feel a profit squeeze because their efforts at continuous improvement (a major source of Japanese supplier profits) are limited to areas such as packaging and factory layout which do not affect product design.[18]

In addition, while Japanese assemblers will let contracts to US-owned suppliers for individual components of a car, they seem reluctant to source subsystems from them. (MacAlinden *et al*. 1991) On the other hand, some US owned firms have found their association with the Japanese quite beneficial: their customers have helped them to adopt sophisticated methods of quality control, and to buy new equipment.

One example is a small plastic injection moulding firm in a small town in western Michigan. When I visited in the spring of 1990, it was in the process of being transformed from a family-run company which competed primarily by providing low-cost, indifferent-quality products, into a firm with a relatively high degree of technical capability. The key change agent was Nippondenso, a large Toyota subsidiary with a factory in nearby Battle Creek. Over a period of almost a year, Nippondenso had sent engineers into the plant to help the supplier restructure its layout, and improve quality and cleanliness. The firm was about to dramatically expand its technical staff by hiring a full-time packaging engineer. This move was made possible by Nippondenso's commitment to providing a stable level of demand; the impact was a reduction in cost (since the firm no longer had to use packaging identical to that used when the parts were shipped all the way from Japan), and reduced lead times, since packaging could now be specially designed to fit into the Battle Creek plant's just-in-time system.

Another example comes from General Motors. Managers at Packard Electric Division credit the assistance they got from Sumitomo Denso as one of the key events in the division's transformation from one of the worst-rated suppliers to NUMMI (the GM-Toyota joint venture in California) into one of the best.[19]

To summarize, many US-owned firms have been able to gain at least a little business with Japanese auto-assemblers in the United States. These firms are likely to be better-performing than average on several dimensions. These firms feel that mutually-beneficial relationships with their Japanese customers are possible, yet there are indications of some doubt as to whether this potential will be realized.

Compared to US firms, transplant supplier facilities are disproportionately located outside of traditional areas. Only 34 per cent of the Japanese firms in my sample were located in Ohio, Michigan or Indiana. However, almost all of the Japanese plants were established in the 1980s. The locational differences disappear if we compare the Japanese plants to 'new' US plants (those which began selling to automakers after 1983). While 66 per cent of old US plants were located in Ohio, Indiana or Michigan, only 27 per cent of new plants were.[20]

According to my data, firms have also chosen less-urban locations recently. Of US-owned business units in my sample in 1983, 71 per cent were located in a metropolitan statistical area (MSA) which had a 1988 population greater than 200,000. Of business units which began supplying automakers after 1983, only 57 per cent were. Similarly, 56 per cent of all the Japanese firms were located in large MSA's. Within the Japanese sample, there has been a marked shift since 1983. Of the twenty-three 'old' firms, 79 per cent were in large MSA's, while of the thirty-eight 'new' firms, only 32 per cent were. A striking 44 per cent of the new Japanese firms were not in MSA's at all, compared to 17 per cent of the old Japanese firms, 18 per cent of the old US firms, and 11 per cent of the new US firms.[21]

This evidence casts doubt on the Florida and Kenney (1991) thesis that 'the Japanese are rebuilding the rust belt [by] . . . making long-term commitments where US business leaders had seemed to give up hope'. The Japanese are not re-building the rust belt in the places where it is crumbling. they are not in most cases hiring workers displaced by the decline of US industry, or firms who have seen their business shrink with the Big Three's market share.[22]

What is the attraction of these new regions? There are two factors. The first is the ability to implement more efficient production methods without having first to unlearn the old.[23] Being in a new region, means workers have little automotive experience. Japanese assemblers have explicitly expressed a preference for such workers. (Fucini and Fucini 1990). The second factor is that new regions offer more opportunities to shift costs to other parties. As Howes (1991) documents, taking advantage of a young, non-union work force gives the transplants a significant cost advantage that is not related to efficiency. When these non-efficiency based cost advantages lead to the contraction of traditional US firms, society suffers a dead-weight loss: Rust Belt plants and workers are left idle while in the Sun Belt, new plants are built and new workers are trained.

Are transplant supplier jobs good jobs?

Japanese transplants demonstrate the highest percentage of high school graduates among their shop workers (99 per cent). After controlling for the complexity of their products and age of their plant, the difference remains statistically significant. The US firms which supply the Big Three or Japanese customers hire roughly the same percentage of high school graduates (80 per cent).

Total training in the Japanese transplant firms is significantly higher for US suppliers, regardless of whether their customer is American or Japanese (45 versus 40 hours). When the age of the plant and complexity of products are taken into account, the transplants continue to provide a significantly higher level of training to their workers with at least one year of experience.

Median wages vary remarkably little by category; in general, skilled workers are paid $13 per hour and unskilled or semi-skilled workers receive $9.00. A union presence is only one-fifth as likely in the transplant firms as in the Big Three suppliers.

However, Japanese-owned suppliers offer more job security. Suppliers to the Big Three are almost three times as likely as the Japanese transplants to agree that 'layoffs are an unfortunate but necessary tool for responding to business uncertainty'.

The percentage of male employees does not differ significantly across the groups. While the percentage of engineers to total employees is not large in any group, the Japanese transplants have a significantly higher percentage, especially after age and complexity are controlled.

Differences in average travelling time for maintenance technician to plant range from 4.8 to 8.7 hours, with the shortest travelling time reported by US suppliers to Japanese customers, and the longest reported by Japanese transplant firms. For General Motors suppliers, the time is about 4.8 hours. The increased travel time for Japanese-owned firms is due to their location outside the traditional auto agglomeration. The need to wait longer for repairs is one important reason why these plants had more inventory. Lack of access to skilled maintenance personnel also hampers efforts to modify machinery to obtain incremental process improvement.

To summarize, Japanese transplants provided more skilled and secure jobs according to the measures of training, attitudes regarding layoffs, and engineering usage. However, these jobs were far less likely to be unionized, and were further away from the traditional auto agglomeration.

Conclusion

Japanese transplants are having two effects on US auto parts firms. First, they promote learning by US firms, by providing 'a lean competitor located right across the road' , who can 'strip away all the cultural and economic explanations of why the other manufacturer is succeeding'. (Womack *et al.* 1990: 257). The survey results show that the demonstration effect has been fairly strong in promoting US automakers' and suppliers' use of voice.

However, the Japanese firms also pose a threat, and not only to those firms who refuse to adopt an attitude of continuous improvement. However, this

Table 10.5 Job characteristic summary results

Loss of good jobs?	US with Big Three	US with Ford/Chrysler	US with Japanese customer	Japan owned	Japanese in Japan
Median % shop workers with High School diploma	80	84	80	99	n/a
Median total training hours	40	40	40	45	n/a
Median Wage, Skilled	13	13	13	13	n/a
Median Wage, Unskilled	9	9	10	9	n/a
% Saying layoffs may be necessary	65.19	66.47	55.88	17.65	n/a
% with union presence	49.49	51.76	32.35	9.804	n/a
Median engineering/total employees	0.02892	0.03038	0.02949	0.03484	n/a
Average percentage of male shop workers	57.32	56.14	61.5	62.5	n/a
Average travelling time (in hours) for maintenance technician to get to plant	6.046	7.793	4.792	8.62	n/a

Table 10.6 Job characteristic regression results

Loss of good jobs?	JOWN	JOWN, JCUST, FC	JOWN, JCUST, FC, complex, age	Ratio of columns 2 and 4
% Shop workers with High School Diploma	15.48 (0.0001)	17.49 (0.0001)	15.33 (0.0002)	0.9903
Total training hours	51 (0.0007)	54.76 (0.0007)	46.43 (0.0047)	0.9104
Wage, skilled	−0.6976 (0.1930)	−0.536 (0.3413)	−0.08032 (0.8921)	0.1151
Wage, unskilled	−0.4901 (0.2933)	−0.5854 (0.2622)	−0.05937 (0.9096)	0.1211
Layoffs may be necessary	−2.122 (0.0001)	−2.006 (0.0001)	−1.895 (0.0001)	0.893
Union presence	−2.058 (0.0001)	−1.695 (0.0008)	−1.14 (0.0316)	0.5539
Engineering/total employees	0.013 (0.0253)	0.01719 (0.0071)	0.01995 (0.0023)	1.535
% of male shop workers	2.164 (0.5621)	0.7536 (0.8542)	4.327 (0.2965)	2
Average travelling time (in hours) for maintenance technician to get to plant	2.675 (0.3006)	3.524 (0.3085)	3.37 (0.3504)	1.26

Notes:
Coefficients on binary dependent variables result from logistic regression
Probability values are in parentheses

threat is posed by all new auto suppliers, not just Japanese entrants. Older firms, even though they may work hard at continuous improvement, face competition due to policies available disproportionately to new firms, such as hiring young workers with low health and pension costs, building plants in low-wage areas, and receiving tax abatements available only to new firms.

It should be emphasized that none of the statements about ill effects of the transplants require evil intent on the part of the Japanese. Now that political and economic pressures have caused the automakers to start producing in the United States, they must walk a tightrope between alienating their hosts in North America, and abandoning their traditional suppliers and employees who cannot easily follow the assemblers to the US.

The combined effects of US institutional structures that give preference to newcomers and Japanese commitments to give preference to long-term suppliers have left traditional US component suppliers in an unfavourable position for reasons that are not entirely due to lack of efficiency. The correct response is not to blame the Japanese for taking advantage of the situation, but to change the situation.

To the extent that the Japanese can be induced to transfer their system here, there is a double benefit: the direct benefit from having high-quality suppliers, and the indirect benefit of diffusion of continuous improvement to US firms as well. To the extent that the Japanese succeed in shifting costs to taxpayers and workers, there is a double cost: the direct cost of lost contributions to wages, fringe benefits, and taxes, and the indirect cost of forcing other firms to match these actions in order to compete.

The key for policymakers is to maximize the learning effect while minimizing regressive cost-shifting. For Womack *et al.* (1990: 255) this is not so much of a problem, since 'once a lean producer starts down the path to assembly in a major regional market, the logic of the (lean production) system tends powerfully to bring the complete complement of production activities, including product development, along as well'. However, it is not clear why this logic is powerful enough to outweigh the disadvantages of disrupting 40-year old ties with key suppliers.

A law requiring domestic content (or pressure for such a law) would simultaneously give Japanese automakers the incentive to buy more parts here, and would give them an excuse to use with their traditional suppliers about why they have reduced sourcing from them. Political pressure has already produced results, in that the Japanese have pledged to increase their US parts purchases from $9 billion in fiscal 1990 to $19 billion in fiscal 1994 (Johnson and Maskery 1992).

The cost of such political pressure will be short term inefficiency, since US suppliers are not by and large familiar with the voice system in general, nor with the ways of a Toyota or a Honda in particular. However, if the intervention is done correctly,[24] the US will eventually be able to learn the system, and embark on a new round of improvements – just as the Japanese did several decades ago, when they simultaneously protected their market and sought out foreign expertise. (Cusumano 1985)

Measures should also be taken to encourage *domestically-owned* suppliers to compete through investments in skill development rather than by seeking to shift costs to taxpayers and workers. As the cases of Mark 1 Plastics and Packard Electric show, Japanese transplants can provide significant insights into how firms can provide effective technical assistance. Public policy could encourage such efforts by providing sectoral training funds, and setting up incentives for firms to encourage employee participation (Levine and Tyson 1990).

Notes

1 Thanks to Elliot Bendoly, Patricia Clifford and Godfrey Chua for research assistance above and beyond the call of duty. Thanks also to Steve Herzenberg, Laura Leete and John Paul MacDuffie for comments. I am grateful for financial support from the Sloan Foundation, through its grant to the International Motor Vehicle Program at MIT, and from the Center for Regional Economic Issues, Case Western Reserve University.

2 By 'efficient production practices', I mean practices which produce the greatest output for the least amount of inputs, where the measures of inputs and outputs take into account all social costs and benefits. For example, suppose firm A produces more output per dollar spent on wages than firm B, and this difference occurs solely because A pays lower wages than B. In this case, A is *not* more efficient than B, because A is not using less labour input; it is simply shifting part of the benefits of production from employees to owners.

3 For more on suppliers' employee participation practices, see Helper and Levine (1994).

4 The number of observations given is for responses to the 1993 sales manager survey; fifteen suppliers did not provide information on their most important automaker customer. As noted above, the data in Japan was collected by Sako; the results presented here are drawn from Helper and Sako (1995). The data from Japan are not included in the data used to estimate regressions.

5 Florida and Kenney (1991) report that two thirds of their respondents established US plants as a result of direct invitations from their customer.

6 Since both assembler and supplier transplants are separate business units from their Japan-located parents, respondents answered this question in terms of their relationship in the United States. Therefore, in most cases the length of relationship regarding a particular product was fairly similar to the age of the plant making that product.

7 This variable was 1 if more than three-quarters of the plant's metal-cutting machinery was computer numerically controlled (CNC), and 0 otherwise. Plants that reported that CNC equipment was not applicable to their product were not included in the statistics calculated for this question.

8 These results were obtained using the Kruskal–Wallis test, a nonparametric statistical test.

9 Unless stated otherwise, all distributions summarized by means are single-peaked, and all differences in means and proportions described as 'significant' have a probability value of 0.05 or less. All statistics cited exclude missing data.

   Only twenty-three of sixty-one Japanese transplants in the 1989 sample were in business in 1984, so it might be that the changes in Japanese practice in 1989 were due to the entry of a different type of firm, rather than to changes by existing firms. However, both t-tests and Kruskal–Wallis tests show that there are no significant differences between new and old Japanese firms in terms of 1989 supplier relations practices.

10 See Dobler *et al*. (1984: ch. 15) for more on value analysis, and Asanuma (1984) for detailed discussion of its application in the Japanese auto industry.

11 More precisely, the mean is 3.10 and standard deviation is 1.021 for 'five years ago' and 3.20 and 1.067 respectively for 'now'; the difference in means is significant only at the 0.18 level.

12 Long-term contracts do not necessarily provide protection against loss of business for this reason, since many of these contracts contain what one Ford executive called 'inferior technology escape clauses'. Indeed, 34 per cent of those with contracts three years or longer thought their customers would switch as soon as technically feasible – not that much lower than the 45 per cent of respondents with contracts lasting a year or less who predicted this outcome.

13 However, the survey data give no indication of the volume of a US supplier's sales accounted for by the transplants; in most cases it is small.

14 The probability of χ^2 is 0.26; a probability of less than 0.05 is generally recognized as statistically significant.

15 Respondents were asked to answer the survey for a 'typical product', and to rate the technical complexity of that product on a 1 to 5 scale, with 5 being 'highly complex'. Of firms with Japanese customers who rated their product at 5, only 36 per cent got their contracts without forming any joint ventures with Japanese firms. Of those whose products were 1s or 2s, 78 per cent did not form joint ventures.

16 Respondents were asked to express their opinions on a 1–5 scale; 'agree' is defined as an answer of '1' or '2'.

17 That is, answered '4' or '5'.

18 On the profit squeeze see Cusumano and Takeishi (1992). Interviews with Honda and Toyota suppliers in 1993 and 1994 indicated that the assemblers were becoming more willing to accept design modifications as they gained confidence in their US operations, and as they began to produce some car models exclusively in the US. However, American managers at both suppliers and automakers described these negotiations as very tough.

19 Interviews at Packard Electric, Warren, Ohio, November 1991. See also Nishiguchi (1990) and Frank Gillett (1992).

20 My 1989 Japanese sample is biased toward firms located in Ohio, so the percentage located in traditional states is biased upward somewhat. The conclusions that can be drawn with a good deal of certainty are two: Japanese plants are less likely to be in Ohio, Indiana, or Michigan than the US average, but the differential shrinks when only new plants are considered.

21 There is no evidence that my Japanese sample is biased in the urban/rural direction.

22 Kenney *et al*. (1988) recognize the rural bias of the Japanese, but this point is not made in their later work.

23 However, to the extent that one of the things which doesn't have to be unlearned in new regions is a belief in bargaining hard with management, 'unlearning' also belongs in the redistribution category below.

24 A place to start might be Howes' (1991) suggestion that for each greenfield plant the Japanese are allowed to build, they must rehabilitate a brownfield plant.

References

Abernathy, W. and Clark, K. (1985) 'Mapping the winds of creative destruction'. *Research Policy* 14 (February): 3–22.

Abernathy, W., Clark, K. and Kantrow, A. (1983) *Industrial Renaissance*, New York: Basic Books.

Abernathy, W. and Wayne, K. (1974) 'The limits of the learning curve'. *Harvard Business Review* 52 (September–October) 109–119.

Andrea, D. Hervey, R. and Luria, D. (1986) 'The capacity explosion: implications for Michigan suppliers', *Auto in Michigan Newsletter* 1 (March): 6–8.

Asanuma, B. (1984) 'A contractual framework for parts supply in the Japanese auto industry', *Japan Economic Studies* Summer: 32–53.

Clark, K. (1989) 'Project scope and project performance: the effects of parts strategy and supplier involvement on product development', *Management Science* 35 (October): 1,247–63.

Cole, R.E. and Yakushiji, T. (eds) (1984) *The American and Japanese Auto Industries in Transition*, Ann Arbor, MI: Joint US-Japan Automotive Study, University of Michigan.

Conover, W. (1971) *Nonparametric Statistics*, New York: Wiley.

Cusumano, M. (1985) *The Japanese Automobile Industry*, Cambridge, MA: Harvard University Press.

Cusumano, M. A. and Takeishi, A. (1991) 'Supplier relations and management: a study of Japanese, Japanese transplant, and US auto plants', *Strategic Management Journal* 12: 563–88.

Dobler, D., Lee, L. and Burt, D. (1984) *Purchasing and Materials Management*, 4th edn, New York: McGraw-Hill.

Economic Strategy Institute (1992) *The Case for Saving the Big Three*, Washington, DC: Economic Strategy Institute.

Fucini, J, and Fucini, S. (1990) *Working for the Japanese: Inside Mazda's American Auto Plant*, New York: Free Press.

Florida, R. and Kenney, M. (1991) 'Transplanted organizations: the transfer of Japanese industrial organization to the US', *Am. Soc. Review* 56 (June): 381–98.

Gillett, F. (1992) 'The integrating supplier', Master's Thesis, MIT Sloan School of Management.

Heim, C. (1986) 'External spheres and the theory of capitalist development', *Social Concept* 3, 2 (December): 3–42.

Helper, S. (1991a) 'How much has really changed between US automakers and their suppliers?', *Sloan Management Review* 32, 4 (Summer): 15–28.

—— (1991b) 'Strategy and irreversibility in supplier relations: the case of the US automobile industry', *Business History Review* 65, 4 (Winter): 781–824.

—— (1994) 'Three steps forward, two steps back in supplier relations', *Technovation* 14, 10 (October): 633–40.

—— (1995) 'Supplier relations and investment in automation: results of survey research in the US auto industry', Cambridge, MA: National Bureau of Economic Research, Working Paper 5278.

—— (1996) 'Incentives for supplier participation in product development', in T. Nishiguchi (ed.) *Managing Product Development*, Oxford: Oxford University Press, pp 165–189.

Helper, S. and Levine, D.I. (1992) 'Long-term supplier relationships and product market structure', *Journal of Law, Economics, and Organization* 8, 3 (October): 561–81.

—— (1994), 'Supplier participation and worker participation: is there a linkage?', Industrial Relations Research Association *Proceedings* pp. 12–25.

Helper, S. and Sako, M. (1995) 'Supplier relations in the auto industry: a limited US-Japan convergence', *Sloan Management Review* 36, 3 (Spring): 77–84.

Herzenberg, S. (1991) 'Continental integration and the future of the North American auto sector', US Department of Labor photocopy.

Hirschman, A. (1950) *The Strategy of Economic Development*, New Haven, CT: Yale University Press.

—— (1970) *Exit, Voice, and Loyalty*, Cambridge, MA: Harvard University Press.

Howes, C.(1991) 'The benefits of youth: the role of Japanese fringe benefit policies in the restructuring of the US motor vehicle industry', *International Contributions to Labour Studies* 1: 113–32.

—— (1993a) *Japanese Auto Transplants and the US Automobile Industry*, Washington: Economic Policy Institute.

—— (1993b) 'Constructing comparative disadvantage: lessons from the US automobile industry', in H. Noponen *et al.* (eds) *Trading Industries, Trading Regions*, New York: Guilford Press.

Johnson, R. and Maskery, M. (1992) 'Japan torpedoes big three hopes', *Automotive News* 13 January: 1.

Kaserman (1978) 'Theories of vertical integration', *Antitrust Bulletin* Fall.

Kearns, R.(1992) *Zaibatsu America*, New York: Free Press.

Kenney, M. and Florida, R. (1991) 'How Japanese industry is rebuilding the rust belt', *Technology Review*, February/March.

—— (1994) *Beyond Mass Production: The Japanese System and its Transfer to the US*, Oxford: Oxford University Press.

Kenney, M., Florida, R. and Mair, A. (1988) 'The transplant phenomenon: Japanese auto manufacturers in the United States', *Economic Development Commentary* 12, 4: 3–9.

Kingsolver, A. (1993) 'Tobacco, textiles, and Toyota: working for MNC's in rural Kentucky', photocopy, Lawrence University.

Levine, D.I. and Tyson, L.D. (1990) 'Participations, productivity, and the firm's environment', in A. Blinder (ed.) *Paying for Productivity*, Washington, DC: Brookings Institution.

Levine, D.I. and Helper, S. (1995) 'A quality policy for America', *Contemporary Economic Policy* 13, 2 (April): 26–37.

Lieberman, M., Helper, S. and Demeester, L. (1995) 'The empirical determinants of inventory levels in high-volume manufacturing', UCLA Anderson Graduate School of Management Working Paper.

McAlinden, S. *et al.* (1991) 'The US Japan automotive bilateral 1994 trade deficit', Ann Arbor, MI: Office for the Study of Automotive Transportation, University of Michigan Transportation Research Institute (UMTRI), Report No. 91–20.

Milward, H. and Newman, H. (1989) 'State incentive packages and the industrial location decision', *Economic Development Quarterly* 3 (August): 203–22.

Monahan, J, and Pickens, B. (1991) *Keiretsu, USA: A Tale of Japanese Power*, Cincinnati: Mid-America Project.

Nishiguchi, T. (1990) *Strategic Industrial Sourcing: The Japanese Advantage*. Oxford: Oxford University Press.

Odaka, K. Ono, K. and Adachi, F. (1988) *The Automobile Industry in Japan: A Study of Ancillary Firm Development*, Oxford: Oxford University Press.

Piore, M, and Sabel, C. (1984) *The Second Industrial Divide*, New York: Basic Books.

Porter, M. (1983) *Cases in Competitive Strategy*, New York: Free Press.

Sako, M. (1992) *Prices, Quality and Trust: Interfirm Relations in Britain and Japan*, Cambridge: Cambridge University Press.

Schonberger, R. (1984) *Japanese Manufacturing Techniques*, New York: Free Press.

Smitka, M. (1991) *Competitive Ties*, New York: Columbia University Press.

Williamson, O.(1975) *Markets and Hierarchies*, New York: Free Press.

—— (1985) *The Economic Institutions of Capitalism*, New York: Free Press.

Womack, J., Jones, D. and Roos, D. (1990) *The Machine that Changed the World*, New York: Rawson Associates.

11

CUSTOMER–SUBCONTRACTOR RELATIONSHIPS†

Emilio Esposito and Mario Raffa

Introduction

Subcontracting has undergone a remarkable development at national and international level in the last 30 years: from the traditional to the current approach.[1]

The traditional approach, dates back to the 1960s and the notion of subcontracting was strictly linked to the notion of development of a certain area. In their original accepted meanings both these notions are related to the possible industrial and territorial effects arising from development policies focused on the large firm as a catalyst for development (Ferrando 1984). In this framework 'Perroux's polarized development theory' was clearly crucial in explaining the subcontracting role within the industrial system. Many authors highlighted different forms of subcontracting (Sallez and Schlegel 1963; Vennin 1975; Sallez 1975, 1977; Chaillou 1977; Barthomieu *et al.* 1983): *capacity subcontracting* ('sous-traitance concurrence – ou de capacité'), when the customer, unable to achieve the desired production level in-house, acquires an additional labour capacity from a subcontractor; *specialization subcontracting* ('sous-traitance complementaire ou de spécialité'), when the subcontractor provides the customer with techniques other than the ones used by the customer itself; *Supply-type subcontracting*, when design, methods,

† This paper was funded by CNR 93.03543.CT11, CNR Strategic Project 'Trasferimento delle tecnologie dei progetti finalizzati', MURST 60 per cent 1992 and 40 per cent 1993.

A previous version of this paper was presented at the workshop of Economia and Management, 'Information technology e nuovi rapporti strategici cliente fornitore', held in Milan on 16 December 1993. This version includes comments by some speakers (M. Colombo, R. Ferrata, A. Grandi, S. Mariotti, G.L. Marzocchi, S. Meregalli and A. Zanoni) and discussants (L. Chevallard from Fiat Auto, A. Neviani from Aermacchi and B. Zuccaro from Benetton Group).

Even though the paper is the result of joint research by the two authors, the sections 'Methodology of the research' and 'Evaluation model of the inter-firm technology transfer channels', are written by M. Raffa, and 'Structural characteristics of the Italian subcontracting system' and 'The trend of the Italian subcontracting system', by E. Esposito.

development and manufacturing are contracted out, this subcontracting is quite similar to what is currently defined as *complex subcontracting* (Del Monte 1991) or *fully developed subcontracting* (Saget 1988; De Maio and Maggiore 1992; Esposito and Raffa 1992, 1993).

In the 1980s, literature on subcontracting issues (current approach) was highly influenced by the debate on inter-firm relationships, particularly on the inter-firm 'vertical relationships' and their 'hybrid forms of management'. Studies on subcontracting were influenced by the transaction costs theory (Williamson 1979, 1985), by the theory of the firm as a set of contracts (Klein *et al.* 1978) and by the co-operative game theory of the firm (Aoki 1984).[2] More recently, many authors devoted much of their attention to the Japanese industrial system based on fully developed strategic alliances between large firms (Fletcher 1993; Teece 1992; Samson 1993), large and small firms (Lawton Smith *et al.* 1991; Minato 1992, MITI 1991) customers and subcontractors (Sako 1988, 1992; Asanuma 1989; David 1990; Imrie and Morris 1992; Morris 1992; Lecler 1992; Oliver and Wilkinson 1992; Morris and Imrie 1993; Colombo and Mariotti 1994). They have also pointed out that in the 1990s the subcontracting phenomenon has developed rapidly and subcontractors have become more and more crucial to the large firms' innovation strategies (Aoki 1988; Lamming 1993).[3] Mutual trust, that develops through shared knowledge and the exchange of information and technology, is the foundation of the organizational and cultural change related to the development of new customer–subcontractor relationships[4]

The research presented in this chapter aims to evaluate the degree to which Italian subcontracting systems are interested in the ongoing transformations of international industrial systems. In particular, the paper analyses the variety and specificity of relationships between the firms involved in the subcontracting chain using an evaluation model of the technology transfer channels developed by the authors (Esposito and Raffa 1991, 1994). It also highlights an issue that has so far been given little attention in studies of subcontracting firms, i.e.: to what extent the size of the subcontracting firm and the specificity of the customer's industrial sectors affect the relationship-based system.

The research carried out by ODISSEO (Centre for Organization and Technological Innovation) started in 1986 and has so far involved seventy-eight Italian subcontractors and their customers. After presenting the research methodology, this chapter illustrates a model to evaluate inter-firm technology transfer and the results of the field-survey. Structural characteristics of the Italian subcontracting system and the trend of the Italian subcontracting systems are then analysed.

Methodology of the research

This chapter is based on research started in 1986 and still in progress. The stages of the research are illustrated in Figure 11.1. The survey was carried out using a structured questionnaire. All data was collected and updated through interviews with the firm's top management and by means of frequent meetings and visits to the companies. For this paper only some items of the questionnaire sections were used.

The subcontractors in the sample carry out subcontracting (parts, components and finished products) for several large customers (Augusta, Alenia, Alfa Avio, Ansaldo, FF.SS., Fiat, Magnaghi, Olivetti, Sip) performing in very different sectors, such as the automobile, the aircraft, the telecommunications and mechanical industries (Table 11.1). In any case, all these customers share the need to manufacture products that must meet demanding requirements of quality, reliability and safety (although with a different mix in each industry).

The customers and subcontractors of the field survey are typical of the 'subcontracting phenomenon in the Italian medium/high-tech industries for several reasons':

- from the 'industrial standpoint': the sample includes subcontractors working for completely different industries. The sample includes the automobile industry, typified by high process innovation and high production lots; the aircraft industry, typified by an intensive research and development activity and low production lots; the telecommunications/ electronics industry with intermediate characteristics between the auto- mobile and aircraft industry (Table 11.1). The sample is highly significant. In fact, in the automobile industry sample there are fifteen firms included in the Fiat automobile's top twenty quality list; in the aircraft industry the sample includes fifteen out of twenty main subcon- tracting firms operating in compliance with specifications and regulations set by the main Italian customers; in the telecommunications/electronics sector, the firms studied in this survey represent about 50 per cent of the main industry's subcontracting firms;
- from the 'territorial standpoint': the sample includes enterprises located throughout the national territory. The subcontracting firms based in Northern Italy are forty-three while the remaining thirty-five are based in Southern Italy (Table 11.2);
- from the 'size standpoint': as regards the distribution by class of employees the sample represents differently sized subcontractors. In fact eighteen firms (out of seventy-eight) have fewer than twenty employees, thirty-one firms have 21–50 employees, eight firms have 51–100 employees and twenty-one firms have more than 100 employees (Table 11.2).
- from the 'type of subcontracting' standpoint: the sample includes both traditional and complex subcontracting. The distribution of the subcon- tractors' production activities, i.e., the range of the technologies used in subcontracting is wide (Table 11.3). Precision mechanical parts manufac- turing is the prevailing activity (twenty-seven firms); this reflects

Figure 11.1 The stages of the research

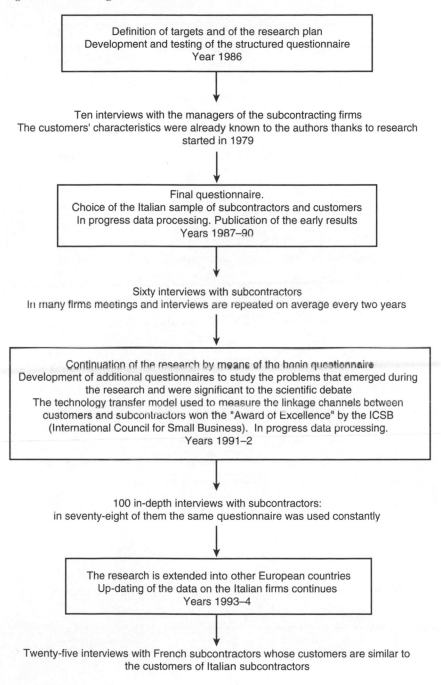

Table 11.1 Main customers of the seventy-eight investigated subcontracting firms

Main customers	Sector	Number of firms	% of firms
Augusta	Aircraft	5	6.4
Alenia Telecommunications	TLC/electronics	8	10.3
Alenia Aircraft	Aircraft	16	20.5
Alfa Avio	Aircraft	4	5.1
Ansaldo	Transportation	5	6.4
FF.SS.	Transportation	4	5.1
Fiat	Automobile	24	30.8
Fiat Iveco	Transportation	3	3.9
Magnaghi	Aircraft	10	12.8
Olivetti	TLC/electronics	7	9.0
Other firms in the:			
Aircraft industry	Aircraft	9	11.5
Automobile industry	Automobile	26	33.3
Agroindustrial machines industry	Mechanical	6	7.7
Electromechanical industry	Mechanical	9	11.5
Mechanical industry	Mechanical	22	28.2
Mechanical-textile industry	Mechanical	6	7.7
Motorcycle industry	Motorcycle	3	3.9
TLC industry	TLC/electronics	11	7.7
Transportation industry	Transportation	6	7.7
Various industries		18	23.1

Source: ODISSEO-DIS, Faculty of Engineering, University of Naples, Italy.

Table 11.2 Distribution of the seventy-eight investigated subcontractors by class of employees and geographical location

Class of employees	Southern Italy	Northern Italy	Total of firms	
			Number	%
up to 20	6	12	18	23.1%
20–50	19	12	31	39.7%
51–100	2	6	8	10.3%
more than 100	8	13	21	26.9%
Total of firms	35	43	78	100.0%
%	44.9%	55.1%	100.0%	

Source: ODISSEO-DIS, Faculty of Engineering, University of Naples, Italy.

subcontracting reality (i.e., firms often manufacture parts and components assembled by the customer). This takes place both in traditional and
high-tech industries; in fact fifteen firms manufacture precision mechanical parts for the aircraft industry. In addition to these firms that supply
manufacturing skills by means of machine tools (numerical control lathes
and cutters, work stations, etc.) there are also several firms supplying
complex technological skills such as assembly of mechanical parts (eight
firms), skilled assembly (five firms), manufacturing of electric and electronic equipment (seven firms), iron powder manufacturing (two firms)
and composite material manufacturing (five firms);[5]

- from the 'customers' strategic projects' standpoint: the sample includes
  subcontractors on which customers rely to establish well-developed
  subcontracting relationships (De Maio, Maggiore 1992);

Table 11.3 Production activities of the seventy-eight investigated subcontracting
firms

Production activities	Number of firms	% of firms
Mechanical parts assembly	8	10.3
Specialized assembly	5	6.4
Equipment	6	7.7
Looms and/or electric assembly	3	3.9
Medium/light carpentry	9	11.5
Electric boards	1	1.3
Electric/electronic equipment manufacturing	7	9.0
Die manufacturing	5	6.4
Rubber manufacturing	2	2.6
Sheet manufacturing	3	3.9
Composite material manufacturing	5	6.4
Plastic material manufacturing	6	7.7
Precision mechanical parts manufacturing	27	34.6
Aircraft precision mechanical parts manufacturing	15	19.2
Light alloy manufacturing	9	11.5
Iron powder manufacturing	2	2.6
Welding	3	3.9
Dies	4	5.1
Aircraft painting	2	2.6
Other	14	18.0

Source: ODISSEO-DIS, Faculty of Engineering, University of Naples, Italy.

- from the 'sample stratification' standpoint: the sample includes subcontractors positioned all along the subcontracting chain.

Evaluation model of the inter-firm technology transfer channels

To analyse the wide range of customer–subcontractor and inter-subcontractor relationships the technology transfer model between two firms was used (Esposito and Raffa 1991, 1994). In this model the channels through which two firms communicate are viewed as vehicles for transferring the various technology components (Allen 1988; Badaracco 1991) (Figure 11.2).

The firm's technology is seen as a set of knowledge embodied in hardware systems, software systems, and human resources (The Technology Atlas Team 1987). This implies a systematic application of various categories: 'machinery', 'professional skills', 'information', and 'organizational rules'. The 'machinery' category includes all technologies embodied in objects, components, parts, equipment and systems; the 'professional skills' category includes all person-embodied technologies, i.e., the whole set of human skills; in the 'information' category, are placed the technologies embodied in the form of ideas and information recorded in manuals, articles, memoranda and any other written documentation; and the 'organizational rules' category includes all technologies embodied in the form of procedures and organizational linkages.

This model allows both 'tangible and intangible technological categories' to be measured. In general by measuring the specificity of the channels content, the model allows us to represent the 'complexity of the inter-firm relationships'. Indeed, even when firms' technologies are homogeneous, relationships are still typified by high specificity, as the firm's history and its managerial characteristics affect the relation development pattern. Moreover, the type of product and service supplied by the customer is related to the characteristics of its subcontracting firms. Even the efficiency and effectiveness of the relationships are linked to the type of channel being used.

The field survey enables us to 'identify eleven channels through which the various technology components are transferred between customer and subcontractor':

- raw materials (i.e., special alloy, composite materials);
- pre-finished parts and components;
- specific processing equipment (i.e., scribing and drilling templates, master and inspection templates, jigs);
- assistance to the subcontractor on specific issues (i.e., production cycle, quality management);
- customer's visits and suggestions (i.e., adoption of new technologies);

- collaboration at the beginning of the order, through which the customer transfers the programme philosophy and receives suggestions;
- written documents (i.e., documents, papers, drawings, and schemes related to the programme);
- meetings held at the customer's site (i.e., to solve specific production cycle problems);
- customer's visits to check the state of the order (and to monitor the subcontractor's capability);
- suggestions by the customer to adopt a quality control system (QCS);
- direct intervention by the customer to improve QCS.

There is no one-to-one relationship between technology transfer channels and technology categories. Each channel usually directly affects more than one technology category as well as indirectly affecting all technology categories. Therefore the relationship is one-to-many.

Through this technology transfer model the different characteristics of the subcontracting system were highlighted.

Structural characteristics of the Italian subcontracting system

The model of Figure 11.2 was used to analyse:

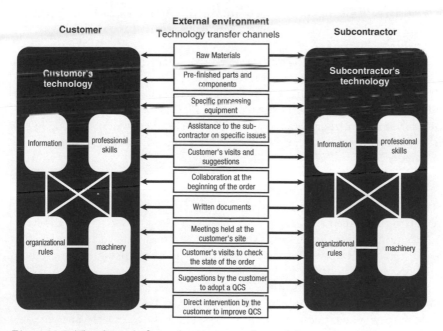

Figure 11.2 The channels for technology-transfer model

a   the intensity of the customer–subcontractor 'collaboration';
b   the relationship asymmetry, by means of examples concerning some major
     Italian industries;
c   the subcontractor's share of turnover which is business from the customer.

Intensity of the customer–subcontractor collaboration

The intensity of the collaborative relationship is the basic factor that differen-
tiates modern subcontracting systems from traditional ones. The intensity of
these linkages was measured by assessing the number and the importance of
technology transfer channels used in the linkage between the two firms. The
following index was used:

$$DOC = (\Sigma_{1.11} \, C_i \times I_i) / 99$$

in which:

DOC: degree of collaboration between customer and subcontractor;
C_i: channel 'i', it is equal to zero (if it is not used) or one (if it is used);
I_i: Importance of the channel 'i' for technology transfer, it takes a value from 1
      (not important) to 9 (very important).

The measurement index ranges from a minimum value of 0, when no
channel is used, to a value of 1 when all channels are used and their importance
is very high.

Tables 11.4 and 11.5 exhibit how the index changes according to the class
of employees and the customer's industry.

Table 11.4 illustrates that the 'intensity of the collaborative relationship is
independent of the subcontractor's size'; in fact, as to the first customer, the
intensity of the collaboration is equal to 0.60 on average, while it is 0.63 in the
firms with more than 100 employees and 0.53 in the firms with fewer than 20
employees.[6]

Table 11.5 illustrates that the intensity of the collaboration between the
subcontractor and the customer is strictly related to the customer's industrial
sector. The collaboration relationship is equal to 0.83 in the aircraft industry,
to 0.66 in the telecommunication/electronics industry and to 0.59 in the automobile industry. Finally the firms subcontracting to several customers, as they
do not establish favoured relationships with a specific customer, have looser
collaboration relationships (0.45).[7]

Synthetically, the results of the survey point out that the 'intensity of the
collaborative relationship is high and independent of the firm's size'. Moreover,
while the new subcontracting phenomenon seems to be transversal and involves
all industrial sectors, the customer's industrial sector, and consequently its

related technologies, 'play a major role in the type and intensity of the collaboration relationship between customer and subcontractors'.

Customer–subcontractor asymmetric relationships

The 'degree of utilization of the technology transfer channels' shows that new subcontracting relationships, unlike traditional ones, are typified by a significant exchange of the four technology components (machinery, organizational rules, professional skills and information). The use of these channels allows the

Table 11.4 Degree of collaboration between the seventy-eight subcontracting firms and the first two customers, by class of employees

Class of employees	Degree of collaboration	
	1° Customer	2° Customer
up to 20	0.53	0.29
20–50	0.62	0.55
51–100	0.59	0.57
more than 100	0.63	0.38
Total of firms	0.60	0.45

Source: ODISSEO-DIS, Faculty of Engineering, University of Naples, Italy.

Note:
Correlation between the subcontractor's size and the degree of customer subcontractor collaboration is not significant (r = 0.18)

Table 11.5 Degree of collaboration between the seventy-eight subcontracting firms and the first two customers, by industries

Industry	Degree of collaboration	
	1° Customer	2° Customer
Aircraft	0.83	0.65
Automobile	0.59	0.34
Telecommunications/electronics	0.66	0.51
Other mechanical industries	0.44	0.38
Others	0.45	0.33
Average	0.60	0.45

Source: ODISSEO-DIS, Faculty of Engineering, University of Naples, Italy.

Note:
The calculated value of Kruskal–Wallis' test ($\chi^2 = 42.4$) has a probability of occurring of less than 0.1 per cent. We conclude therefore that the observed difference between the five industries is statistically significant

customer to manage all of the co-ordination mechanisms (direct monitoring, mutual adjustment, process standardization) needed to run a complex system where firms with different characteristics and experience are involved (Table 11.6).

Table 11.6 Degree of utilization of the technology transfer channels between the subcontractor and its first two most important customers by industry

Technology transfer channels	Industry	Aircraft		Automobile		TLC/electronics		Other mechanical	
		Customer		Customer		Customer		Customer	
		First	Second	First	Second	First	Second	First	Second
Raw materials		0.90	0.75	0.16	0.21	0.29	0.00	0.18	0.14
Pre-finished parts and components		0.70	0.50	0.21	0.11	0.57	0.14	0.27	0.14
Specific processing equipment		0.60	0.45	0.26	0.16	0.43	0.29	0.23	0.09
Assistance to the subcontractor on specific issue		0.65	0.30	0.42	0.16	0.29	0.29	0.09	0.09
Customer's visit and suggestions		0.75	0.55	0.68	0.37	0.86	0.57	0.55	0.41
Collaboration at the beginning of the order		0.80	0.70	0.95	0.58	0.86	0.86	0.82	0.68
Written documents		1.00	0.90	0.89	0.53	1.00	1.00	0.86	0.82
Meetings held at the customer's site		0.85	0.75	0.84	0.47	0.71	0.71	0.32	0.41
Customer's visit to check the state of the order		1.00	0.85	0.89	0.58	0.71	0.86	0.82	0.73
Suggestions by the customer to adopt a QCS		1.00	0.75	0.63	0.32	0.57	0.29	0.27	0.32
Direct intervention by the customer to improve QCS		0.90	0.65	0.58	0.32	1.00	0.57	0.45	0.41

Source: ODISSEO-DIS, Faculty of Engineering, University of Naples, Italy.

Note:
The index equals 0 if no firms uses the channel or 1 if all firms use it

In particular, it emerges that:

- 'in the subcontracting relationships soft channels' (collaboration at the beginning of the order, customer's visits and suggestions, customer's visits to check the state of the order, assistance to the subcontractor on specific issues, meetings held at the customer's site, suggestions by the customer to adopt a quality control system, direct intervention by the customer to improve QCS) 'are as used as hard channels' (raw materials, pre-finished parts and components, specific processing equipment, written documents). This means that 'both tangible and intangible technology components are crucial';
- 'collaboration is not limited to the first stages of the order' (collaboration at the beginning of the order, written documents) but 'continues in the successive stages' as well (assistance to the subcontractor on specific issues, meetings held at the customer's site);
- even though the main linkage channel is represented by 'written documents', through which the subcontractors receive drawings and specifications for the order, the high usage of the 'visit and suggestion' channel shows the stability of the new relationship and the 'mutual participation and involvement' needed to obtain a quality product;
- while subcontracting relationships are stable and close it must be emphasized that subcontractors establish 'asymmetrical relationships' with the various customers: that is, the relationship with the first customer is usually closer than the relationship with their second and third customer, by so doing subcontractors may use the know-how acquired and/or developed through the collaboration with their 'first customer' to obtain a greater bargaining power with their 'second customer'. The subcontractor thus becomes a vehicle for the circulation of technological skills.

Table 11.6 also shows that the evolution and transformation of subcontracting differs according to the industrial sector. Applying the technology transfer model to different industrial sectors it emerges that the structural differences of the industrial sectors and thus of the various customers, affect the type of collaboration with subcontractors.

For example, in the 'automobile industry',[8] collaboration is high in the first stages of the order and declines slightly in the following stages. The most frequent technology-transfer channels used between the customer and the subcontractor are written documents defining the order and collaboration at the beginning of the order. Both these channels are crucial in the first stages of subcontracting, when standards, specifications and other issues are analysed. The customer also gives suggestions and/or directly intervenes to implement the quality system. This indicates that the customer-subcontractor relationship in the automobile industry is oriented towards forms of collaboration which are typical of the new subcontracting relationship.

In the 'aircraft industry', [9] the consistently high usage of all the technology-transfer channels denotes a high technology exchange between customer and subcontractor. Unlike the automobile industry, collaboration is high also during order execution. A major role is played by written documents and suggestions to adopt and improve the subcontractor's quality system.

The customer's weight in the subcontractor's turnover

The literature agrees that relationships between subcontractors and customers are more balanced than in the past (Hallén et al. 1991; Lamming 1993; Raffa 1992; Scott and Westbrook 1991). Nevertheless, when the specificity of the relational investment is high (Williamson 1979) and the subcontracting demand is focused on a few customers, subcontractors' dependence is high.

The data from our survey confirms that subcontracting is focused on a few large customers although the weight of the first two customers in the subcontractors' turnover is not homogeneous (Table 11.7). Specifically, the first two customers play a major role in the aircraft and automobile industries. In fact, allowing for the weight of the first two customers in the turnover of the subcontractors investigated, it emerges that it amounts to 78.4 per cent in the aircraft industry and to 82.1 per cent in the automobile industry, while it is lower in the telecommunications/electronics industry (57.8 per cent) and in other mechanical sectors (63.6 per cent).[10]

Moreover, our survey shows that the weight of the customer in the subcontractor's turnover has not modified in the last few years. In fact, five years before the weight of the first customer was 56.1 per cent in the aircraft industry, 63.8 per cent in the automobile sector, 37.0 per cent in the

Table 11.7 Weight of the first two customers on the seventy-eight subcontractors' turnover by industries

Industry	% Sales turnover	
	1° Customer	2° Customer
Aircraft	59.1	19.3
Automobile	67.2	14.9
Telecommunications/electronic	36,4	21.4
Other mechanical industries	44.5	19.1
Others	17.8	12.2
Average	49.6	17.6

Source: ODISSEO-DIS, Faculty of Engineering, University of Naples, Italy.

Note:
The calculated value of Kruskal–Wallis' test ($\chi^2 = 35.7$) has a probability of occurring of less than 0.1 per cent. We conclude therefore that the observed difference between the five industries is statistically significant

telecommunications/electronics industry and 44.4 per cent in the other mechanical sectors.

This last fact shows that, although the process of focusing of the subcontractor's turnover on a few large customers involves all industries, it does not emerge as an overall tendency towards a higher focusing.

Table 11.8 shows that, on average, the weight of the first two customers is high (about 67 per cent of the subcontractor's turnover) and independent of the subcontractor's size. This clearly shows that, even though to different weight, subcontractors because of technical reasons (need to get adjusted to the customer's technologies, quality system and culture) and economic reasons (hope of getting constant orders through favoured relationships) focus their activities on a few customers.

Obviously, subcontractors to win constant orders try to establish close relationships with the first customer. Also, customers need reliable firms to establish long-term relationships. Consequently, relational investment is high, as is mutual dependence. To offset this dependence subcontractors try to achieve a position within the subcontracting chain corresponding to their strategy.

The trend of the Italian subcontracting system

Subcontracting stratification

Relationships among subcontractors are increasingly structured as a pyramid at whose summit there are a few co-maker firms that have close collaboration relationships with the customers (Sako 1988). The customer usually intervenes

Table 11.8 Weight of the first two customers in the seventy-eight subcontractors' turnover by class of employees

Class of employees	% Sales turnover	
	1° Customer	2° Customer
up to 20	49.3	18.8
20–50	43.4	18.2
51–100	42.4	15.9
more than 100	62.7	16.4
Total of firms	49.6	17.6

Source: ODISSEO-DIS, Faculty of Engineering, University of Naples, Italy.

Note:
Correlation between subcontractor's size and percentage of sales turnover is not significant ($r = 0.16$)

directly in its dealings with the first level firms of the subcontracting chain by pressing for the implementation of manufacturing and quality management systems that are consistent with its own. It also stimulates such implementation through the various technology transfers (i.e., suggestions, direct intervention, training). These subcontractors manufacture – and sometimes even design – complex components for the customer. Some of them establish collaborative relationships with other subcontractors and are positioned at the summit of the chain, thus co-ordinating a network at whose base there are many other subcontractors (Esposito and lo Storto 1992). The field survey shows that these relationships involve the following: transfer of a significant share of the production cycle (fifty-one firms out of seventy-eight) from one subcontractor to another; exchange of technical information (twenty-six firms); collaboration for product development (twenty-eight firms); establishment of consortia (seventeen firms). The firm decides to contract out some stages of its production cycle because of technological and economic factors, the need to be lean, and temporary saturation of its own production capacity.

The transfer of production activities from one subcontractor to another implies the transfer of technical specifications, of support for quality management and, in some cases, of technicians. The stratification of the subcontracting relationship, and the strong collaboration between the parties involved, indicate a dynamic and heterogeneous subcontracting system where the firms play different roles, implement different strategies and have different behaviour. To the single subcontractor, climbing up to the summit of the subcontracting chain is neither easy nor linear. Furthermore it implies a 'strategy envisaging collaborative and competitive relationships with the other subcontractors'. A firm, climbing the subcontracting chain, achieves strategic positions vis-à-vis its customer, thus gaining a competitive edge over the lower level subcontractors. This competitive edge is useful also during economic crises when the customer – in a period of stagnation and declining orders – will reduce, or even get rid of non strategic linkages, while carefully avoiding getting rid of relationships whose re-establishment would take a long time and might strongly affect the customer's activity in the economic recovery stage.

From manufacturing to design

As suggested by many authors, in order to analyse how subcontracting is shifting from simple 'manufacturing' to 'design', we broke down the subcontractor's activity into its business functions: design, manufacturing, marketing (Barthomieu et al. 1983; Chaillou 1977; Asanuma 1989). Tables 11.9 and 11.10 illustrate the outcomes by industrial sector and class of employees and show that fifty-six subcontractors out of seventy-eight perform only the manufacturing function (traditional subcontracting)[11]; fourteen firms perform design of parts and components as well (complex subcontracting)[12];

eight firms perform the whole cycle, from component design to manufacturing and marketing (from complex subcontracting to supply).

The phenomenon of some firms going through various subcontracting forms (from traditional to fully developed subcontracting and supply) is taking hold in Italy as well. Eight firms of our sample followed this path and are now performing the marketing function that supports the selling on the market of components designed and manufactured by them. This is important as it summarizes the growth process undergone by some subcontractors that through their relationship with the customer grow, develop design activities, and finally enter the market autonomously. This is the case, for example, with several component manufacturers in the automobile industry.

As to the design function, Table 11.9 shows the specificity of the various industrial sectors.[13] In the aircraft industry eighteen firms out of twenty perform only manufacturing, while two also design some components ordered by the customer. In the automobile industry the situation is just the opposite: out of nineteen firms that can be ranked as subcontractors for the industry, seven perform only manufacturing and twelve perform design functions as well (four out of these twelve also perform the marketing function).[14]

Table 11.10 highlights diversities as to class of employees. Smaller firms with fewer than twenty employees are focused on manufacturing, while larger firms with more than 100 employees develop the design function as well; in our case thirteen firms out of twenty-one.

Empirical evidence shows that Italian subcontracting is not homogeneous. There are remarkable 'sectorial asymmetries'.

In the aircraft industry, that is characterized by small production lots, high quality standards and high technology level. Subcontracting is mainly focused on manufacturing and the exchange of technology plays a major role. In the automobile industry, that is characterized by enormous lots of production and a lower level of quality and technology, subcontracting firms are deeply rooted in the production cycle of the large customer (in fact they are even involved in the design of some parts and components) and delivery time plays a major role.

These differences indicate the difficulties that may meet a model of vertical relationship – successful under specific industrial conditions – when applied to other industrial conditions. In particular, many difficulties may arise when the models of vertical relationship being used in the automobile industry (e.g., the 'lean supply model') are applied to other industries (e.g., the aircraft industry). Difficulties will be greater when the structural characteristics of the subcontracting system of the application sector are very different from the subcontracting system of the automobile industry.

Results and conclusion

This research shows that subcontracting in Italy has undergone a significant evolution that involves all industrial sectors, although to a different extent.

Table 11.9 Firm's functions in the seventy-eight subcontractors by industries

Industry	Number of firms		
	Manufacturing	Design	Marketing
Aircraft	20	2	0
Automobile	19	12	4
Telecommunications/electronics	7	3	1
Other mechanical industries	22	4	2
Others	10	1	1
Total	78	22	8

Source: ODISSEO-DIS, Faculty of Engineering, University of Naples, Italy.

Note:
The Fisher test, between automobile and aircraft industry, shows that a significant difference is proven (test value better than P = 1 per cent)

Table 11.10 Firm's functions in the seventy-eight subcontractors by class of employees

Class of employees	Number of firms		
	Manufacturing	Design	Marketing
up to 20	18	1	2
20–50	31	5	2
51–100	8	3	1
more than 100	21	13	3
Total of firms	78	22	8

Source: ODISSEO-DIS, Faculty of Engineering, University of Naples, Italy.

Differences depend on the subcontractors' typology (size, design skills, capability to meet the customer's demand, etc.) and that of the customers (technology specificity, industrial sector within which it performs its activity, international regulations as to safety and reliability, etc.).

In the past customers played a prevailing role in the inter-firm relationship: by contracting out parts and components to small and medium firms they monitored the whole production process. The subcontracting system was then a 'star-shaped' organization at whose core stood the customer that established relationships with several subcontractors.

Now relationships are no longer bilateral only; they include many hierarchical relationships developed along the subcontracting chain. Customers, while developing collaboration with subcontractors, carry out a selection of them resulting in a stratification of the subcontracting system shaped as a pyramid at whose summit there are the first-tier subcontractors acting as a liaison between the customer and the second/third-tier subcontractors.

The intense relationships between the parties involved in the subcontracting system facilitates the inter-firm technology and information transfer and guarantees the customer constant improvements in quality, price and delivery times. Thus, subcontracting is becoming a strategic lever for the Italian industrial system to be competitive.

Specifically, the technology transfer model used to evaluate changes in inter-firm relationships shows that:

- new subcontracting relationships, unlike traditional ones, are characterized by high exchanges of the four technology components (machinery, organizational rules, professional skills, information). In fact the degree of utilization of the technology transfer channels by subcontractors is remarkable;
- the high usage of the technology transfer channels highlights that subcontracting relationships are characterized by an intense involvement of the subcontractors in the customer activities;
- in the new subcontracting relationships soft channels (information, human resources) are as used as hard channels (machinery, equipment). This means that both tangible and intangible technology components are crucial;
- collaborative relationships are close both at the beginning of the order and during the execution of the order and they enable the customer to co-ordinate all mechanisms (direct monitoring, mutual adjustment, process standardization) needed to manage a complex system involving firms with different characteristics and experience;
- the degree of collaboration between customer and subcontractor is independent of the subcontractor's size. This outcome highlights the growing strategic role played by subcontractors.
- subcontractors, regardless of their size, because of technical reasons (technological structure, quality system, customer's culture, etc.) and economic reasons (orders, etc.) focus their activities on a few customers. By so doing the subcontractor's turnover mainly depends on the orders from the first two customers;
- even though subcontractor's turnover is focused on a few large customers, it does not emerge a tendency towards a higher focusing;
- subcontracting involves both manufacturing and design functions. This means that in the current subcontracting system an increasing role is played both by specialization subcontracting and by new forms of developed subcontracting while capacity subcontracting is declining. Nevertheless there are sectorial asymmetries and differences related to the subcontractors' size. Smaller firms are mainly involved in manufacturing activities while smaller firms develop design functions as well.

251

Subcontracting in the aircraft industry is still manufacturing-oriented, while in the automobile industry firms are deeply rooted in the customer's production cycle (even performing design activities as to parts and components).

In conclusion, this chapter, after pointing out the importance of analysing the specificity of the subcontracting system in the main industrial sectors, wants to stress the difficulties that may meet a model of vertical relationship – successful under specific industrial conditions – when applied to other industrial situations. In particular many difficulties may arise when the models of vertical relationship being used in the automobile industry (e.g., the 'lean supply model') are applied to other industries (e.g., the aircraft industry). Difficulties will be greater when the structural characteristics of the application sector are very different from the automobile industry's characteristics.

Notes

1 These two approaches summarize how subcontracting has been changing in the last few decades. Nevertheless, a synthesis is never exhaustive of the issues it aims to analyse; in fact the need for a choice implies the exclusion of studies and contributions being developed in the same research area. To fill this gap reference is made to contributions mentioned below and to the attached bibliography. As to the various issues related to the inter-firm collaboration and network firm models reference is made to the proceedings of the international meeting organized by the RSO Institute 'The network firm: identify, design and manage it' (RSO 1988) and to the theoretical review of Fletcher's strategic alliances (1993). As to the organizational choices made by smaller firms in their development processes, reference is made to Lorenzoni (1988, 1992). To probe into the debate on the new configurations of the firm, relationship typologies and issues related to vertical and horizontal relationships, see the papers sent to the AiIG meeting held in Bari, 'Le nuove configurazioni dell'impresa e dei mercati' (Dioguardi 1994).

2 For a useful review of the latest contributions on the theory of the firm see Del Monte (1994) and Dosi et al. (1992). A critical review of theories and contributions related to the interpretation of the subcontracting system can be found in Mariotti (1994).

3 Lamming (1993), in his study of the automobile industry, highlights the partnership strategic role in the subcontracting chain and points out that the customer's standpoint is still prevailing in the relationship. The author underlines the development of lean supply that goes beyond partnership. Lean supply is characterized by a dynamic relationship based on collaboration and competitiveness between peers; this demands a deep organizational and cultural change by all of the firms involved in the relationship.

4 The importance of mutual trust is maintained by many scholars. In particular Lamming highlights that lean supply implementation requires close inter-firm collaboration and new honesty in supply chain relationships (Lamming 1993: 238–9). La Sako (1992: 36–48) identifies three types of trust (contractual trust, competence trust, goodwill trust) and points out its positive impact on buyer–supplier relationships both from the X efficiency (Leibenstein 1966) and from the transaction cost standpoint (Coase 1937; Williamson 1975, 1979).

5 An example of mechanical parts assembly is the manufacturing and assembly by the subcontractor of components for automobile engines. An example of skilled part assembly is the assembly of aircraft parts in the aircraft industry.

6 By correlating the subcontractors' size with the collaboration intensity no meaningful connection emerges.

7 Kruskal-Wellis' test is equal to 2.4 and it is better than the critical value 9.5 corresponding to P=5 per cent probability. Thus we can conclude that differences in the 5 industries are not incidental.

8 The automobile industry is undergoing a high automation of its manufacturing process and just-in-time and time-to-market philosophies are developing.

9 The aircraft industry is characterized by high-tech products and, often, by artisanal manufacturing processes where quality is much oriented towards demanding reliability and safety requirements.

10 The heterogeneity of the clusters is confirmed by Kruskal–Wallis' test taking a value equal to 35.7, much higher than the critical value equal to 9.5 corresponding to probability P = 5 per cent. Then the differences between the clusters are not incidental but they are due to real differences in the samples from which they are drawn.

11 Subcontracting focused on manufacturing has been defined here as *traditional subcontracting* as it corresponds to the subcontracting definition by Sallez (1975), Chaillou (1977), Barthomieu *et al.* (1983).

12 Complex subcontracting definition corresponds to Del Monte's definition (1991); in any case it corresponds to Chaillou's specialization supply (1977) and, partly, to Asanuma's drawings approved (1989).

13 The combination of the subcontractor to the customer's industry allowed for the share of turnover that is business from the first customer's industry (not lower than 40 per cent).

14 Fisher's test was used to analyse any big difference between the automobile and the aircraft industry. Fisher's test value corresponds to a probability level lower than 1 per cent, much lower than the critical value of 5 per cent. Thus we can conclude that the two industries are likely very different with respect to their design activity.

References

Allen, T.J. (1988) *Managing the Flow of Technology*, Cambridge, MA: MIT Press.

Aoki, M. (1984) *The Cooperative Game Theory of the Firm*, Oxford: Oxford University Press.

—— (1988) *Information, Incentives, and Bargaining in the Japanese Economy*, New York: Cambridge University Press.

Asanuma, B. (1989) 'Manufacturer–supply relationships in Japan and the concept of relation-specific skill', *Journal of the Japanese and International Economies* 3: 1–30.

Badaracco, J.L. (1991) *The Knowledge Link – How Firms Compete Through Strategic Alliances*, Boston, MA: Harvard Business School.

Berthomieu, C., Chanel-Reynaud, C., Guighard, J.P., Hanaut, A. and Longhi, A. (1983) *Structure industrielle et sous-traitance*, Paris: Presses Universitaires de France.

Chaillou, B. (1977) 'Définition et typologie de la sous-traitance', *Revue économique* 2: 262–85.

Coase, R.H. (1937) 'The nature of the firm', *Economica* 4 (November): 386–405.

Colombo, M. and Mariotti, S. (1994), 'L'eccellenza nelle relazioni cliente fornitore. Osservazioni sul modello giapponese', *Economia & Management* 4.

David, A.J. (1990) 'The customer/supplier relationship. The Nissan way', *Total Quality Management* 1, 1: 59–67.

Del Monte, A. (1991) 'Alcuni modelli di interpretazione nei rapporti fra grandi e piccole imprese', *Workshop: Rapporti di collaborazione tra grandi e piccole imprese*, Naples, May.

—— (1994) *Manuale di organizzazione e politica industriale*, Turin: Utet.

De Maio, A. and Maggiore, E. (eds) (1992) *Organizzare per innovare. Rapporti evolutivi cliente-fornitore*, Milan: Etaslibri.

Dioguardi, G. (ed.) (1994) *Sistemi di imprese. Le nuove configurazioni dell'impresa e dei mercati,* Milan: Etaslibri.

Dosi, G., Giannetti, R. and Toninelli, P.A. (1992) *Technology and Enterprise in a Historical Perspective*, Oxford: Clarendon Press.

Eccles, R.G. (1981) 'Bureaucratic versus craft administration: the relationship of market structure to the construction firms', *Administrative Science Quarterly* 26: 449–69.

Esposito, E. and lo Storto, C. (1992) 'Qualitative and structural changes of the subcontracting firms: a micro-analytical approach to the study of inter-firms relationships', *EIASM RENT VI – Research in Entrepreneurship 6th Workshop*, Barcelona, 26–7 November.

Esposito, E. and Raffa, M. (1991) 'Supply in hi-tech industry: the role of the small businesses', *Proceedings of the 36th ICSB World Conference*, Vienna, 24–6 June.

—— (1992) 'Qualité et sous-traitance dans l'industrie italienne: quelques résultats d'une étude empirique', *Revue internationale P.M.I.* 5, 2: 57–82.

—— (1993) 'The evolution of subcontracting firms. Empirical evidence', *23rd European Small Business Seminar*, Northern Ireland, 15–17 September, pp. 840–58.

—— (1994) 'The evolution of Italian subcontracting firms. Empirical evidence', *European Journal of Purchasing and Supply Management* 1, 2: 67–76.

Ferrando, P.M. (1984) *Subfornitura e approvvigionamenti nell'evoluzione del sistema aziendale*, Milan: Franco Angeli.

Fletcher, D. (1993) 'Strategic alliances and value adding networks. A critical review', *EIASM RENT VII Research in Entrepreneurship 7th Workshop*, Budapest, 25–6 November.

Hallén, L., Johanson, J. and Seyed-Mohamed, N. (1991) 'Interfirm adaptation in business relationships', *Journal of Marketing* 55 (April): 29–37.

Imrie, R. and Morris, J. (1992) 'A review of recent changes in buyer–supplier relations', *Omega* 20, 5/6: 641–52.

Klein, B., Crawford, R. and Alchian, A. (1978) 'Vertical integration, appropriable rents, and the competitive contracting process', *The Journal of Law and Economics* 21: 297–326.

Lamming, R. (1993) *Beyond Partnership, Strategies for Innovation and Lean Supply*, New York: Prentice Hall.

Lawton Smith, H., Dickson, K. and Lloyd Smith, S. (1991) 'There are two sides to every story: innovation and collaboration within networks of large and small firms', *Research Policy* 20: 457–69.

Lecler, Y. (1992) 'L'avenir du partenariat à la Japonaise', *Revue Francaise de Gestion* November–December: 51–63.

Leibenstein, H. (1966) 'Allocative efficiency versus X-efficiency', *American Economic Review* 56: 383–415.

Lorenzoni, G. and Ornati, O.A. (1988) 'Constellations of firms and new ventures', *Journal of Business Venturing* 3, 3: 41–57.

Lorenzoni, G. (ed.) (1992) *Accordi reti e vantaggio competitivo*, Milan: EtasLibri.

Mariotti, S. (1994) 'Rapporti verticali tra imprese, mercati organizzati ed economia della cooperazione: una rassegna critica', in G. Dioguardi (ed.) *Sistemi di imprese. Le nuove configurazioni dell'impresa e dei mercati*, Milan: Etaslibri, pp. 65–97.

Minato, T. (1992) 'Strategic alliance between small and large business', *The First International Federation of Scholarly Associations of Management (IFSAM) Conference*, Tokyo, 7–9 September 1992, pp. 66–9.

MITI (1991) *White Paper on Small and Medium Enterprises in Japan*, Tokyo: MITI.

Morris, J. (1992) 'Organization in an alien environment: Japanese style sub contracting relations in the U.K.,' *The First International Federation of Scholarly Associations of Management (IFSAM) Conference*, Tokyo, 7–9 September 1992, pp. 78–81.

Morris, J. and Imrie, R. (1993) 'Japanese style subcontracting. Its impact on European industries', *Long Range Planning* 26, 4: 53–8.

Oliver, N. and Wilkinson, B. (1992) *The Japanization of British Industry*, Oxford: Blackwell.

Perroux, F. (1966) *L'Economie du XX Siècle* (Italian translation) *L'economia del XX secolo*, Milan: Etas Kompass.

Raffa, M. (1992) 'Strategie di cooperazione: l'evoluzione della subfornitura nei settori a tecnologia sistemica', in R. Filippini, G. Pagliarani and G. Petroni (eds) *Progettare e gestire l'impresa innovativa*, Milan: Etaslibri.

Rothwell, R. and Whiston, T.G. (1990) 'Design, innovation and corporate integration', *R&D Management* 20, 3: 193–201.

RSO (1988) Proceedings of the international meeting *The network firm: identify, design and manage it*, organized by the RSO Institute, Camogli, 12–14 October.

Saget, F. (1988) 'Partnership between small and large firms: what does it entail? How is it developing?', in *Partnership Between Small and Large Firms*, London: Graham and Trotman, pp. 49–64.

Sako, M. (1988) 'Partnership between small and large firms: the case of Japan', in *Partnership Between Small and Large Firms*, London: Graham and Trotman, pp. 66–79.

—— (1992) *Price, Quality and Trust. Inter-firm Relations in Britain and Japan*, Cambridge: Cambridge University Press.

Sallez, A. and Schlegel, J. (1963) *La sous-traitance dans l'industrie. Modalités, lacunes, prospectives*, Paris: Dunod.

Sallez, A. (1975) 'Sous-traitance, productivité économique et croissance régionale', *Economie appliquée* 2/3: 459–96.

—— (1977) 'De l'analyse structurelle de la firme à la division spatiale du travail', *Economie appliquée* 2: 319–61.

Samson, R. (1993) 'Competing with the Japanese strategies for European business', *Long Range Planning* 26, 4: 59–65.

Scott, C.S. and Westbrook, R. (1993) 'New strategic tools for supply chain management', *International Journal of Physical Distribution and Logistics Management* 1, 1991 (Italian translation), *Problemi di Gestione* XIX, 2: 105–137.

Teece, D.J. (1992) 'Competition, cooperation, and innovation – organizational arrangements for regimes of rapid technological progress', *Journal of Economic Behavior and Organization* 18: 1–25.

The Technology Atlas Team (1987) 'Components of technology for resources transformation', *Technological Forecasting and Social Change* 32, 1: 19–35.

Vennin, B. (1975) 'Pratiques et signification de la sous-traitance dans l'industrie automobile en France', *Revue économique* 2: 280–306.

Williamson, O.E. (1975) *Markets and Hierarchies: Analysis and Antitrust Implication*, New York: Free Press.

—— (1979) 'Transaction-cost economics: the governance of contractual relations', *The Journal of Law and Economics* 2: 233–61.

—— (1985) *The Economic Institutions of Capitalism*, New York: Free Press.

INDEX

Note: italic page numbers refer to figures and tables